The Rise and Fall of the UK Film Council

The Rise and Fall of the UK Film Council

Gillian Doyle, Philip Schlesinger,
Raymond Boyle and Lisa W. Kelly

EDINBURGH
University Press

© Gillian Doyle, Philip Schlesinger, Raymond Boyle and Lisa W. Kelly, 2015

Edinburgh University Press Ltd
The Tun – Holyrood Road
12 (2f) Jackson's Entry
Edinburgh EH8 8PJ
www.euppublishing.com

Typeset in 11/13 Adobe Sabon by
IDSUK (DataConnection) Ltd, and
printed and bound in Great Britain by
CPI Group (UK) Ltd, Croydon CR0 4YY

A CIP record for this book is available from the British Library

ISBN 978 0 7486 9823 3 (hardback)
ISBN 978 0 7486 9824 0 (webready PDF)
ISBN 978 1 4744 0366 5 (epub)

The right of Gillian Doyle, Philip Schlesinger, Raymond Boyle and Lisa W. Kelly
to be identified as authors of this work has been asserted in accordance with the
Copyright, Designs and Patents Act 1988 and the Copyright and Related Rights
Regulations 2003 (SI No. 2498).

Contents

Tables and Figures

Tables

Figures

Preface

This book is based on findings from a research project entitled *The UK Film Council (UKFC): A Case Study of Film Policy in Transition*, which was led by Professor Gillian Doyle (principal investigator) and conducted by her and a team comprising co-investigators Professor Philip Schlesinger, Professor Raymond Boyle and Research Associate Dr Lisa Kelly, all based at the Centre for Cultural Policy Research (CCPR) at the University of Glasgow. We gratefully acknowledge the support of the Arts & Humanities Research Council (AHRC) (Reference AH/J00457X/1). The broad objectives of our study, which ran from September 2012 until March 2015, were to investigate the history of the UK Film Council (UKFC), to examine its effectiveness as a model of public support for film and also to analyse what lessons can be drawn from its experience.

Established in April 2000 but wound up at the end of March 2011, the UKFC was the key strategic body responsible for supporting the film industry and film culture in Britain for more than a decade. Our project investigated the UKFC's short-lived experience as lead support body for film and the fundamental questions raised, in the wake of the Council's demise, about how strategic interventions for film in the twenty-first century may be framed and put into operation.

It is important to understand the scope and limitations of the present work. The Film Council became the head of a so-called 'family' of partner organisations – see Appendix 1. There is a separate tale to be told about this extensive network and how it operated. The present study, however, confines itself to what we have judged to be central aspects of the UKFC's operations. There is no shortage of further work to be done.

Our investigation involved extensive fieldwork, including some fifty interviews with key policy-makers, former UKFC personnel, industry analysts, leading film-makers and other prominent film industry stakeholders. Our interviews (that, with only three exceptions, were conducted by telephone or Skype) were generally all audio-recorded face to face. All were professionally transcribed with full confidentiality observed where requested. We have provided the dates on which these interviews took place as well as their locations. In some cases, we have given sparser details than others. That is because about one-third of our interviewees chose not to go on the record attributably, a sure indication that for not a few the closure of the Film Council remains a highly sensitive topic. We have in all cases respected the wishes of contributors and in instances where we have been unable to directly cite our sources they have nonetheless very valuably informed our study. A small number of others – prominent players in the saga – chose either not to respond to our requests for interviews or were unavailable. In the fullness of time, we may expect further testimony to emerge – perhaps even in response to the pages that follow.

We also conducted analysis of policy and strategy documents, board minutes, internal UKFC documents and reports (where accessible) and relevant academic literature. We gratefully acknowledge that several of the charts and figures presented in this monograph draw on data from secondary sources, including the UKFC, the British Film Institute (BFI) and consultants Olsberg SPI.

In the course of conducting this study, we were struck by the extraordinary fact that no comprehensive archive had been compiled of the UKFC's paper record to be handed over to its legacy organisation, the BFI. Nobody either at the Department for Culture, Media and Sport (DCMS) or the BFI knew how to lay hands on a full account of the Film Council's decision making, despite repeated requests for information. Eventually, we did find that some material was held at the BFI and we are grateful to those who sought to provide us with access to this. However, as indicated in what follows, there are further documents, not least those relating to the tense merger negotiations between the UKFC and BFI in 2009–10, that we have simply not been able to see. We would recommend that, in the interests of improved public understanding of the workings and records of our publicly funded institutions, where possible better care be taken in procedures for record keeping and archiving in the future.

We are very grateful to interviewees, including the following, who kindly consented to participate in our research: Chris Auty, Tim Bevan, Jenny Borgars, Stephen Bristow, Bill Bush, Tim Cagney, Chris Chandler, Rob Cheek, Phil Clapp, Tom Clarke MP, Will Clarke, Fiona Clarke-Hackston, Carol Comley, Lenny Crooks, Jonathan Davis, Andrew Eaton, Jane Glastonbury, Professor John Hill, Thomas Hoegh, Robert

Jones, Sir Gerald Kaufman, Philip Knatchbull, James Lee, Dan McCrae, Tina McFarling, John McVay, Agnieszka Moody, Amanda Nevill, John Newbigin, Rebecca O'Brien, Jonathan Olsberg, Alan Parker, Steve Perrin, Simon Perry, James Purnell, Paul Richardson, Marc Samuelson, Tanya Seghatchian, Lord Chris Smith, Iain Smith, Lord Wilf Stevenson, Heather Stewart, Stewart Till, Paul Trijbits, Neil Watson, Peter Watson, Paul Webster and, last but not least, John Woodward.

Earlier versions of some of the material in this book have appeared in the following: Boyle, R. (forthcoming), 'Digital Divides? The UKFC and the Digital Screen Network', *The International Journal for Media and Cultural Politics*; Doyle 2014a; Kelly, L. W. (forthcoming), 'Professionalising the British Film Industry: The UK Film Council and Public Support for Film Production', *The International Journal of Cultural Policy*; Schlesinger 2015a and 2015b.

We thank Richard Paterson of the BFI, film producer Bob Last and Professor John Caughie of the University of Glasgow who, over the course of the project, provided invaluable guidance and advice. We thank our proofreader Clare Edwards. Thanks also to Gillian Leslie and the team at Edinburgh University Press.

Part I
Background

CHAPTER 1

Why Does Film Policy Matter?

> Discussion of film policy, past and present, revolves around three main themes: that Hollywood dominates the market: that the film trade has distinctive *economic* features, and that the film trade has distinctive *cultural* characteristics.
>
> (Dickinson and Harvey 2005: 420; emphasis added)

This chapter introduces the context within which the UK Film Council (UKFC) was conceived and would operate during its lifetime from 2000 to 2011. It asks: why does film policy matter? In seeking to address this question we analyse some of the key themes and concepts that are developed throughout the book, including the challenge for policy-makers of addressing both the economic and cultural aspirations for the medium of film and the film industry.

In this opening part of our study, we explain why film policy is significant and assess the complex range of objectives surrounding public policy intervention to support film. Later in the chapter, we examine some international models of film support, specifically the French model, and contrast differing approaches, in particular the Hollywood model, towards sustaining national production industries. The final part of the chapter outlines the structure of the book.

Policy as Politics

Film policy does not exist in a vacuum. Throughout this book we argue that the particular political context and culture of the UK has played a key role in shaping aspects of film policy over the years. We concur with Des Freedman who suggests:

> There is nothing predetermined about the personality of the media systems to which we are exposed. While the form a media system assumes at any one time is by no means the direct expression of the state's political priorities, it makes little sense to ignore the impact of political actors and political values on the character of the wider media environment. (Freedman 2008: 1)

To that end, the role of politics, both in terms of party politics and in the wider sense of how power is organised in a society, is an important part of the narratives that surround the development of film policy in the UK. Rather than viewing policy formation as a rather dry, technocratic process, we suggest that it is an often highly charged process, involving a range of political actors, stakeholders and lobbying interests. Understanding this context and the elements of both continuity and change in the political environment framing policy are all-important elements that run throughout this study and are examined in some detail in Chapter 3.

The tension between framing film policy either through primarily an industrial or cultural lens has often bedeviled interventions in the film policy arena. As Maud Mansfield argued in 2009 in her report on film policy for the HM Minister for Culture, Communications and Creative Industries Ed Vaizey:

> Film policy has rarely been able to square the economic and political desirability of a self supporting industry with a shared language market and an acknowledged dependence on inward investment from the Hollywood majors and/or their controlling of the market. (Mansfield 2009: 5)

State intervention in the arena of film has been complicated somewhat due to the nature of an industry that has particular sectors of production, distribution and exhibition that, while part of the one value chain, often have complex and differing needs and priorities.

Policy interventions also have a long history as a result of the international and complex structure of the film industry, providing as it does employment across a range of sectors from craft and manufacturing to the service sector. Yet the cultural importance of film, with its potential as a medium for projecting a range of distinct representations of nations and identities onto a global stage, has always been the underlying factor that has heightened its industrial importance in policy terms. As John Hill has argued:

> In this respect, UK film policy, for all its apparent industrial hard-headedness, has typically possessed implicit cultural underpinnings. (Hill 2004: 33)

As we note later in this chapter, some institutions, such as the European Commission (EC), have rhetorically at least prioritised the cultural dimension of film in attempts to mobilise it as part of a cultural space in which a European identity can be expressed. But even in this policy environment, the industrial position of the film industry in Europe and its ability to act as a bulwark against Hollywood's domination of the sector is also deemed a policy priority.

Interestingly, whether or not the UK state should actually have a film policy has never been seriously questioned by the political class except, perhaps, during the 1980s when 'rolling back the state' in all its forms became, in rhetorical terms at least, the new political orthodoxy. For some scholars, such as Jeremy Tunstall (Tunstall and Machin 1999), the dependent nature of the UK film industry on Hollywood capital or US capital has resulted in policy formation being broadly defensive in strategy, as the UK attempts to deal with an economically more powerful industry in the US with which it shares a common language. While the shadow of Hollywood has unquestionably been a commanding factor in shaping policy interventions over the years, it has not been the only one.

The Culture–Commerce Dichotomy

The perceived economic importance of UK film has been at the core of most UK state intervention in the industry from the start of the twentieth century. To explain why film policy matters in this part of the book, it is, to put it simply, because politicians (of all political persuasions) broadly believe that is an industry that matters to the British economy and Britain's image abroad. Politicians and sections of the industry (more often than not the production sector) have always been keen to provide the evidence that substantiates this type of thinking. That means that film policy has always been, in part at least, an economic policy. In Chapters 2 and 3, we discuss in more detail how the Treasury has been either directly or indirectly a key Whitehall player in shaping film and film-related policy.

In 2012 a report by Oxford Economics titled *The Economic Impact of the UK Film Industry (Third Edition)* commissioned by the British Film Institute (BFI), Pinewood Shepperton plc, the British Film Commission (BFC) and Creative England argued:

> Today the core UK film industry is a substantial industry, directly generating 43,900 full time equivalent (FTE) jobs and contributing £1.6 billion to national GDP [gross domestic product]. In employment terms, the industry is larger than fund management and the pharmaceutical and manufacturing sector. Furthermore, the overall trend is very positive with employment increasing since 1995, mirroring film production levels (particularly inward investment). Overall, when considering the film industry's procurement, spending effects

from those directly and indirectly employed and its contribution to UK tourism, trade and merchandise sales, the core UK film industry supported a total of 117,400 FTE jobs, contributed over £4.6 billion to UK GDP and over £1.3 billion to the Exchequer (gross of tax relief and other fiscal support) in 2011. (Oxford Economics 2012: 6)

Fiscal intervention in film policy has tended to have a focus on boosting indigenous film production and capturing inward investment (usually in the form of US capital) to bolster film production and post-production activity.

In the UK context, we trace the historical pattern of these interventions in more detail in Chapters 2 and 3. At this point, it is worth highlighting that the industrial or economic focus on film policy has often been in tension with a more cultural or educational dimension regarding the value and worth of film in society. In this connection, Margaret Dickinson and Sylvia Harvey have argued:

> Until the 1980s Britain followed the practice common in many states in Europe of operating parallel support mechanisms for film as industry and film as culture, justified by a mixture of economic and cultural arguments. (Dickinson and Harvey 2005: 421)

Yet, the broader policy dichotomy between positioning film as an industry and framing film as a distinct cultural and artistic form has often bedeviled organisations and institutions set up to deliver what in practical terms have often become competing and contradictory goals and policy objectives.

John Hill has suggested that embedded in these debates are also deeply rooted cultural assumptions around the status of film in contrast to other cultural and artistic forms. He argues:

> The ambivalent status of film – as industry, entertainment and, in some cases, 'art' – has also been evident in the application of film policy in the UK. Unlike the traditional arts, the cultural value or aesthetic worth of cinema has not been a given and film has therefore not automatically fallen within the domain of 'arts policy' (or, following its establishment the Arts Council). As a result, government policy and legislation directed at film has been driven by a variety of imperatives. (Hill 2004: 32)

For example, the British Film Institute (BFI), set up in 1933, has viewed its remit as being that of a broad cultural agency, with educational and archival goals focused on nurturing and valuing a deeper understanding and support for British and international cinema. In contrast, the task of sustaining and growing the economic and industrial development of the British film industry has been allocated to a range of other organisations and institutions, resulting in an often fragmented and complex policy landscape with multiple agencies responsible for differing aspects of industrial and cultural policy.

Over the years, of course, the BFI has had to adapt with changes in the political, economic and cultural environment within which film production, distribution and exhibition takes place. The BFI's *Film Forever* plan,when laying out its strategic priorities for 2012–17 stated:

> Supporting British film and filmmakers is core to what we do. We will back new voices, new stories, new ideas and skills, enriching and diversifying British film production. (BFI 2012a: 4)

In one sense, this ambitious aim for the BFI had been given new impetus by its change of status to become a funding body given the earlier abolition of the UK Film Council. This involved the transfer of new funding responsibilities to an established organisation that had been a cultural film agency, which in the past had itself allocated funds for specific types of British film. We return to these issues later in the book.

In historical terms, intervention in film policy has mattered because of its perceived economic and cultural importance, not least to the various sectors of the industry that have lobbied to have their interests taken up by politicians.The challenge has been in realising often diverse goals through an at times cluttered landscape of institutions and organisations tasked with delivering on differing aspects of industrial and cultural policy related to film. Chapter 3 pays particular attention to this aspect of the policy landscape as we outline the particular policy context of the 1990s that led to the creation of the UKFC.

Digital Challenges and Policy Complexity

The shift from analogue to digital has been one of the epoch changing moments across the media landscape in the last decade or so (Meikle and Young 2011). The challenges and opportunities of the digital environment for the media industries have also raised issues for policy-makers as the pace of technological innovation has driven regulatory change across the communications industry. As we argue in Chapter 7, digital transformation for the film industry was initially viewed primarily as something that would alter the economics of production and perhaps, latterly, distribution. However, the complexity of the digital environment and the ways in which patterns of media creation, consumption and engagement are changing have resulted in policy thinking having to stretch across a range of issues from new modes of content creation to distribution and intellectual property (IP) related matters.

In the dying months of Gordon Brown's Labour Government in 2009, Lord Carter's report *Digital Britain* attempted to shape a policy framework for government engagement across a range of areas being reshaped by digital technologies. It argued:

> The public policy objectives in film remain the same in the digital world as in the analogue: widening the audience for cultural film and enhancing the sustainability of culturally-specific British films. But the emergence of digital technology in recent years has provided a vital opportunity to create a dramatic change in the cinematic experience, through greater access to an even wider range of films and other cultural experiences such as opera and music concerts. Crucially, it allows the deployment of new and developing technologies such as the re-emergence of 3D film. (DCMS & BIS 2009: 123)

However, this general ambition actually masked a myriad of policy challenges being faced in a converging media environment for the screen industries, not least what is meant by the term 'film' in a digital era increasingly characterised by 'screens', 'platforms' and 'content'.

The complex policy challenges facing any state intervention to support the film industry, which could range across IP debates and into the relative merits of new distribution platforms and business models, was highlighted from an economic perspective by Oxford Economics' report into the film industry in 2012:

> The rapid technological change in the creative industries presents both huge opportunities and challenges for the film sector. As noted in the *Film Policy Review* '*digital technologies create the possibility of a paradigm shift in the creative and commercial potential of film*'. The sector's future will depend in many ways on its ability to react to, manage and exploit these changes, and succeeding in its efforts to reconcile the many emerging forms of content distribution and consumption with robust means of securing and appropriating the associated revenue streams. (Oxford Economics 2012: 92; emphasis added)

An example of the interplay between the cultural and the commercial as drivers of policy can also be identified in aspects of the *Digital Britain* report of 2009, where it was held:

> In film a system of cultural tax credits has long helped to sustain a wide range of films that speak to a British narrative, rather than the cultural perspectives of Hollywood or multinational collaborations. Other countries such as Canada, for similar reasons, extend the model of cultural tax relief beyond the film industry to the interactive and online worlds. CGI [Computer generated imagery], electronic games and simulation also have a significant role in Britain's digital content ecology and in our international competitiveness. Each of these has the same capability as the more traditional sectors, such as film, to engage us and reflect our cultural particularism. They may in future have a cultural relevance to rival that of film. **The Government has therefore committed to work with the industry to collect and review the evidence for a tax relief to promote the sustainable production for online or physical sale of culturally British video games.** This work will balance any potential support with the need for fair competition and ensure value for money for taxpayers. (DCMS & BIS 2009: 121; emphasis in the original)

One of the key shifts in focus concerning film policy promoted by the shift to digital has been a greater awareness of the audience and the changing patterns of media consumption and their implications for content producers. The UK's Film Policy Review (FPRP 2012), for example, argues that it is only by better understanding the audience for film and how that audience is evolving in the digital age that the industry can succeed. While a concern about the audience is of course not new, and often has been central to policy on film education, for instance, it is interesting how the shift from analogue to digital has increased the importance of the audience in policy rhetoric around film, even if this has often been in terms of ensuring the commercial viability of the industry.

Unquestionably, the digital context has ultimately increased the policy focus on the distribution and exhibition of film-related content, even if this shift has been some time in coming. The European Commission, in its *European Film in the Digital Era: Bridging Cultural Diversity and Competitiveness* report for the European Parliament, notes:

> The digital revolution offers more possibilities and flexibility for distribution and is having a fundamental impact on audience behaviour. (EC 2014: 2)

Indeed, as is discussed later in this chapter, when we turn our attention to European models of support for film, the 2014 EC report notes how, historically, the overwhelming focus of state aid in Europe for film has been focused on production with, in 2009, only 8.4 per cent of this aid spent on distribution and 3.6 per cent on promotion (EC 2014: 7). So, in policy terms, digital technology and the ways in which it is becoming embedded in aspects of production, distribution and exhibition of film have forced a reshaping of any public intervention in this policy arena. It has also highlighted the growing issue of 'policy lag', where technological innovation and change are happening at such a pace that policy formation or intervention struggles to remain relevant in addressing an evolving sector or industry.

In his introduction to the sequel to the Film Policy Review published in 2014, the former Labour Secretary of State for Culture, Media and Sport Lord (Chris) Smith notes how:

> [t]he Internet – once a perceived enemy, spawning huge piracy – is becoming a primary revenue source. Whilst piracy remains very much a live issue, the statistics are encouraging: in 2008 around 12% of consumer spending on media and entertainment was devoted to digital; by 2017 that is expected to have risen to around 50%. (Smith cited in FPRP 2014: 4)

In other words, even two years on from the Film Policy Review (DCMS 2012), the nature of the impact of the Internet (as both a threat and an opportunity) and evolving patterns of media consumption make the future-proofing of any policy intervention even more difficult. When the gestation period for policy formation is particularly long, as is the case, in say, European Union (EU) media policy, then the likelihood of serious 'policy lag' increases. While the shift to digital both in the UK and across Europe has reframed some of the detail concerning policy intervention, the major paradigm shift since the 1990s has of course been in positioning film within the broader frame of creative industries policy.

Creative Industries and Economic and Cultural Renewal (or Back to the Future)

Despite the vagaries of political and cultural shifts that see some policy areas consistently given a high political or media profile while others become less important, the dominance since the 1990s of the creative industries paradigm in the UK policy arena has seen film remain positioned as a key part of the creative economy (Schlesinger 2007, 2009).

Dickinson and Harvey, preferring the alternative term the 'cultural industries', rather than the New Labour coinage, the 'creative industries',wrote in the 2000s that

> [t]he [UK] government has been clearer about the economic goals of film policy than cultural ones. And film has increasingly been seen as part of the broader strategy for growing the cultural industries and promoting the cultural industries. (Dickinson and Harvey 2005: 423)

The key paradigm shift that took place in the 1990s that saw film policy become part of the broader policy narrative about the importance of the creative industries in re-energising the UK economy is discussed in more detail in Chapter 3. In particular, we focus on the importance this thinking had on shaping the form and nature of what would eventually become the UKFC.

As we noted earlier, the move from analogue to digital across media and communications has been one of the defining characteristics (and policy challenges) faced by these industries over the last two decades. So while film policy has remained distinct, it has also become part of a wider discourse on the role that the creative industries play in the broader economic and cultural life of the UK. The Film Policy Review of 2012 argued:

> [This] has been undertaken in the context of an extremely challenging economic climate, in the UK and globally. The recommendations in this Review are designed to help ensure that film, as a key part of the creative industries, is one of the sectors which plays a full role in driving growth, creating jobs and stimulating inward investments and exports. (DCMS 2012: 6)

While the role that film plays in the cultural life of the UK is acknowledged and addressed in the review, the leading edge of the report focuses on the ongoing economic impact that film as part of the creative industries plays in the economy. In part, this emphasis also reflects the shift during the 1990s that saw the Department for Culture, Media and Sport (DCMS) become the policy home for UK film-related matters. However, the Treasury remained an important part of the policy picture. For those in the DCMS who were fighting for its budget with other government departments in Whitehall, the economic arguments regarding the importance of culture in all its forms were always likely to gain more traction with the Treasury than arguments based on the intrinsic cultural value generated by film.

Shifts in political emphasis that inevitably take place over time contribute to defining policy priorities. So, for example, in the EU, the industrial strength of the European film industry (specifically in relation to the challenge from Hollywood) may be a policy priority but the cultural dimension of film is commonly prioritised, as befits an organisation deeply concerned with European identity. Thus, the Commission argues:

> The audiovisual sector has substantial cultural, social and economic significance. It shapes identities, projects values and can be a driver of European integration by contributing to our shared European identity. The sector contributes to growth and jobs in Europe and is a driver for innovation. (EC2014: 2)

Fundamentally, at a European level we may note a reordering of the cultural and commercial policy drivers that have been part of the UK policy context for film. It is evident that the policy dichotomy between commerce and culture has not disappeared in the digital age.

It is also important to observe that even within any supposedly UK-wide policy environment, there is a need to factor in the diverse devolved politics of the UK. In 2010, there was a merger of the Scottish Arts Council (a cultural agency) and Scottish Screen (a screen industries development agency) into a new body, Creative Scotland. One result has been to make a distinct film policy in Scotland increasingly invisible. As a result, the production sector in Scotland has lobbied consistently since 2010 in an attempt to secure a higher policy profile for film within Creative Scotland. *Review of the Film Sector in Scotland*, commissioned by Creative Scotland, published in 2014, noted the cultural importance of film, but identified an industry at 'something of a crisis point, with levels of production that are too low to sustain a viable domestic industry' (BOP Consulting 2014: 1). It also argued that in the digital environment with a converging landscape

> [a] film agency – or even one focused just on television and film – would feel out of date. Markets and audiences have shifted considerably, even since the days of Scottish Screen, to a complex and changing pattern of content consumption. (BOP Consulting 2014: 3)

The report called for increased Scottish Government policy intervention and leadership across a range of agencies in this converged sector including Creative Scotland.

What this discussion highlights is the continual complexity of the film (or screen) support landscape, as differing support models move in and out of fashion (or simply return in a new format) and the recognition, particularly acute in small countries such as Scotland, that some form of public investment is crucial if these sectors are to flourish both economically and culturally. As Robin MacPherson has argued:

> What counts as a successful film (industry) inevitably means different things to different people. Nonetheless, when it comes to building a sustainable domestic film sector for cultural or economic reasons or both, small countries around the world face similar challenges in countering the hegemony of regional and global film 'superpowers'. (MacPherson 2011)

While the media landscape and the position of film within that environment is unrecognisable from the era of early state intervention at the start of the twentieth century, the core political reasons for intervention, or why film policy continues to matter, remain remarkably similar.

International Models of Film Support

As noted earlier, the international aspects of the film industry and the potential global reach of cinematic representations mean that many states choose to intervene in this area for a combination of industrial and cultural reasons. This section briefly situates the UK experience in relation to other international models of film support and alternative approaches to film policy. It examines and contrasts the UK approach with, in particular, the approach of the French state to film industry intervention, which in many ways has come to symbolise a broader European tradition of film policy.

At the core of the historical and contemporary challenge for film industries across Europe is how best to compete with the economically and culturally powerful vertically integrated film industry that is Hollywood. A very notable characteristic of global markets for film is the predominance of output from the US (WTO 2010) and more particularly of films made by the Hollywood-based 'majors'. The exceptional track record of the major studios in consistently dominating global trade in film or, more generally, the success of the Hollywood model reflects the fact that the major studios – Disney, Twentieth Century Fox Film Corporation, Paramount Pictures Corporation, Sony/Columbia Pictures, Universal Pictures/Universal Studios Inc. and Warner Bros. Entertainment Inc. – are large, well-resourced and vertically integrated film companies with extensive control over film distribution activities in virtually all territories around the world (Doyle 2013: 105–10). With assured access to distribution, the majors are able to commit significant resources both to production and to marketing or P&A (prints and advertising) so as to build awareness of and audience demand for a steady stream of big budget film releases. Strategies of risk reduction, including reliance on repetition (sequels) and stars, are commonplace (De Vany 2004). But, in essence, the key to the commercial success of the Hollywood majors is their ability to finance their own film productions, use their own international distribution networks, exhibit widely and often in outlets that they own, and then channel a proportion of profits back into new production in order to keep the virtuous circle going.

To that end, public intervention in film industries across Europe has been an accepted part of the political landscape for decades. In some cases the cultural protectionist argument around language has been a driver of industrial policy and intervention in the provision of subsidy/investment in the production sector of the film industries across Europe. Thus, the challenge of creating and sustaining an indigenous film industry through direct state support and production incentive schemes is not unique to the UK but is one that is being faced by countries across the globe. Tunstall and Machin pointed out that '[Europe] has 101 separate industries – each with its own separate policy – across Europe's more than thirty countries' and, as such, 'Europe's national "film industries" have long had difficulty competing with the Hollywood "movie industry"' due to a difference in 'vertical scale'(1999: 215).

Yet, although the economic and cultural domination of the US has long influenced not only UK but also European and global approaches to film policy, Hollywood is itself experiencing problems as 'generous incentive schemes offered by other states and countries' have resulted in half as many feature films being produced in Los Angeles in 2013 as in 1996 (*The Economist* 2014). It can be argued that with individual US states now implementing industrial film policies, the benefits of interventions and incentives are recognised even in the most self-sustaining of film industries. As Scott suggests, this is not necessarily a new situation:

Even in the Hollywood film industry, which on first examination looks like the essence of free-wheeling market capitalism, there is considerable collective order in the form of influential business associations, powerful professional guilds, indurated social networks, conventionalized behaviours, and mechanisms for public provision of supportive infrastructures and subsidies, all of which help to strengthen the bases of the industry's competitive advantages. (Scott 2000: 12)

The French Model

The French model for film support provides an interesting case to examine, as not only has France succeeded in developing 'the most prolific film industry in Europe' but its approach differs from that of both the UK and the US in a number of ways (Albertazzi and Cobley 2010: 194). As noted by Broche *et al.*, between 2002 and 2005 the EU member states 'provided over €6.5 billion of state aid for film production, which helped to produce over 3,600 films' (2007: 44). Of these, France provided the highest overall amount of state aid for film, followed by the UK and Germany, while more than 600 film support schemes were in operation across the EU (ibid.). Table 1.1 demonstrates that by 2010 to 2011, France produced more films than the UK and, perhaps more importantly, secured a domestic film share of more than 40 per cent in 2011. This is in stark contrast to the UK's 12.8 per cent and Germany's 21.8 per cent.

Table 1.1 Country indicators.

Output	Production volume 2010/11 (€m)	Number of films 2010/11	Average budget 2010/11 (€m)	Domestic film share 2011 (%)
Australia	89	17	5.3	3.9
Brazil	138	98	1.4	2.4
France	1390	272	5.1	41.6
Germany	463	71	2.73	21.8
Singapore	n/a	14	n/a	2
Sweden	23.7	21	2.6	19.8
UK	1540	237	6.52	12.8

Source: Olsberg SPI (2012: 39–42).

For Albertazzi and Cobley (2010: 194), the French support system has offered a 'viable alternative to Hollywood for a long time'. Based on an overall commitment to film culture, Olsberg SPI notes how 'France has developed a mature, stable and highly evolved system for the support of its film industry, with backing across the political spectrum'(2012: 43). This has largely been achieved through a consistent and 'carefully crafted policy of support' over a number of years that has been implemented by both the French Government and the French national film agency, LeCentre national ducinéma et de l'image animée (CNC) (the National Centre for Cinema and the Moving Image), which was established in 1946 as a 'quasi-autonomous administrative body' (Scott 2000: 2, 13).

L'exception culturelle (the cultural exception) is applied to French film in order to protect it against competition from the international market and is supported not only by regulation but also by public opinion. While France has what can be understood as a medium-sized film industry, other smaller nations adopt a similar approach. For example, on outlining Danish film policy and support, Hjort (2005: 120) highlights how the Danish Film Institute (DFI) seeks to 'assure the availability of artistically varied offerings within Danish film, which in turn will contribute to the articulation and development of cultural identity, Danish culture and language'.

UK film policy differs from the French model in a number of ways, with four key reasons outlined in a comparative report carried out in 2013 by Creative Screen Associates. These are based on the UK:

- Being made up of four nations – England, Wales, Scotland and Northern Ireland;
- Sharing a common language, English, which is also the official language of more countries than any other across the globe, spoken fluently by more than 25% of the world's population;
- [having] limited public and political priority placed on the arts and culture;
- [being] an economy built on free market economics with state intervention determined by market failure. (Creative Screen Associates 2013: 2)

The shared language between the UK and the US, as we note in Chapter 2, has been a key factor in shaping the often close economic and production links between these countries – although in reality it has often been an uneven relationship, one that has been characterised by a UK dependency on American capital and finance. The shared language has been both beneficial to the UK film industry and to its detriment. For instance, without a need to protect its national language the UK has acted as a subordinate to Hollywood over the years and been overly reliant on US capital to sustain its production base.

Concerns about the subordination of the UK industry are reflected in the emphasis on 'sustainability' (as opposed to film as a form of cultural expression) that, as we will argue, strongly influenced the UK Film Council's sense of mission, particularly in its early years. Moreover, rather than apply a consistent approach to film policy and support in the manner of the CNC in France, our account of both the creation and closure of the UKFC and its relationship with the long-running BFI, illustrates the problems, contradictions and irrationality of film policy-making processes and practices in Britain. In this sense we suggest that understanding the particular trajectories of any policy intervention require an understanding of the often nationally specific political and cultural contexts within which these policy formations are legitimised and sustained.

Film funds in France are generated through taxes collected on all films (not just French productions) shown across all platforms (including cinema tickets and Internet distribution) and a mandatory requirement for French broadcasters to invest substantially in indigenous films (see Creative Screen Associates 2013; Olsberg SPI 2012; Scott 2000). Indeed, part of the success of the French model can be attributed to a consistent and innovative approach in 'adapting its regulations' to help deal with the numerous threats that cinema has faced over the years in the form of television, video and online platforms (Albertazzi and Cobley 2010: 194). Not only has this helped sustain film production in France but the overall commitment to film culture has cultivated a substantial audience for indigenous film both in cinemas and on television (see Table 1.1).

As UK film funding is reliant on a government grant-in-aid derived from general taxation alongside proceeds from the National Lottery, with no mandatory involvement from broadcasters, it is much more 'vulnerable to changing government priorities, political orientations and economic recession' (Creative Screen Associates 2013: 3). In 2010, UK public investment totalled £347 million while in France the total was £578 million due to both CNC and broadcaster support (ibid.). It is also the case that the cultural and commercial aspects of film appear more difficult to reconcile in the UK than within the French model. For example, in France there is a 'refusal to distinguish between "cultural" cinema which would benefit from [state] aid, and "commercial" cinema, which would not benefit from it, starting from the assumption that every film is a cultural product' (Bellucci 2010: 219). While this assumption may have informed the rhetoric of the UKFC, it did not necessarily translate into practice.

With regard to film support schemes, France has a system of both automatic and selective subsidies for production funding. As outlined by Olsberg SPI (2012), automatic funding for French film production comes in two forms, both administered by the CNC. The first, *le compte de soutien*, is based on the market performance of a producer's last film (in terms of French box office, DVD and TV sales) and paid out €66 million in 2010. The second, *le crédit d'impôt*, 'is a 20 per cent tax credit on eligible French production costs (up to a maximum of 80 per cent of the budget), which is capped at €1 million per project; this was worth €40.4 million to French productions in 2010' (ibid.). It should be noted that unlike the UK, in which only those films in receipt of National Lottery funding are now able to share in recoupment income, the French *compte de soutien* 'benefits all French producers with films released on some or all platforms in the French market' (Creative Screen Associates 2013: 7). By rewarding market success across platforms, this is just one method by which French subsidy schemes help support and create a sustainable independent production sector in a way that has so far eluded the UK. There is also the more recent addition of the French Tax Rebate for International Production (TRIP) incentive scheme for foreign productions shooting in France, which again offer a 20 per cent rebate but has a higher cap of €4 million per project.

Selective funding, on the other hand, involves an advance against receipts, or *l'avance sur recettes*, which is an interest-free loan recoupable from income and can be awarded either before or after production. The CNC's budget for this was €28 million in 2010 and €30 million for 2011. This is in addition to various other selective schemes aimed at supporting 'development, co-production (German, Canadian), Third World cinema, or specific genres, including music and animation', which total about €4.5 million a year (Olsberg SPI 2012: 44). Overall, it has traditionally been easier to access film financing in France, largely through the availability of 'soft' money, than in the UK, meaning that while the latter produces many more films on an annual basis, they tend to be low or micro-budget in scale. In contrast, French films have higher median budgets while overall production spend within the market is also greater than that of the UK (Creative Screen Associates 2013: 3).

Approaches to co-production and inward investment also vary in both countries, with France creating an environment that supports the former while the UK has been particularly successful in recent years at encouraging the latter. France is a member of Eurimages, the Council of Europe's cultural support fund, which was established in 1986 and 'aims at promoting co-productions and the circulation of audio-visual works within Europe' (Littoz-Monnet 2007: 52). At present, Eurimages has a total annual budget of €25 million (Council of Europe 2014) and, according to Creative Screen Associates (2013: 4), France's membership of the scheme 'generates a 400% return on its estimated membership fee in terms of the film finance investment secured for French co-productions'. The UK, on the other hand, joined the scheme in 1992 only to withdraw in 1996 despite protests from British film-makers (Magor and Schlesinger 2009: 304). So far, successive governments of different political persuasions have failed to make a clear commitment to rejoin. Both countries are members of the European Convention on Cinematographic Co-production, however, along with forty-one other countries, with the BFI and CNC currently offering £1 million and €4.19 million, respectively, for co-production support (Creative Screen Associates 2013: 4). While these amounts are indicative of the different priorities placed on co-production by each country, co-production levels in the UK have also dropped significantly since the introduction of the new film tax credit in 2006.

The revised UK tax credit system has led to the UK devoting more effort than France towards encouraging inward investment, largely in the form of big-budget productions backed by US studios but qualifying for UK tax breaks. This approach ties in with the UKFC's (2007a: 2) latter goal 'to help make the UK a global hub for film in the digital age, with the world's most imaginative, diverse and vibrant film culture, underpinned by a flourishing, competitive film industry'. A clear focus has thus been placed on skills, facilities and infrastructure that, along with financial incentives, seek to attract high-profile foreign productions. According to Creative Screen Associates (2013: 4), France is a 'far less appealing destination than the UK for US inward investment productions' for the following reasons: the UK production system has 'closer synergies' with the US than France; French crew rates are similar to those in the UK but 'French fringes are expensive adding an additional 55 to 65% of costs' in some departments; and the production process should be undertaken in the French language if effective communication is to take place across the entire project. As noted above, similarities with the US in terms of language and systems of production has in this case been beneficial to the UK film industry in successfully encouraging inward investment.

It can be argued that the UK and French models of film policy are indicative of economic and cultural approaches to film, respectively. For example, Scott (2000: 31) notes how the fact that the French film industry is also regarded as 'an institution embodying cultural values and perspectives that well merit public support ... is a political judgement that French society has already made, firmly and unambiguously'. While the same cannot always be said of the UK, Hill (2012: 337) nevertheless states that it is 'possible to argue that [UK] film policy has rarely been a matter of economics alone but has also depended upon cultural assumptions about the significance of film for the projection of national culture at home and abroad'. Indeed, he goes on to state that this 'interweaving of policy objectives' became more evident during the UKFC's tenure as lead support body for film (ibid.).

Competing cultural and commercial objectives noted earlier within national approaches to film policy is something that we will engage with throughout the book, but it is important to note that Scott (2000: 27) believes that one of the problems to occur in relation to the French model of film support is a dramatic reduction in 'entrepreneurial risk' that 'has been notably less forthcoming in helping to shape new competitive strategies or to create new synergies of a type that might promote superior levels of economic performance'. With the continued development of new media platforms and modes of delivery for films, along with 'France's generous support system to cinema ... coming under the scrutiny of outsiders (the European Commission and the WTO)', these are just some reasons why Albertazzi and Cobley (2010: 195) describe the French model 'as a system "running out of steam"', a view shared 'even by its supporters'.

It also worth noting that some film historians such as Jens Ulff-Moller (2001) argue that equating the success of the French film industry with the state's 'cultural' policy does not stand up to detailed empirical investigation. Moller argues that the post-World War I grip that Hollywood exerted on the European (and French market in particular) through a combination of politics, diplomacy and aggressive monopolistic trade practices has never truly been challenged and that the quota system remains a blunt instrument in attempts to counter-balance Hollywood hegemony.

At a European level, the EC's review of the industry in 2014 noted that most of Europe's film industry are in fact national film industries, with little significant movement of films produced in one market crossing over into another and that there are still 'limited opportunities and incentives to internationalise projects and to target several [European] markets' (EC 2014: 7). Thus, while film polices play out within often very specific national contexts, the generic challenge of competing with a vertically integrated monopolistic industry characterised by the US model casts a long shadow over film industries across Europe, both large and small.

Conclusion: Mapping Out the Research and Book Structure

Against these broader policy debates this volume offers a specific case study of the UK Film Council and provides a probing analysis into the operation, politics, governance and performance of a public body devoted to advancing public support for film in the UK. Our study seeks to provide an engaging account of the differing passions, aspirations and hopes surrounding film policy and public funding mechanisms in the UK.

We also examine competing cultural and economic objectives and address the various tensions between regional, national, European and international interests in an increasingly transnational film industry. We aim to provide an innovative and up-to-date analysis of how a cultural funding body had to negotiate competing policy objectives over time and through shifting economic and political conditions.

At a time of political change across the UK and unprecedented advances in the technologies of film production, distribution and exhibition, this book also provides an innovative searching examination of the key implications of changing pressures, and circumstances that are often unexpected and unpredictable, affecting models of public support for film. In doing so, it unravels the strategic role that frameworks of public support can play in helping both the film industry and film audiences exploit the advantages offered by the digital age.

The book's contents are arranged under four thematic headings that build logically from one to the next: Background; Agenda for the UK Film Council; Impact; and Strategic Lessons. This chapter and the one that follows form Part I, setting out key elements of the debate and, necessarily, a historical perspective.

Part II – *Agenda for the UK Film Council* – builds on the opening two chapters by analysing the particular circumstances that precipitated and gave rise to the perceived need, in the late 1990s, for a new organisation to support film in the UK. Drawing on a wealth of original interviews with senior politicians, film executives, independent producers, industry experts and leading film-makers, it examines the key players, forces and assumptions that shaped the inception of the new body and its original sense of mission. Interviewees include Lord (Chris) Smith (former Secretary of State for Culture, Media and Sport); all three chairmen of the UKFC, Sir Alan Parker (film-maker), Stewart Till (distributor) and Tim Bevan (producer); and John Woodward (the UKFC's CEO). Chapters 3 and 4 thus trace the history of the UK Film Council (UKFC) by investigating those who drove its agenda, which objectives were prioritised and how and why the weighting of these changed over time. In particular, it examines how a national film agency relates to transnational political, economic and cultural spaces.

Part III – *Impact* – investigates and analyses the performance of the Council across a number of key parameters. Chapter 5 assesses how effective this organisation was in fulfilling its remit, in negotiating competing economic and cultural objectives and in satisfying the varying constituencies of interest that form the landscape of film provision. Chapter 6 focuses specifically on how successful the UKFC's key funding schemes and initiatives were and asks whether the organisation offered good value for money as a support body for film. Chapter 7 considers the role played by the Council in helping the UK film industry adjust to a digital environment. Chapter 8 presents a probing analysis of the Council's performance over its lifetime in relation to its key strategic objectives of advancing the economic prospects of the film production sector, promoting film culture and helping industry and audiences exploit the advantages offered by the digital age.

Part IV – *Strategic Lessons* – analyses the circumstances surrounding the decision announced in 2010 to close down the UK Film Council. Chapter 9 draws on many revealing insights provided by leading film executives, politicians and industry stakeholders, reflecting on the significance of political contexts in shaping film policy outcomes and assessing the strategic lessons for the future design of film policy offered by the experience of the UK Film Council. Finally, in Chapter 10 we draw the book together by analysing the challenges faced by cultural funding bodies in negotiating competing policy objectives over time and through shifting economic and political conditions.

Thus, the book as a whole offers a significant and timely critical overview of the contemporary policy environment for film in the twenty-first century. UK film policy has always been driven by economic and cultural concerns, with the emphasis often on the former. As new technologies and patterns of media consumption disrupt the media environment (the digital revolution) and policy paradigms move in and out of fashion (for instance, the creative industries) then the focus in film policy has reflected these broader shifts of context. The challenge for those organisations tasked with delivering on policy aspirations, has been that the state tends to expend more energy on measuring activity across short-term political cycles rather than long-term time frames.

Film policy continues to matter because it feeds into larger policy concerns regarding economic development as well as domestic and international projections of national and cultural identity. These are policy issues that resonate with the political class, which in one sense is where this chapter began. The next two chapters in the book look in more detail at the broader historical contours of UK film policy and the gestation and creation of the UK Film Council in the years up to 2000.

CHAPTER 2

Film Policy in the UK: 1920s–1979

Mr Cohen asked the Prime Minister if he will make a statement on the Report of the Working Party on the Future of the British Film Industry.

The Prime Minister: The Report of the Working Party, chaired by Mr John Terry, was published as Cmnd. 6372 in mid-January. Since then we have given careful consideration to its analysis of the position of the film industry in this country and to its proposals. The Government accepts the value of a strong British film industry, able to take its place in a competitive international market and providing audiences, here and abroad, with an up-to-date image of our society and of the quality and power of our creative artists.

We have been particularly impressed by the two principal recommendations in the Terry Report, namely the need to strengthen the industry's financial position and the need for a single new body charged with overall responsibility for all aspects of the industry's activities.

(House of Commons Debate, 29 March 1976)

The Hollywood switch has tended to turn the British film industry on for one decade and off for the next.

(Tunstall and Machin 1999: 134)

Introduction

The long forgotten Terry Report on *The Future of the British Film Industry* (HMSO 1976), set up by Prime Minister Harold Wilson almost forty years ago, highlighted the fact that the relationship between the British state and the film industry had at its core a concern with both the economic importance and the cultural role of film in British society. It is no surprise, then, to find that since the early part of the twentieth century that state intervention in the policy arena has, at differing moments, reflected and grappled with these often competing concerns. This chapter maps out some of the significant moments in the evolution of film policy as it relates to the business and infrastructure of the industry in the UK and takes us up to the late 1970s. Over this period, a clear pattern is evident in that the film industry and its specific relationship to Hollywood shaped various state interventions that were mostly aimed at buttressing an indigenous industry and also focused on growing and developing the UK's capacity to compete internationally.

The first substantial state intervention in the film industry was the inclusion of cinema in the Entertainment Tax of 1916. This positioned cinema with other areas of popular culture such as the music hall. The state was keen to derive additional revenue from the popularity of cinema through a tax on cinema tickets, yet it would not be long before various British governments realised that the state would be required to put money into supporting the industry rather than see it solely as a source of revenue for the Treasury.

The shared language with the US has clearly been critical in the relationship between the UK and US industries since the arrival of the 'talkies' in the 1920s. The UK has often been an economic bridgehead for the Hollywood industry as it strove to maximise revenues in the European market and beyond. The shared language has also become a touchstone for debates about the relationship between the film industry and aspects of British national identity, or indeed the importance or otherwise of creating a distinct 'national cinema' (Aldgate and Richards 2002; Leach 2004; Street 1997). The arrival of the talkies in the late 1920s had of course acted as an impetus for the UK industry as it could compete in the US market in a manner that was difficult for other language-bound industries, such as the French. By this time we already had significant intervention in the industry through the Cinematograph Films Act of 1927.

1920s–1950s: Managing the Market

The 1927 Act recognised the interrelationship between production, distribution and exhibition in the film industry and was driven by a need to protect the industry in Britain. In their seminal study, Dickinson and Street (1985) note how previous interventions by the state had been concerned with censorship or safety, but the 1927 Act under the auspices of the commercially orientated Board of Trade, with its imposition of quotas guaranteeing screen time for films produced in Britain, marked a sea-change in the relationship between government and industry. The Act was a response to a crisis that had seen the volume of British films being screened in the UK fall as US films became increasingly popular. British film production had fallen to a low of only thirty-seven films by 1926 (the figure had been 150 films just five years earlier) (Dickinson and Street 1985: 5). Film production would not reach such depths again until 1989, when only thirty films were made in the UK. By imposing screen quotas on exhibitors to carry British films, the 'quota quickies' were born. A British film industry that, Tunstall (Tunstall and Machin

1999: 134) argues, did not exist to any extent because of American influence in the 1920s, enjoyed an uneven period of growth into the 1930s, before flourishing in production terms during World War II as it benefited from considerable state support.

The 1927 Act was the first significant state intervention that attempted to grapple with what would become a major structural issue for film policy over the coming decades (Low 1985). The problem was that Britain lacked the industrial scale and capacity necessary in its production and distribution companies to compete with the economic might of the American industry. While The Rank Organisation perhaps came closest to competing with the US conglomerates, particularly in the 1940s, ironically it would be fatally wounded, not by the market, but by the actions of British government policy (Dickinson and Street 1985; Murphy 1992).

The post-war British Government of 1947 was experiencing a dollar crisis and as a result only allowed the Hollywood studios to extract 25 per cent of their profits from the UK economy. Given his later interest in the British film industry when Prime Minister, it was Harold Wilson, then President of the Board of Trade, who ironically was responsible for the import duty imposed on Hollywood films as Britain in the grip of a Sterling crisis attempted to retain as many dollars as it could. An American ban followed on sending US films to Britain, with Rank significantly increasing its level of film production in order to fill the gap only for the dispute to be settled and a flood of backdated Hollywood films then re-entering the UK market in 1948–9. As a result, Rank's production arm lost £3 million (Harper and Porter 2003; Macnab 1992) and the organisation learned an important lesson in attempting to compete with the US major studios. As an organisation it never took such risks again after this crisis. Andrew Marr argues that this fiasco was part of a wider political pattern becoming increasingly common in post-war Britain where

> [a]gain and again, Britain's deep dependency on the United States was simply underestimated by politicians. (Marr 2007: 108)

It also highlighted the often disjointed nature of governmental intervention into areas that impacted on the British film industry.

1936: The Moyne Committee

Dickinson and Street (1985: 47–52) document in detail the deep rooted tensions between the commercial film 'trade' and other sectors of the film industry as well as those parts of government that wanted to enhance and develop the educational and cultural dimension of film in national life, particularly during the setting up of the BFI in the 1930s. This unresolved tension between viewing film from within the frame of either economic and industrial policy or educational and cultural policy is played out again and again over the years in policy circles.

Policy also impacted on the industry in other more tangential ways. For example, the nascent years of television in the UK in the 1930s saw growing links between film companies and the new medium of television with the Gaumont-British Picture Corporation keen in 1937 to install a number of large television screens in its cinema theatres. However, while the film industry lobbied the government during the 1930s to allow it to broadcast television in its cinemas, this was rebuffed by the stronger lobby from the British Broadcasting Corporation (BBC) that viewed theatre television as a direct threat to its broadcast monopoly (Stokes 1999: 25). Significantly, it would be funding from public service television in the 1980s that would help prevent the film production sector from being wiped out as post-1979 Conservative Governments rolled back the state's role in funding and financially underpinning the film industry in the UK.

What is striking when reviewing the broad sweep of governmental intervention in the industry is the manner in which the arguments have a familiar ring regarding their key policy concerns. The Moyne Committee of 1936, for example, tasked by the Board of Trade with reviewing the success or otherwise of the 1927 Act, drew attention to financial and structural concerns that still resonate in policy circles. It noted:

> The British film producing industry has an insufficient supply of capital for its needs and … the cost of production of British films has been increased by the necessary money being obtainable only at a high rate of interest … Lack of finance is a powerful factor in enabling foreign interests to obtain control and is certainly an impediment to the industry's continued and satisfactory expansion … The Government should, as soon as may be, take such steps as may be practicable to encourage financial interests to constitute one or more organizations to finance British film production, in approved cases, on reasonable terms. (Moyne Committee Report 1936: Recommendations)

The committee was concerned with what it saw as the exhibition sector, in particular, being controlled largely by US finance; however, at the same time it sought to encourage US companies to make bigger-budget films in the UK (many US majors such as Warner Bros. Entertainment Inc. had well-established British subsidiary companies). The Cinematographic Films Act 1938 reflected the committee's thinking by extending the quota system but with greater emphasis on raising the quality of film produced in the UK. In reality, the 1938 Act had two main consequences. First, it enabled bigger budgets for British production, encouraging competition in the international film market. Second, and more significantly, it enhanced the trend for US-based film companies to set up subsidiary companies in the UK. For example, Metro-Goldwyn-Mayer Studios Inc. (MGM) quickly followed Warner Bros. Entertainment Inc. and Twentieth Century Fox Film Corporation by establishing themselves in the UK and quickly enjoyed success with films such as *A Yank at Oxford* (1938; dir. Jack Conway) and *Goodbye, Mr. Chips* (1939; dir. Sam Wood) (HL SCC 2010: 8).

1940s–1950s: British Film Success

World War II resulted in increased government support for the industry and was a period in which a number of iconic British films were released, such as *In Which We Serve* (1942; dir. Noël Coward), *We Dive at Dawn* (1943; dir. Anthony Asquith) and *Millions Like Us* (1943; dirs Sidney Gilliat and Frank Launder). These films both reflected and significantly shaped British national identity in this time of crisis (Aldgate and Richards 1994; Landy 1991; Murphy 2000). For the duration of the war, film under the Ministry of Information (MOI) was viewed as key part of the broader cultural war effort, tasked with both maintaining morale on the home front and helping people make sense of the conflict within a framework that reinforced British values and identity. Perhaps for the only time in the century, the economic value of the industry was less important from a policy perspective than the impact that cinematic representations of the war and British identity may have on a growing cinema audience that, by the end of the war in 1945, was running at 30 million spectators a week (the figure had been 19 million in 1938).

However, by the later part of the 1940s, some familiar concerns about the industry were resurfacing and again driving state policy interventions. The combination of a lack of private finance for the production of British films allied with the ever present concern at the dominance of the UK market by the US film industry helped shape the Labour Government's Cinematograph Film Production (Special Loans) Act of 1949. This Act led to the establishment of the Eady Levy, which was a tax (initially voluntary, but made compulsory by 1957) on UK box office cinema receipts with proceeds divided between the exhibitor and reinvestment in new productions. The National Film Finance Corporation (NFFC), which was to facilitate loans for indigenous film production, was the main institution to emerge after passage of the 1949 Act.

Despite these interventions and encouragement for international growth of the British industry the 1950s was a period dominated by a focus on a majority of films that tended to be either domestic comedies or war dramas. In retrospect, given the trauma of war, the success of the comedies that came from Ealing Studios (Barr 1980) was not surprising. It is also worth noting that a key figure in their success, producer Michael Balcon, was also credited as being instrumental in shaping the image they presented of Britain during the 1940s and 1950s. Andrew Marr argues:

> [Balcon] was the great interpreter of these years, second only to Churchill in crafting how the British remember themselves in the middle of the twentieth century. (Marr 2007: 119)

Most of the cinemas that attracted the growing audience in the early 1950s were US-owned ABC Picture House, run by Warner and MGM, and Odeon and Gaumont, managed by Rank, which had become closely linked with Twentieth Century Fox Film Corporation (Sandbrook 2005: 118). This was the decade that saw Hollywood investment in overseas film production decline. In addition, television was starting to establish itself as the key domestic entertainment medium, and within a decade with a public service ethos embedded in both the BBC and ITV, television offered a range of domestic drama that would mean that the cinema audience wanted something different. This alternative was of course often provided by Hollywood drama and escapism. Yet despite these challenges Murphy argues that the period after 1949 was not as bleak for the film industry as is sometimes portrayed.

> The bid to make Britain's film industry a serious rival to Hollywood failed, but there was a long and relatively prosperous Indian summer before serious disintegration set in at the end of the 1960s. (Murphy 1992: 230)

It was the start of a new environment for film-makers in the UK, one in which television would play an increasingly important role. Tunstall, commenting in the 1990s, characterised the film-makers' environment as one in which

> [they] live in the twin shadows of the Hollywood big six companies and British television. These individual British film-makers do make quite a lot of films, but their 'films' are typically low-budget productions only seen by small audiences. (Tunstall and Machin 1999: 132)

By the late 1950s, the US industry was in a position to start investing again in overseas film production with the UK once again a preferred and favoured location. As result the 1960s saw one of the periodic booms in the UK film industry, albeit one financed by US capital. The era began of what film critic Alexander Walker (1974) has called 'Hollywood England'.

At the Whim of Hollywood: The 1960s and 1970s

The 1960s offer us an insight into the paradox of the British film industry and its relationship to film policy objectives intended to sustain an industry. At one level, it is a decade of considerable success. It would be the era that introduced a number of international British movie stars such as Sean Connery, with the launch of the James Bond franchise in 1962 with *Dr. No* (dir. Terence Young) (although it would be the 1963 film *From Russia with Love* (dir. Terence Young) that would make Connery an international superstar). Other British actors were also transformed into film stars in the 1960s. Michael Caine's break came with *Zulu* (1964; dir. Cy Endfield) and *The Ipcress File* (1965; dir. Sidney J. Furie); Peter O'Toole's with *Lawrence of Arabia* (1962; dir. David Lean) and Richard Burton's with *The Spy Who Came in from the Cold* (1965; dir. Martin Ritt). British directors, such as David Lean, enjoyed further international success with films such as *Doctor Zhivago* (1965), while American directors were keen to work in Britain, often helping to consolidate the reputation of the production craft industry in the UK with films such as Stanley Kubrick's *2001: A Space Odyssey* (1968). Thus, at one level here was the international British film industry mobilising indigenous talent and often bringing a 'British' perspective to films that were successful in the US. Indeed four of the Best Picture Oscars of the 1960s were 'British' films, including *My Fair Lady* (1964; dir. George Cukor) and the musical *Oliver!* (1968; dir. Carol Reed).

Yet if one applies other criteria to measuring the success of the British film industry, it is evident that by 1967, 90 per cent of funding for 'British' films was dependent on US capital. Dickinson and Street (1985) note how the policy debates on film in the 1960s, from the 1960 Films Act onwards, were driven by Treasury concerns. They note how Lord Willis, President of the Writers' Guild of Great Britain and director of two independent film companies, when speaking in a House of Lords debate in 1966, highlighted the paradox at the core of state intervention in film policy. He argued:

> Most of our film legislation has had the effect which is the precise opposite of its intentions. Far from giving British film producers greater independence and finance, it has weakened them. And far from preventing American domination of the British film industry,

American domination was never so complete and overwhelming as it is today. (Lord Willis cited in Dickinson and Street 1985: 239)

Other film and social critics (Sandbrook 2006; Walker 1974) have viewed the 1960s success of US-funded British films as a short-lived, rather self-indulgent interlude in a long-term relationship of dependency with American capital. Sandbrook (2006: 382) argues that by 1967 the British film industry 'was in serious trouble'. While Walker (1974: 395) quotes one Paramount executive as saying, 'When the money began to vanish the American studios simply packed up and went home.' The impact of this withdrawal of US capital was evident in the decline of production across the UK film industry in the 1970s. Not for the first time this financial dependency on US capital meant that as ever the position of the industry in the UK would be subject to the vagaries and whims of the domestic US film industry.

As Dickinson and Street (1985: 240) note, from 1965 to 1971, on average the US flow of capital for film-making in the UK was running at £19 million per annum. However, from 1972 to 1979 the average flow of US capital was only £6 million. The reason for this shift was a combination of factors, including the near bankruptcy of Hollywood in the late 1960s as well as an increasing investment focus from the US studios in American television, as they attempted to alter their business model while domestic cinema audiences declined and the popularity of television continued to grow. In addition, a range of tax changes in the US meant lower returns on foreign investment and a greater focus on the domestic US market. In short, the 1970s was a difficult decade for the American film industry and, as a result, the investment that had buttressed and underpinned much of the British industry in the previous decade disappeared.

In addition to the domestic crisis in the US film industry, the 1970s was also the decade when television became the centrepiece of domestic popular culture in Britain and cinema attendances dropped and at one point appeared to be in terminal decline. The film industry in the UK became a source of location sites for US films, still keen from time to time to use studios and highly developed craft skills in Britain. It was also a location for post-production work on films, not least those with special effects at their core, such as *Star Wars* (1977; dir. George Lucas) (later retitled *Star Wars Episode IV: A New Hope*) and the lucrative James Bond franchise.

As already noted, the Labour Governments of the 1970s showed a greater interest in film policy than their Conservative counterparts, with Prime Minister Harold Wilson, in particular, keen to intervene in reshaping the policy environment. However, the broader economic crisis that faced the UK economy during this decade, and the lack of available public finance overpowered any opportunity to develop a sustained policy focus on the area of film. The Terry Report of 1976 (John Terry was managing director of the NFFC from 1958 to 1978), with its call for a British Film Authority (a forerunner of the Film Council) indicates the direction of travel with regard to policy thinking in terms of support for the industry during this period. However, these initiatives failed to find support at that time, in part due to the wider economic crisis that the Labour Government was struggling with.

Also by the 1970s, public service television drama, rather than film, was the medium that offered the dominant representations of British society, making sense of a country experiencing both economic decline and decreasing political influence in the rest of the world. While the idea of a 'national cinema' still existed in the 1970s in discussions of the role and influence of British cinema (although the supposed clarity of the meaning of Britishness would begin increasingly to unravel in this decade), the existence of a vibrant industry operating across production, distribution and exhibition was equally problematic and indeed the survival prospects of cinema in the age of television were equally unclear as the 1970s drew to a close.

Conclusions: A Complex Policy Field

We have argued in this chapter that policy intervention in the UK film industry has been sporadic and uneven over the decades. It has often been defensive in nature and shaped by the role and influence that the US industry has played both internationally but also within the UK domestic market. Policy thinking by the British state has also tended to focus on the production base of the film industry rather than on the distribution and exhibition sectors of the industry. As Jeremy Tunstall in his analysis of the UK screen industries has argued:

> British film and TV entertainment has been defensive for the very good reason that Britain from 1920 was targeted by the American film industry as a key, or the key, export market. However, although the British film industry, and later both the BBC and ITV, adopted defensive tactics, there was never (and there still is not) an effective overall British defensive strategy for confronting Hollywood. (Tunstall cited in Tunstall and Machin 1999: 129)

Another factor has been the unresolved tension within elite policy circles over the positioning of film as a distinct cultural form related to aspects of national identity and the framing of film as part of economic or industrial policy. Indeed, this division runs like a fault line through much policy thinking. The classic dichotomy between film as art or film as commerce – while remaining unresolved – has tended to mean that policy interventions for the former are often made in terms that underline the importance of the latter, not least when it has been the Treasury that requires to be convinced of the value of film.

British experience up to the 1970s suggests that the BFI had a marginal policy influence on the infrastructure of the industry (this was anyway beyond its remit), and despite various skirmishes over the direction of travel of policy, the overwhelming policy focus has been on the economics of the industry with the Treasury as one of the key shapers of film policy intervention in the UK. Despite any interventions by the British state, the film industry in the UK has never enjoyed the special status afforded it in some other European states, such as France, but neither has it been totally left to find its feet in the unforgiving environment of the marketplace.

This is not to suggest that cultural concerns are excluded entirely from the Treasury's approach. Economic logic alone may have suggested that there was not a purely financial case for any sustained support for the industry, given US dominance of the market and the lack of risk-taking in the City to support the industry. Attendant cultural arguments about international prestige have hardly been absent.

We began this chapter with a quotation from an exchange in the House of Commons about the future of the industry. The proposal, in 1976, by the Labour Government to set up a single film policy agency, the British Film Authority, that would make economic and cultural interventions (including defining British as opposed to Anglo-American films) faced opposition from various quarters and disappeared when Labour lost the general election of 1979 (Dickinson and Street 1985: 246). However, as we have argued in this chapter, when examining the policy relationship between various British governments and the film industry, it appears that if we wait long enough certain policy ideas will inevitably resurface. The next chapter traces the steps taken towards the creation of the Film Council by examining the shifts in film policy thinking that took place in the UK during the 1980s and the 1990s.

Part II
Agenda for the UK Film Council

CHAPTER 3

The Creation of the Film Council

Rationalisation of Government Support Machinery
In the longer term, the roles of the Government support bodies will be reviewed in order to ensure that their strategies are coherent and well-targeted, with a stronger emphasis on developing the film industry.

(FPRG 1998: 7)

But the worst thing, in my view, is that there ... was a pluralism and a very effective British way of working that got lost. The fact of having activity in an unorganised or not over-organised way I think is ... very helpful. And the British are very good at kind of ad hoc structures, much better than trying to design the overall body that will run everything.

(Simon Perry, film producer and formerly CEO of British
Screen Finance, Telephone interview, September 2014)

Introduction

Cultural agencies such as the Film Council may be conjured into life by governments of one colour and unceremoniously interred by those of another. The Film Council's creation owed much to the personal commitment of Secretary of State for Culture, Media and Sport Lord (Chris) Smith in the 'New' Labour Government that took office in May 1997.[1] As we shall later recount in more detail, another Culture Secretary – the Conservative Jeremy Hunt – was responsible for its peremptory demise, as a member of the Conservative-Liberal Democrat cabinet installed in May 2010.[2] These individuals' actions need to be set in the broader context of the history of British film policy outlined in Chapter 2, as well as the particular conjunctures in which they took their decisions.

The present chapter focuses on the creation of the Film Council and its immediate pre-history. In significant measure, it is a tale of the role of policy-making elites and the use of favoured forms of expertise in determining the function of public bodies in shaping the film industry. As we have seen, film policy has a distinctive, long history, in line with two persistent governing assumptions: first, an emphasis on promoting national identity through cultural expression and, second, a need to keep inventing new forms of economic intervention in order to keep the film industry alive (Magor and Schlesinger 2009). Immediately after the May 1997 election, film became a special case of a wider creative industries policy (Schlesinger 2009).

Before and After the Downing Street Seminar?[3]

A significant change in policy came in 1979 when the Conservatives entered office and Margaret Thatcher became Prime Minister. Over the course of its first five years in power, the new government set about removing economic support, thus transforming how cultural subsidies were distributed for film production. In 1981, the National Film Finance Corporation (NFFC) was restructured and its state funding dramatically reduced. In January 1983, the quota system was suspended. Then, in July 1984, the White Paper on *Film Policy* suggested scrapping the Eady Levy and the NFFC altogether to further rid the film industry of 'the paraphernalia of Government intervention' (cited in Hill 1996: 103–4). These proposals were subsequently implemented in the 1985 Films Act along with the abolition of the Cinematograph Films Council (CFC). The NFFC's assets were transferred to a private company, British Screen Finance Ltd, in which Channel 4, Cannon and Rank initially invested. Finally, in 1986, a fiscal measure, which had made films eligible for 100 per cent capital allowances in the first year, was phased out (Hill 1996: 103–4).

As John Hill (1996: 103) has argued, the removal of economic support for film production 'was not simply destructive' because the effectiveness of the Eady Levy and the quota system had become increasingly questionable. The NFFC had long been regarded as an organisation constrained by 'inadequate funding resources and ... having to function strictly on commercial lines' (Dickinson and Street 1985: 241), although it provided an important lifeline for independent producers. Meanwhile, the value of the Eady Levy fund, determined by cinema admissions, had decreased with the decline in cinema going. As producers received a proportion of the fund in relation to the box office success of a film, the fund tended to pay out to the more successful film-makers rather than those most in need. Similarly, the quota system had never proved to be particularly effective. During the 1970s, when the number of registered 'British' films dropped by half, largely due to the withdrawal of the US studios from British film production, many cinemas failed to screen the required percentage of indigenous productions (Hill 1996: 103). Meanwhile, some argued that the phasing out of the 100 per cent capital allowances tax shelter encouraged 'those with gumption and ingenuity to [find] imaginative ways out of a desubsidised environment' (Stanbrook 1984: 173).

However, as economic subsidies for film were dismantled, no alternatives were proposed. It would seem that, taken in the round, economic measures did have an impact on output as, following their complete withdrawal, film production went into decline and in 1989 only thirty films were produced in Britain (Hill 1996: 109). The US studios had returned during the 1980s to make their own films but not to invest in British films. In 1986, £270.1 million was invested in British film production but this fell to £135.7 million in 1988 and declined further to £49.6 million in 1989 (Hill 1993: 209), with film-makers relying in the main on two key funding sources – British Screen Finance and Channel 4.

On 15 June 1990, a seminar was held at Downing Street, chaired by Prime Minister Margaret Thatcher, to review the film industry and consider future issues. According to the prominent film producer David Puttnam, twenty 'senior representatives of the British film world' attended and this meeting was a turning-point for the relationship between government and the film industry.

> The seminar generated a series of proposals that eventually resulted in the establishment of a new quango [quasi-autonomous non-governmental organization], the British Film Commission, along with a £5m European Co-Production Fund and a dedicated tax break. A few years later, at the urging of Richard Attenborough, the then Prime Minister, John Major, agreed to National Lottery funds being used to support film production. (Puttnam 2010: 1)

The seminar included discussions on US inward investment and the promotion of British films abroad. The head of Universal Studios, Lew Wasserman, was invited, indicating the importance of Hollywood in any debates on the UK film industry. Moreover, the position of the industry in Europe was also considered, given the launch of pan-European initiatives. Eurimages, the Council of Europe's fund to support co-productions (Jäckel 2003: 79) began in 1988 and MEDIA I (the programme to stimulate growth and competition among Europe's audio-visual industries) in December 1990. The government subsequently set up working groups to discuss the key matters, one being the use of fiscal incentives for production investment (Headland and Relph 1991: 1).

In 1991, with the active backing of its director, Wilf Stevenson, to stimulate wider debate the BFI produced the 'UK Film Initiatives' series of pamphlets. This included Michael Prescott's *The Need for Tax Incentives*, which argued that fiscal support was essential, alongside other forms of state aid, to encourage investment in British film production and enable British film-makers to compete on a 'level playing field' with other countries offering these incentives in Europe, Canada and Australia (Prescott 1991: 4–5).

It has been argued that the momentum for change in British film policy slowed down when John Major replaced Margaret Thatcher as Conservative Prime Minister in 1991, reflecting uncertainties in the government about how best to proceed (Hill 1993: 220). Nonetheless, the initiatives put in place by Major's administration during the 1990s had a far-reaching impact on film policy into the next century. In 1992, the Chancellor of the Exchequer, Norman Lamont, introduced fiscal support for the film industry in the form of tax relief covered by a clause in the Finance (No. 2) Act. Section 42 was also referred to as 'large budget tax relief' and provided incentives for films with budgets in excess of £15 million. Also in 1992, the Department of National Heritage (DNH) was established, with responsibility for policy in culture and the arts, leisure, tourism and sport. Funding opportunities for the arts expanded with the new National Lottery established by the National Lottery. Act in 1993. Regional Arts Councils were in charge of allocating the Lottery money to film projects. The distribution of Lottery funds was initially confined to capital projects and it took intense lobbying from some, such as Wilf Stevenson, director of the BFI, to have film accepted as a capital asset.

However, the lack of private investment in the British film industry was an enduring problem and, in 1995, the then Secretary of State for Heritage, Stephen Dorrell, set up an advisory committee to explore the main obstacles to industry growth. The Advisory Committee on Film Finance, led by the banker Sir Peter Middleton, was subsequently formed with members from the worlds of finance and film. The committee reported in July 1996, pointing to structural problems in how the industry was organised, financial matters (including lack of expertise on film finance in the City) and an overall lack of communication between the industry and the City (Middleton 1996: 3). Meanwhile, the Arts Council of England (ACE) commissioned a report by Spectrum Strategy Consultants, published in May 1996. This explored the feasibility of film franchises 'expressly designed to create vertically-integrated companies' with a sustained level of output to encourage investment (BSAC/PACT 2005: 9). Following film producers' lobbying, ACE subsequently invited bids for £96 million of Lottery money. Just after the election of the 'New' Labour Government, these funds were distributed to three film franchises over a six-year period. The awards were made to The

Film Consortium, Pathé Pictures and DNA Films, which were set up in May 1997.

In retrospect, the Lottery allocated significant (but, as it turned out, insufficient) funding to support the work of the franchises. Pathé Pictures, the Film Consortium and DNA Films were part of the attempt to create mini-studios (Caterer 2011: 63; Magor and Schlesinger 2009: 303–5). The idea was to establish stable frameworks for the production, distribution and exhibition of slates of films. Vainly as it turned out, hopes were invested in the successful vertical reintegration of Pathé Pictures, the largest of the franchises, as a counterweight to the US majors (Caterer 2011: 64–8). If the would-be British studio model was highly under-capitalised, it still paid homage to the US.

Regarding the franchises, James Caterer (2011: 50) has noted that 'competition with Europe seemed to be a prime motivating factor' for the creation of this funding stream. As we have seen from the way in which Hollywood has loomed large in its history, British film policy is not conceived in isolation from external considerations, although Europe is, and has been, of secondary importance to the US. Caterer (2011: 55) further observed that 'building links with Europe or sustaining an infrastructure to sustain Hollywood blockbusters were only partial solutions to the industry's difficulties, with the big question remaining: what measures could be taken to stimulate home-grown film production?'

A New Body for New Times?

In the period that immediately preceded the birth of the Film Council, policy discussion about film in the UK frequently referred to the underperformance of British films in domestic and international markets and to how 'difficult it is for smaller countries to try and compete with the Americans' (Middleton 1996: 2.2). So the immediate context in which the idea of establishing a new body began to take shape was one in which it was widely recognised that the vertically disaggregated structure of the UK industry, with little or no integration between production and distribution, and also the generally small scale of operations of UK film companies, placed the British production sector at a disadvantage. But despite widespread agreement about the existence of these problems, there was little consensus about how they ought to be addressed (Pratten and Deakin 1999).

The incoming Labour Government had inherited Conservative policies, with the most significant one taking the shape of Lottery support for film. The establishment of a National Lottery in the mid-1990s meant that additional funds had become available to support film. Responsibility for awarding these funds was initially vested with the Arts Councils of England, Wales, Scotland and Northern Ireland. However, few of the films that received support via the Arts Councils achieved success and the predominant perception was one of general under-performance on the part of Lottery-subsidised films (Hill 2012: 336). Concern grew about what the leading Hollywood film director, Alan Parker,[4] who became the first chairman of the Film Council, has described as

> the ridiculous way that they had allocated money ... which ... led to an enormous number of really horrible films being made. Worse than that, a lot of films made that were not even actually distributed, which is the greatest tragedy of all really and an enormous waste of public money. (Alan Parker, Interview, London, March 2013)

Critical coverage in the press, led by the *Evening Standard*'s film critic Alexander Walker, whose denunciations of the Arts Council's approach to funding films were frequent and vigorous, fuelled a growing sense that the mechanisms for public support for film were in need of overhaul. Dissatisfied with how this was working, and concerned about the effectiveness of the wider agency landscape, Labour decided to pursue institutional change.

The new government immediately rebadged the DNH as the Department for Culture, Media and Sport (DCMS). In his first budget in 1997, the new Chancellor of the Exchequer, Gordon Brown, reintroduced tax reliefs for films produced in Britain with budgets of less than £15 million. At the same time, Chris Smith, the incoming Secretary of State for Culture, Media and Sport, announced the establishment of a Film Policy Review Group (FPRG) to consider and report on UK film policy (Dickinson and Harvey 2005: 420; Pratten and Deakin 1999: 43).

The FPRG was co-chaired by the new Film Minister, Tom Clarke, and – significantly – by Stewart Till, President of International, PolyGram Filmed Entertainment, whose appointment reflected the special status that global trade and distributor interests were given in the review (Dickinson and Harvey 2005; Magor and Schlesinger 2009).

As we have already noted, there is a back-story to this move. The idea of a unitary film body had been discussed in Labour Party circles in the 1970s. The committee chaired by John Terry, managing director of the NFFC – appointed by Labour Prime Minister Harold Wilson – had recommended the creation of a British Film Authority in 1976. But despite further work pursued under James Callaghan, Wilson's Labour successor as Prime Minister, the opportunity to reshape the support landscape disappeared when Labour lost the 1979 general election.

The director of the BFI, Wilf Stevenson, later to become a Labour peer,[5] revived the idea again in 1996, shortly before the new government set up the FPRG. As he recounted:

> It was the feeling that at a sort of macro level, the government of the day was trying to take too many decisions close up to themselves and they could easily be devolved if there were an agency around that could do it, and the model was the CNC (Centre national du cinéma) in France. Secondly, since the development of the Downing Street Seminar [in June 1990], we had a number of additional film bodies ... there was all sorts of activity ... There was ... to my mind an unhealthy split between the commercial sector and ... those who call themselves the film industry and the BFI was very much seen as an educational charity but not really able to speak for ... the industry. (Wilf Stevenson, Interview, London, February 2013)

In the run-up to Labour's election, Stevenson thought that the idea's time had come, especially given the party's strong creative industries policy focus, a receptive civil service and key advisers in place to follow through on this:

> The funny thing is you do these ... exercises a lot of the time and nothing much happens. But it just so happened there was the right combination of people in the department [the DNH] at the time [with whom] I shared frustrations about the way things were being done and handled. And I think, you know, [in the DNH] they were anticipating a change in government and were looking for stuff so that they can offer [something to] the incoming ministers, who had arrived, by delivery through [Chris Smith's special adviser] John Newbigin on creative industries. So, you know, there was a happy relationship but you couldn't have foreseen that would be the case. (Wilf Stevenson, Interview, London, February 2013)

Stevenson's ideal, then, was for more coherence in film policy, with a unitary body as the means to bring this about. But there were also other behind-the-scenes initiatives. One of these involved John Woodward who, after being appointed director of the BFI in February 1998, later became the Film Council's first CEO in October 1999. However, prior to running the BFI, Woodward was already a key player as the

CEO, since 1991, of the Producers Alliance for Cinema and Television (PACT). According to John Woodward, before Labour was elected, he had a

> conversation with Chris Smith where Chris said to me, 'What do you think about all these different bodies, the BFI, British Screen?' ... At that point, they had the Film Commission. And he [Smith] said, 'Well, wouldn't it make more sense to pool all the stuff together?' And we had the Arts Council, of course, by that time, obviously distributing the Lottery money ... and Chris said, 'Well, ... could you write me a paper about how you might rationalise it all?' Which I did ... It was a model for one overarching film organisation for the industry. (John Woodward, Interview, London, February 2013)

Woodward, acting on Smith's behalf, was quick off the mark. He commissioned a report from the well-known consultancy Hydra Associates, the month after Labour took office. In fact, this report did not recommend what Woodward described as 'a model for one overarching film organisation for the industry'. Indeed, it was much more equivocal about setting up a single, dominant agency and canvassed several options. The consultants described their remit as follows:

> In June 1997, the Department for Culture, Media and Sport (DCMS) asked the Producers Association [sic] for Cinema and Television (PACT) to carry out a study reviewing the current structure of public support for the UK film industry and evaluating its effectiveness against a number of other structural models, from a producer's perspective. (Hydra Associates 1997: 1)

Given later producer discontent with the Film Council, it is worth noting the emphasis on the 'producer's perspective' at this point. The entire report was intended to test producers' experience of the current support system and identify its shortcomings, as well as to establish their possible 'receptiveness to other potential structures of support for the industry'. The consultants were asked to test three options: the status quo; a single agency with separate commercial and cultural divisions; and the 'French model' of a fully integrated agency. These choices were a good indication of how the wind was blowing (Hydra Associates 1997: 45). Despite an implicit steer towards a more centralised model, the consultants noted that it was not their aim to make 'a single recommendation' concerning public support but that they had instead considered possible models drawn from the comparator group of Australia, Canada, Denmark, France and Ireland (Hydra Associates 1997: 1). The report also reflected the evident shift of government policy towards 'a more commercially focused sector' as opposed to 'producing largely cultural product' (Hydra Associates 1997: 9). On the basis of their interviews, the consultants had concluded that producers' overriding concern was with 'obtaining finance for their next production' and that 'recurring themes' were as follows:

- The need to maintain several distinct access points for development and production funding;
- The need for a co-ordinated and well-funded training policy;
- Clarification of the responsibility of all public film bodies and removal of duplication in their activities;
- The importance of having people with industry knowledge and credibility managing public film bodies;
- The importance of maintaining low-budget film-making in order to encourage the development of new talent. (Hydra Associates 1997: 5)

It will be instructive to bear these views in mind when we later come to consider some of the sources of dispute between the Film Council and disaffected producers. The consultants found considerable discontent with the Arts Council's existing approach to Lottery funding, concern at the lack of clarity about what the various existing bodies did and a desire for more coordination. But, running against the evident desire for reform,

> [t]he clear majority view was that the current fragmented structure of support suited British producers because it avoided the creative agenda that a single power base may have. (Hydra Associates 1997: 7)

According to the consultants, the producers interviewed had dismissed as not suitable for the UK as a whole the model of Scottish Screen, a body based in Glasgow set up by the outgoing Conservative Government earlier in 1997. This new agency had combined four smaller bodies, bringing together industrial and cultural development roles in one agency (Hydra Associates 1996).

Indeed, intense producer concern about the possible power exercised by a single body or dominant CEO pervades the Hydra report. We should recall that this consultancy was essentially a private taking of the temperature among one key interest group – a very vociferous one whose views would be critical to the Film Council's reputation. Producers' wish for change but only in ways that suited their interests best was also evident in the next, public iteration of recommendations about how film support should be structured.

The Film Policy Review Group (FPRG)

The creation of the FPRG was a crucial step in establishing the Film Council. As noted, the FPRG had two co-chairmen: the Labour politician and first Films Minister Tom Clarke, and Stewart Till, President of International, PolyGram Filmed Entertainment (then part of Philips, the Dutch multi-national corporation).

Tom Clarke had apparently expected to be appointed to a Cabinet post at Secretary of State level in Tony Blair's first government but, instead, he told us, was offered his pick of Minister of State posts. In his youth, he had been president of the British Amateur Cinematographers' Society. He had also been deputy director of the Scottish Film Council. He believed that the post of Minister for Film could benefit from his experience and he opted for that. For him, the objective of the Review Group was to help place the UK sector on to a more competitive footing with the US film industry (Interview, Coatbridge, March 2013).

By sharp contrast with Clarke's public sector background, Stewart Till personally embodied a rather short-lived European attempt to set up a studio on the Hollywood model. He had emerged as a key industry player in the policy field earlier in the 1990s, alongside former Columbia Pictures CEO (1986–8) David Puttnam, producer, inter alia, of *Chariots of Fire* (1981) and *The Killing Fields* (1984). Puttnam was actively involved both in background discussion of policy matters and in giving advice on the allocation of Arts Council of England film funding in the 1990s. Indeed, Puttnam's policy influence under New Labour extended across several fields (Oakley *et al.* 2014).[6]

In 1997, the year that Labour returned to power, Puttnam had sounded the alarm-bell of cultural and industrial struggle with the US film industry in his book *The Undeclared War* (Puttnam with Watson 1997). Using terms redolent of successive post-war French governments, as well as the activist leadership of the European Commission under Jacques Delors (1994), Puttnam stated that it is 'frankly dangerous to allow Hollywood's extraordinary dominance in the field of filmed entertainment' (Puttnam with Watson 1997: 349). Noting the interconnections between Hollywood and Washington and how this sold both values and goods, he advocated a similar posture for the UK and the European Union. His intervention was completely aligned with Labour's soon to be published thinking on the creative industries (CITF 1998) when he argued that 'the distinguishing characteristics of any nation or community today lie in the quality of its intellectual property' (Puttnam with Watson 1997: 353). It was time, he maintained, to exploit Europe's cultural assets as part of a global economic struggle.

Recalling the immediate context of his own appointment – rather pointedly in light of the direction of travel eventually taken by the Film Council over whose creation he had ostensibly presided – Tom Clarke approvingly cited Puttnam's critique of US domination of the international film industry: 'We had the elephant in the room in whatever we were trying to achieve. And what was that? It was the American film industry' (Interview, Coatbridge, March 2013).

As his position chimed so well with Chris Smith's views, Puttnam's opinions carried considerable weight in his background discussions with the Culture Secretary. Our informants told us that Puttnam had influenced the appointment of key players to the new Film Council's Board of Directors. Moreover, two of David Puttnam's close advisers supported work for the FPRG, and later continued to exercise major influence in policy-making circles. These were John Newbigin, then a key policy adviser at the DCMS, and Neil Watson, who became the main strategy adviser at the UKFC. It was Puttnam who, we have been told, recommended Stewart Till as co-chairman of the film policy review to Chris Smith, who described this appointment – and how these things are done – as follows:

> I hosted a reception for the British film industry and I met with a lot of the key players at that time. I decided to establish the Film Policy Review Group and to ask Stewart Till to chair it, and I announced that at the [Cannes] Film Festival [1997]. (Chris Smith, Interview, London, March 2013)

Published in March 1998, the FPRG's report *A Bigger Picture* set the scene for future change. Its main recommendations included the introduction of a voluntary industry-wide levy to support British production, placing considerable emphasis on the need to foster an industry that was more commercially self-sustaining (FPRG 1998: 4, 13). However, whereas the levy never came into force, a small clause towards the end of *A Bigger Picture* heralded what was actually to become the most significant outcome of the FPRG – the creation of a single new support organisation for film.

> In the longer term, the Government will review the machinery for providing Government support to film in light of the recommendations of the British Screen Advisory Council and other bodies. Its aim will be to establish structures which:
>
> • provide strategic leadership for the film industry and a clearer focus on its development;

- achieve greater coherence by ensuring that the allocation of resources reflects priorities and that gaps and areas of overlap in provision are eliminated;
- ensure that discretionary funding decisions are not all taken by one person or group of people.

It will look at how the roles of all the national and regional publicly funded bodies fit together and will consider whether any changes are needed in order to maximize the benefits for the UK as a whole. (FPRG 1998: 50)

Launching the Film Council

The Film Council was launched on 2 May 2000 as a non-departmental public body (NDPB), working at 'arm's length' from government, with the status of a company limited by guarantee (the sum guaranteed being the £1 provided by the DCMS). It absorbed the other public and semi-public bodies concerned with film, namely the Arts Council of England's Lottery Film Department, the BFI's Production Department as well as its regional funding role, British Screen Finance and the British Film Commission.

The creation of a new funding body offered an expedient springboard for putting into operation the chief and central aspiration highlighted in *A Bigger Picture* – 'to create a self-sustaining commercial film industry' (FPRG 1998: 4). The replacement of several film agencies with a single new body was intended to bring coherence and make oversight of a sector characterised by multiple constituencies of interest more straightforward. A highly sensitive and crucial issue surrounding the establishment of any new body with responsibilities straddling both industrial and cultural aspects of film policy was how to integrate the BFI (Doyle 2014a).

The BFI, which was awarded a Royal Charter in 1983, had been the main support body for British film since 1933 and was much respected as a cultural institution. However, by the late 1990s the BFI was struggling with a range of well-documented management and funding problems (Nowell-Smith and Dupin 2012). For instance, recurrent problems in financing the Museum of the Moving Image led to its closure. Other projects, such as the proposed National Cinema Centre, did not attract funding.

The DCMS hoped that the appointment, in January 1998, of the commercially experienced and successful film director Alan Parker as Chairman of the BFI and, a month later, of John Woodward from PACT as CEO, could help resolve these issues. Parker had two Best Director nominations, for *Midnight Express* (1978) and *Mississippi Burning* (1988), as well as being noted for directing *Bugsy Malone* (1976) and *Fame* (1980) and much else besides. He was a highly credible figure in Hollywood.

Aside from the Production Fund, now shifted to the Film Council, all remaining activities in the BFI came under the Film Council's control. Although the BFI retained its formal autonomy, it now received government funding through the Film Council, which also appointed the chairman of its board. One well-placed source believed that from the start Chris Smith had wanted to fold the BFI into the new body but was persuaded not to do so by some of its highly influential defenders (Interview 18, 2013). Whatever the truth of this, the BFI was definitely seen as needing to be leapfrogged in pursuit of the new Labour strategy. Geoffrey Nowell-Smith has argued:

> Given that focus, it was never likely that that the BFI, whose interests were, in the eyes of the modernisers, positively antiquarian, could be put at the centre of a strategy whose main aim was the development of a sustainable domestic film industry with that of film culture firmly in second place. (Nowell-Smith 2012a: 300)

The rationalisation was incomplete in other respects, too, as the devolution of political powers to the UK's 'nations' meant that – alongside the BFI – separate screen support agencies existed in Scotland, Wales and Northern Ireland. Together with the BFI, Scottish Screen, Sgrîn Cymru Wales and the Northern Ireland Film and Television Commission were all to be brought into what the new Film Council initially characterised as 'partnerships' (FC 2001) and would later describe as its 'family' (UKFC 2009b).

The basis for institutional change, plainly, had been laid prior to Labour's assumption of office, and was rapidly implemented. John Woodward told us he had been 'amused' to find the idea of a new lead agency resurfacing in the FPRG's report. His account provides an insight into how decisions, while seemingly taken as a result of recommendations made after a due process of inquiry, may in fact be largely predetermined:

> When this [*A Bigger Picture*] was published, there was a page at the back which basically, literally in the small print, that said, by the way, we are going to rationalize [the] machinery – which was never discussed at any point in the Film Policy Review by anyone. And that was a decision that had clearly been made privately. (John Woodward, Interview, London, February 2013)

Woodward recollected that he and his chairman, Alan Parker, were one day summoned to Chris Smith's office where the Culture Secretary told them that he wanted to act on the recommendation to create a unified film body. Discussions about the shape of the new body and the role of the BFI 'went back and forth' and in the end it was decided that the BFI should retain responsibility for cultural aspects of film support but be overseen by the newly established Film Council that would receive the annual grant-in-aid and pass on funding to the BFI, thus relegating that established institution to the status of a second-tier body. As John Woodward put it:

> I think that Chris was quite keen ... to get away from this kind of situation where everyone would turn up from these different organisations each year and lobby for their bit of the pie ... [T]here had to be a better and a more coherent and objective way to look at what the priorities were. Undertaken by an expert body [with an understanding of the complexities of the film industry] was going to be far better than by the Secretary of State and three civil servants. (John Woodward, Interview, London, February 2013)

Stewart Till, who had co-chaired the FPRG and subsequently joined the Board of the Film Council as deputy chairman, confirmed that it was Chris Smith who 'absolutely saw the logic of one body and simply said to the civil servants at the DCMS, I think, "Let's create it"' (Interview, London, March 2013).

Woodward believed that the merger of most existing film agencies was Chris Smith's way of demonstrating to the Treasury that there would be 'efficiency savings' in government (Interview, London, February 2013). His account suggests that Smith had been advised to rationalise existing bodies. A reasonable inference is that Smith then asked Woodward to figure out how to produce a new model, used the somewhat equivocal ideas floated through the Hydra Associates' report as a justification for change, and with the proposal now firmly lodged in his private circle, had something to drop into the FPRG's recommendations via his appointees. Setting up the FPRG, therefore, did not so much instigate a process of discovery but rather endorsed a policy position already privately established. However, this interpretation certainly is not in keeping with Smith's own retrospective account:

> We didn't come into government with the idea of creating a Film Council – it emerged out of the work of the *Bigger Picture* group, my response to the rather chaotic landscape of support for film, and the need to bring some coherence to it. (Chris Smith, Interview, London, March 2013)

Smith emphasised his pursuit of a rational process to arrive at a suitable conclusion. Inside the DCMS there was a strong sense that film policy delivery lacked coordination and that it needed strategic leadership (Interview 20, 2013). A strong lead in this direction had come from Smith's special adviser in the DCMS, John Newbigin, as well as from Neil Watson, a very close associate of David Puttnam's, who became a key strategy adviser to the UKFC and subsequently the BFI.

John Newbigin observed that what came out of *A Bigger Picture* was the idea of 'one big organisation', and, furthermore, he thought that Chris Smith knew what he was looking for and believed the Film Policy Review Group was set up with that in mind (Interview, London, February 2013). Prior to this, there had been 'high-level involvement' in the rethinking of structures by key film industry figures such as David Puttnam and also Richard Attenborough,[7] one of the UK's foremost film industry leaders and a former chairman of the BFI Governors. This underlines the importance of private conversations outside the formal review process. We may conclude, therefore, that the direction of travel was set well before the FPRG's deliberations occurred.

Rationalisation and Expertise

Reflecting on the UKFC's origins in 2010, just as Jeremy Hunt, his eventual Conservative successor, was dismantling that body, Chris Smith remarked:

> I felt there was a need for two things. One was much greater coherence – hence the idea of bringing everything together under one roof. Second, I wanted to make sure that we brought what one might call the artistic side of British film-making together with the more commercial side so that each could usefully feed off the other. (Smith cited in Macnab 2010: 3)

This encapsulates the logic of institutional rationalisation. It is based on the belief that one agency is better than many because it may concentrate resources and pursue more effective strategic action. This logic also involves a process of disavowal and of taking a distance from superseded bodies judged to be ineffective.

The pursuit of 'coherence' came about because the existing patchwork of funding arrangements was found wanting by the new Secretary of State and his advisers. But the goal of creating a single agency was not finally achieved because, as noted, the creation of the Film Council – while sweeping up some smaller bodies – left the BFI reduced and weakened, with much of the cultural remit of film policy sub-contracted by the Film Council to the older body. This affected the achievement of Smith's second goal: that of making the industrial and the cultural wings of the film sector interact. This proved difficult, Geoffrey Nowell-Smith (2012a: 300, 298) has suggested, because New Labour strategy 'really was about the creative industries', putting 'film culture firmly in second place', removing 'production from the BFI's brief' and leading to 'the subordination of the BFI to a new organisation of a totally different type'.

A Bigger Picture, with its rationalising recommendation, was published in March 1998. Woodward recalled that he and Alan Parker had met Chris Smith at the DCMS some six or seven months after he had been appointed as director of the BFI. It was made clear at this meeting that soon a new agency would be set up and that it would 'have oversight of all the film funding ... At which point, the BFI would not be getting its money direct from government ... It was a fundamental shift in the power relationship' (Interview, London, February 2013). Shortly thereafter, in August 1999, Parker was appointed chairman of the Film Council by Smith, with Woodward named as its CEO. The creation of the Film Council was a tremendous blow to the BFI, which at one fell swoop both lost its chairman and its director to the new body. During the 'shadow' period from October 1999 to April 2000, when the Film Council was finally established, the BFI's top leadership was apparently unable to come to terms with the change and ill prepared for the coming change in status, according to one key insider (Interview 22, 2013).

The decapitation of the BFI's leadership was at least in part shaped by the value accorded to the role of expertise in government by the tyros of the New Labour project, not least as so many of its leading lights either came from, or relied heavily upon, think tanks or policy advising. The creation of the Film Council was of a piece with New Labour's drive to develop the creative industries, with think tanks and input by leading industry figures mobilised to that end (Schlesinger 2007, 2009). It also came at a moment of wider institutional reinvention. This period was marked by the setting up of other bodies, such as, in 1998, the innovation-focused National Endowment for Science Technology and the Arts (NESTA, now known as Nesta) (Oakley *et al.* 2014) and, in 2003, the 'converged' communications regulator, the Office of Communications (Ofcom). In common with these, the Film Council represented what one policy adviser called 'an iconic New Labour creation' whereby an array of industry bodies was replaced by a single entity intended to bring greater strategic coherence and efficiency (Interview 18, 2013).

The installation of new forms of expertise under Labour's reform of film policy delivery entailed, first, finding fault with (and disavowing) the know-how and practice of existing agencies, and, second, placing a value on specific kinds of expertise as especially credible and effective, thus legitimising them. The next task was to find the right exemplars of the requisite embodied knowledge by choosing particular individuals to undertake the necessary task of transformation.

Chris Smith has described how he set about creating the framework for change:

> [When] I became Secretary of State – one of the very first engagements I had was to go to the Cannes Film Festival [in May 1997] and I hosted a reception for the British film industry and I met with a lot of the key players at that time. And, sort of, on the spur of the moment – it wasn't quite on the spur of the moment, but it was only, sort of, two or three days in the gestation – I decided to establish the Film Policy Review Group and to ask Stewart Till to chair it. And I announced that at the Film Festival. (Chris Smith, Interview, London, March 2013)

Stewart Till, who after his stint co-chairing the FPRG would become deputy chairman, and subsequently the second chairman of the Film Council's Board, described his recruitment thus:

> It was ... 1997, and Chris Smith was the Secretary of State for the Department of Culture, Media and Sport and he went to David Puttnam and said, 'Look, I want to review the British film industry and I want to have the Film Minister, Tom Clarke, to co-chair with someone from the industry.' And Puttnam put me forward. I had a thirty-second interview with Chris Smith on the beach in Cannes. And Chris said, would I chair it with Tom [Clarke], chair the Review Group. (Stewart Till, Interview, London, November 2008)

David Puttnam's advice was evidently crucial in identifying the required experts. Puttnam had a complex and contradictory relationship to Hollywood. He was marked by the immense influence of what – following Pierre Bourdieu (1984: 101) – we may label the 'Hollywood entertainment film habitus'. This was shared in distinct ways by several of the UKFC's board members, and certainly by all three of its chairmen (Schlesinger 2015b). Till – with his PolyGram Filmed Entertainment role (until the company folded in 1999) – represented a European attempt to create a quasi-studio-system. His deputy chairmanship of the Film Council, along with the appointment of Alan Parker as chairman, gave a strong inflection to major production house and distributor values.

Within the DCMS, Chris Smith's special adviser, John Newbigin, had led the input from senior officials. One key move by civil servants was to identify clear role specifications for the Film Council's chairman and

CEO posts to inform the development of a strategic vision and the first business plan (Interview 20, 2013). The search was on for a strong CEO and a chairman who had the weight and confidence to say what he thought. So far as the CEO was concerned, good communication skills, a strategic sense and knowledge of commercial film-making was what the Culture Secretary had in mind. The DCMS was looking for a pair that could work in a strong partnership in implementing the new turn. John Woodward and Alan Parker were deemed to fit the bill (Personal communication, 14 January 2014). Once the leadership was in place, the DCMS turned its attention to finding members for the new Film Council's board of directors. Smith was particularly keen on securing know-how and the capacity to think strategically from selected high-flyers in the film industry. Whereas the government invoked process, thereby legitimising the search for appropriate expertise in terms of explicit criteria, Stewart Till emphasised personal connections:

> I mean from the get-go, Chris Smith recruited, put together the first board almost, well, totally himself, taking some members of the Film Policy Review Group and just people he'd come across. (Stewart Till, Interview, London, November 2008)

Midway through the UK Film Council's life, Margaret Dickinson and Sylvia Harvey (2005: 425) criticised the closed process whereby the UKFC was established and noted the 'relatively limited range of interests represented on its governing body'. This stricture is borne out by our research. Moreover, its leading lights were drawn from a network of contacts around Chris Smith and his key advisers, what one very close observer described rather tellingly as a 'sort of ascendancy' (Interview 47, 2014). On the evidence, it seems, the UKFC's creation was largely decided prior to the public process that led to its official birth.

The creation of a single support body did little to ameliorate the inherently complex and multi-faceted nature of the policy aspirations surrounding support for the film sector. The Film Council made it clear that its primary mission would be to promote the industry's sustainability whereas the cultural remit was generally devolved to the BFI (FC 2001). However, tension between these differing aspects of the rationale for public support of film was inscribed from the outset in the institutional architecture of the Film Council and 'epitomised or symbolised by the awkward and very difficult relationship between the BFI and UKFC', which was to remain 'a fault line' throughout the lifetime of the UKFC (Interview 18, 2013). Attention is turned in the following chapter to the initial challenges the organisation faced as it began to find its feet and as its policy focus evolved over its lifetime.

CHAPTER 4

From 'Sustainability' to 'Competitive Industry'

Introduction

The impetus to support film is widespread internationally and has resulted in the formation of a variety of models of intervention and of agencies dedicated to implementing film policies. Such agencies, wherever they are located, are subject to expectations that reflect the complex and multi-faceted nature of the sector they are tasked with supporting. At the same time, the orientation and the sense of purpose of national film agencies is shaped by specific local circumstances and histories. This chapter focuses on the agenda pursued by the Film Council, where its sense of purpose emerged from, and how its sense of mission developed and shifted over time.

The new lead support body for film that came into operation in April 2000 was initially shaped by a distinctive and powerful sense of mission, which entailed promoting the 'sustainability' of the UK film industry (Doyle 2014a). However, this sense of purpose was to evolve over time. Reflecting a plethora of differing expectations in relation to the purposes behind public support for film, the UKFC's agenda shifted and broadened considerably over the organisation's lifetime from 2000 to 2011. In this chapter, we examine how the Council's sense of strategic direction was determined and exactly how and why the balance of objectives it pursued gradually changed. What were the key forces and assumptions that shaped and recalibrated the Council's sense of mission throughout its lifetime? In later chapters, we consider what these shifts tell us about the nature of film policy and the challenges facing bodies that are charged with enacting it in the twenty-first century.

The Original Mission

In the UK, as in many other European countries, a key issue that has traditionally shaped public policy interventions in the film industry has been concern about the dominance of Hollywood and the comparative weakness of indigenous film production. Such concerns were evident in the period leading up to the establishment of the Film Council, when, for example, the Middleton Report bemoaned the under-performance of British films and the fact that, on account of the difficulty of competing with Hollywood, '[i]n many countries, the film industry has tended to turn inwards, concentrating on making small-budget films of cultural relevance to the domestic audience without much consideration given to their wider international appeal' (Middleton 1996: 2.2). Middleton highlighted the fact that British films failed to do well in domestic and international markets, despite the potential opportunities enjoyed by UK producers since, unlike their continental counterparts, they make film 'in the international language of the cinema' (ibid.). Against this background, *A Bigger Picture* laid down a clear marker that Britain now needed to create 'a self-sustaining commercial film industry' (FPRG 1998: 4). A new and unified support body for film was to provide the means of achieving this.

So although, from the outset, the Film Council was charged with overall responsibility for both industrial *and* cultural aspects of film policy, it was universally understood that the primary mission for the new organisation was to promote industry sustainability. The goal of prioritising commercial sustainability had been set by the FPRG but this strategy was fully supported by Chris Smith, according to Stewart Till (Interview, London, March 2013). For Till, the initial focus on sustainability both reflected, and was a response to, the preceding period when allocation of support for production had been conducted with little or no positive commercial outturns and many Lottery-funded films failed to achieve any form of distribution. According to Woodward, it was essential that the new body should 'turn around' perceptions as otherwise there was a risk that Lottery funding for film may be discontinued (Interview, London, February 2013). For Till, adopting sustainability as the goal was not so much about literally trying to wean UK independent producers off public subsidies as establishing 'the right sort of aspiration' or the general sense of direction for film support policies (Interview, London, March 2013).

Phase 1: 2000–2004

At the start of its life in May 2000 and every three to four years thereafter, the Council published an outline of its strategic priorities for the next few years. The goals set out for each of the three key phases of the organisation's lifetime offer useful landmarks in relation to how the Film Council's sense of mission changed and evolved over time.

The agenda for the initial three-year phase was published in a strategic policy statement titled *Towards a Sustainable UK Film Industry* (Film Council 2000b). This document confirmed that, while the cultural role of the organisation was 'largely delegated to the BFI and its regional partners', the Film Council would itself take charge of the industrial remit. A two-stage plan of action focused on, first, using 'public money to make better, more popular and more profitable films in real partnership with the private sector' and, second, over the longer term, creating 'change within the industry at a structural level in order to create a truly durable sector' (ibid. p. 1).

Although tasked with a remit of promoting sustainability, the Council was not burdened by any historical legacy in relation to how exactly it should use its funds and so, in contrast with the funding bodies it replaced, it enjoyed an exceptional level of freedom and independence in interpreting its mission and defining its own course. As one of the initial members of the Council's board put it, the Film Council was 'given a kind of *carte blanche*' to decide what it wanted to do with Lottery funds, subject to the Lottery rules (Interview 14, 2013). But the board was composed of individuals whose viewpoints and sectorial affiliations differed, some of whom wanted to encourage more alliances between British producers and Hollywood studios and 'would have almost put all the production money into big budget stuff' and others who were more inclined to protect cultural film-making (ibid.). Nonetheless, the board played a key role in shaping the organisation's funding priorities, as explained by Alan Parker, its first chairman:

> The one significant thing I did was to help with its creation and that part of it was not easy because the industry is made up of a lot of disparate groups ... who are always at each other's throats ... The great strength of the Film Council was the fact that particularly the first board was made up of cutting-edge professional film-makers, producers, directors, distributors ... It was a single body responsible for every single aspect of film ... The stature of [people on the first board] was really significant and people listened. [T]he fundamental thing we decided was ... how we allocated funds ... We came to the conclusion that three funds and not just one were necessary. First, the Premiere Fund, which was meant to make commercial films that made a profit. Second, the ... New Cinema Fund was for cutting-edge films, which were not expected to make a profit but actually were meant to encourage film-makers who didn't really fit into the normal commercial bag. And then the third and most important thing ... the Development Fund, which was to develop screenplays. (Alan Parker, Interview, London, March 2013)

The creation of the Premiere and Development Funds signalled a marked shift in the emphasis of film support towards fostering a more business-minded and market-led approach to new production. These initiatives responded to the prognosis in the FPRG Report that the sector was too production-led and fragmented (Pratten and Deakin 1999). At the same time, the establishment of a New Cinema Fund whose purpose was to back radical and innovative film-making showed that the new body was also committed to the wider and more culturally based remit surrounding public support for film.

As chairman of the Council, Parker played a significant role in guiding the organisation through its first phase and a speech titled 'Building a Sustainable UK Film Industry', delivered to an audience of film executives in November 2002, was to become an important landmark. Parker praised the UK industry's 'world-class filmmaking talents' and argued for more skills development and investment in infrastructure and facilities. But the main thrust of his speech was that the industry suffered from having too many small companies making 'parochial British films' of limited interest to international audiences (Parker 2002: 8). He urged the adoption of a more distribution-focused approach that would enable UK film-makers to realise their commercial potential and compete more effectively in international markets. Parker also called for tax incentives to encourage greater inward investment in UK film production.

This call to focus public support more on distribution and on inward investment rather than on culturally relevant local film-making suggested a radical turnaround in where the main emphasis of public support was placed, compared with when Lottery funding for film had been dispensed via the Arts Councils. However, as Parker points out, the film industry is made up of different areas:

> We've had two industries from the very beginning and it's not a bad thing. [...] You have inward investment which relies upon our tax incentives to encourage films, mostly from the United States – very large budget films that fill our studios, and most importantly, create an incredibly qualified workforce of technicians who then can feed into, though not at the same rate of pay, but can feed into the indigenous industry. And you have the indigenous industry, which is the one that cannot survive – not just in the United Kingdom. Nowhere in Europe can it survive without government subsidy of some kind. (Alan Parker, Interview, London, March 2013)

Others on the board of the Film Council shared the view that support ought to be focused on encouraging a more distribution-led approach and, in evidence to a Parliamentary Committee concerned with film policy in September 2003, the organisation's CEO John Woodward pleaded with the Committee, saying: 'For God's sake let us make sure that production is properly harnessed to distribution' (HC CMSC 2003: 30). Evidence to that same Committee from successful UK film company Working Title Films, a subsidiary of Universal, reinforced the argument that distribution is vital to the prospects of the UK film sector:

> We believe that if you are going to be competitive in the motion picture business, not only within your own market but within a worldwide context, there is one thing that you have to tap and that is distribution. The distribution business, like many other businesses, for the film business is run out of America by the majors and that has been the case for the last 50 or 60 years. If you cannot harness that distribution, then you do not really stand a chance. (HC CMSC 2003: 21)

Phase 2: 2004–2007

The development of a sustainable and distribution-led industry remained a central objective in the Council's next strategic plan (UKFC 2004b). Publication of *The Second Three Year Plan: Funding and Policy Priorities April 2004–March 2007* coincided with the appointment of Stewart Till, until then deputy chairman, to replace Alan Parker as chairman of the board and it followed on from a consultation conducted by the organisation that suggested that its first three-year plan was viewed as being 'overwhelmingly successful' (UKFC 2004b: 5). But, for the second phase of the Council's existence (2004–7), the funding and policy priorities began to widen and a hint of this was to be found in the organisation's change of title in May 2003 from Film Council to UK Film Council. John Woodward explains that Phase 2 was when the Council was able to move beyond remedying a variety of high-profile problems that were associated with the earlier systems of Lottery support for film so that, instead, it could now adopt

> a more sophisticated structure to pump-prime the parts of the industry where we thought relatively small amounts of money could make a big difference, training and skills being an obvious one, regional development and activity being another obvious one. (John Woodward, Interview, London, February 2013)

The policy priorities espoused for the second phase of the Council's lifetime – 'to help secure economic growth and a lively and strong film culture in the UK' (Woodward cited in UKFC 2004b: 4) – exhibited much continuity with Phase 1. Once again, the BFI was allocated some

£16 million per year to perform its educational and cultural remit while substantial resources were set aside for the Council's Premiere, Development and New Cinema Funds. A new scheme to promote distribution and exhibition (for example, through specialised prints and advertising) was introduced and, following the winding down of the Lottery-funded production franchises, more funds were made available to support film at regional level via English regional screen agencies and to support the partner agency, Skillset, in delivering skills training for industry professionals. But, consistent with the aim of building industry sustainability, chief among the stated aims for Phase 2 was negotiation of long-term fiscal supports for the sector and promotion of greater inward investment in film production.

However, during this second phase of its lifetime, a key event that was to redefine the Council's sense of mission was the decision by the government to reform fiscal incentives for film. The tax relief measures introduced back in 1997 (Sections 42 and 48) to encourage more investment in production had been warmly welcomed by industry and extended twice in the 1998 and 2001 budgets (Magor and Schlesinger 2009: 12). But manipulation and abuse of the schemes was widespread and the cost of providing these reliefs was high – in the order of £600–700 million per year. According to one industry advisor, 'what went on in 2003–4 was nothing short of a scandal' (Interview 18, 2013). Critics also noted that, among legitimate film investors, the prime beneficiaries of generous UK tax relief schemes were the major US studios.

In 2004, the Treasury announced that loopholes in the existing tax arrangements for film would be closed off and that it would seek approval from the European Commission for a new and more effective form of tax break aimed at film producers. The news that existing reliefs were to be removed caused dismay among film investors and prompted Michael Kuhn of Qwerty Films in a speech to PACT in May 2005 to criticise the Council for failing to foresee and failing to adequately defend the interests of the film industry against this unwelcome shift in policy:

> To many of us it seems that this Janus-like body, representing us to the government but not representing us; representing government to the industry but helpless in light of, and blindsided by, recent tax changes, not hearing criticism, is in need of reform itself. (Kuhn cited in Gibson 2005)

The controversy surrounding a potential withdrawal from tax breaks for film had a decisive influence over how the UKFC articulated its primary role and sense of allegiance from this stage onwards. Tax reliefs were an issue concerning which many people, including some members of the Film Council's board, felt that the organisation should 'stand up to government' (Interview 18, 2013). However, a letter from Woodward, responding to Kuhn's speech, was leaked to the trade press in July 2005. It revealed that although the Council's vision for 'a more sustainable industry' included support for more efficiently designed tax breaks, the organisation had no intention of defending the existing discredited arrangements, and was 'never going to be privy to private scams perpetrated between accountants, tax funds and producers' (Woodward cited in Macnab 2005). A tension existed between those who thought that the UKFC should be the 'hand-maiden of industry' versus others 'who understood that quite properly we were an organisation operating in the public interest, funded by government' (Interview 18, 2013). This prompted John Woodward to clarify in a conference speech in 2005 that, rather than existing primarily to promote the interests and commercial strength of the film industry, the Council's main purpose was to serve the wider public interest:

> We sit between government and industry but we are not an industry body. We are a government body ... Our job is to give the government impartial advice about what is sensible ... and to try and mediate between the aspirations and ambitions of a rapacious film industry and what is achievable and realistic. (Woodward cited in Macnab 2010)

Although the withdrawal of Section 42 and 48 tax reliefs precipitated some criticism of the UKFC, the organisation's work with the Treasury to ensure continuity in this broad form of support is regarded by many as one of the Council's most significant achievements. The Film Act 2006 was to introduce a new scheme of Film Tax Credits for qualifying UK films under £20 million. According to film historian and former UKFC board member (1999–2004) Professor John Hill, 'the fact that the Treasury were persuaded to carry on with tax credits ... has a lot to do with the work of John Woodward, Alan Parker and Stewart Till' (Interview, Glasgow, March 2013). Former Secretary of State for Culture, Media and Sport James Purnell also commended the role of the Council in negotiating the introduction of suitable alternatives to Section 42 and 48 reliefs and took the view that 'getting tax breaks sorted out' was the area in which the UKFC was at its strongest (Interview, Glasgow, May 2013).

Phase 3: 2007–2011

A new planning period from April 2007 to March 2010 marked the start of Phase 3 of the Council's life, one characterised by a further widening in the organisation's interpretation of its role and responsibilities. At this stage, '[n]ot only did we decide to continue with all of our existing funding priorities, we also decided to invest an additional £5.5 million in a UK Film Festivals Fund; a UK Digital Film Archives Fund; a Partnership Challenge Fund and Digitisation and Marketing Fund' (Woodward cited in UKFC 2007b: 6–7). New support schemes announced in *Film in the Digital Age* (UKFC 2007a: 3), added to an existing array of commitments, provided testament to how the Council was progressively broadening its mandate and embracing a growing set of economic and industry imperatives, greater responsibility for cultural aspects of the film remit, as well as a more sustained focus on digital technology.

By the time of publication of the 2007 strategic plan, references to fostering a 'sustainable' industry had been dropped entirely from the rhetoric. Instead, this document spoke of developing an internationally 'competitive' industry built on skills and creativity. The Council's third strategic plan declared that '[o]ur goal is to help make the UK a global hub for film in the digital age, with the world's most imaginative, diverse and vibrant film culture, underpinned by a flourishing, competitive film industry' (UKFC 2007a: 2).

Another key development in Phase 3 was that the approach taken by the Council on allowing producers to share in the proceeds from successful Lottery-funded film projects was changed. The recoupment terms surrounding grants awarded by the Film Council were a longstanding area of concern for independent producers. The Council had traditionally taken a relatively 'aggressive' stance, insisting that any commercially successful films must repay all or most of the Lottery-funding awarded to them in the first instance, a state of affairs that was not popular with independent producers (Dawtrey 2011). However, this stance softened in the last couple of years of the organisation's lifetime from 2009 onwards.

Criticisms of the UKFC's approach to recouping returns from Lottery-funded films were based on concerns that the funding structures offered too little in the way of financial incentives for producers. According to John McVay of PACT, when the Film Council was first set up, his organisation had advocated that

> [t]his new agency should look at financing indigenous films on preferential terms to allow producers get [*sic*] corridors in their revenues

from the movies to make them more sustainable, to give them working capital, to give them money for development so eventually, over
time, if that [strategy] is successful, you get them off the public teat.
(John McVay, Interview, London, March 2013)

However, the Council had a different opinion on this matter and believed
that, as a body dispensing public funds, it was obliged to maximise
recoupment and manage carefully the reinvestment of returns from any
film projects it had funded earlier that turned out to be successful. For
John Woodward, the inclination to recoup and recycle funds into new
projects is exactly what is expected of public support bodies:

People who run profit-making companies and get subsidy to invest
in what are potentially profit-making entities, if their activities then
start to generate revenue, it seems not unreasonable for the public
purse to get that money back so it can reinvest it in other activities.
(John Woodward, Interview, London, April 2013)

Many independent producers felt aggrieved by this hard line on retaining recoupments and thought that, instead, the Council should have
offered producers access to a share in earnings recouped by the Council
on those of their film projects, which had managed to achieve some
financial success (Interview, London, March, 2013). The adoption of
a tough stance on recoupment by the Film Council – one that made it
more rather than less difficult for UK producers to earn profits from
their films – flatly contradicted the organisation's espoused mission of
boosting the financial viability of the UK industry, as far as McVay was
concerned (Interview, London, March 2013).

PACT lobbied for change and, in 2009, the introduction of a 30 per
cent 'corridor' for producers on recoupment was announced – that is, a
30 per cent proportion of profits recouped by the Council from Lottery-
funded film projects that were successful would now go to producers,
rather than all being recycled back into the UKFC's budget. This soften-
ing in the Council's position partly reflected a broader process of evolutionary change as, over time, the organisation negotiated and sought
to accommodate an ever-wider array of pressures and concerns from
across the film industry and beyond. But another catalyst was change in
the profile of the UKFC's board of directors.

The introduction of a softer line on recoupment targets coincided with the appointment of Tim Bevan as chairman of the UKFC
(2009–11). A co-chair of the leading production company Working
Title Films, Bevan was perceived as a more sympathetic advocate of
the interests of the local film-making community, having started his

own career as an independent producer. Bevan's term brought not only a more relaxed approach to recoupment but also, significantly, a much more energetic approach to digital priorities and promoting innovation and creativity. A final strategic plan covering the period from 2010 to 2013 emphasised the need 'to help ensure a successful transition into the digital age for UK film' (UKFC 2010a:8). This marked a notable reweighting of priorities, as Bevan has explained:

> When the Film Council was set up ... the Internet was young at that point. But by 2009 it [was having an impact] and so I felt when I took over ... the whole Film Council needed to have a re-evaluation – a look at what its function was and how it sat within the media landscape at that point ... I felt ...putting public money into film production should really be directed as much as possible at first and second time film-makers ... We also felt ... what needed looking at was how the new world of [digital] distribution was ... going to affect the film industry ... [We wanted to set up] an 'Innovation Fund' where people working in areas [related to new technologies] that would have substantial impact on our industry ... could apply for funding to support that. Now that never actually came to fruition, that fund, because by the time we had just elected to proceed with it, we got shut down! (Tim Bevan, Interview, London, April 2013)

At the end of a ten-year evolutionary path, the UKFC had freshly taken stock and was about to proceed with what many regarded as a more balanced and realistic appreciation of the priorities for a support body for film in the twenty-first century. However, just two months after the election of the new Conservative-led Coalition Government in May 2010, it was decided to close the UKFC with responsibility for its activities being transferred elsewhere. Bevan, whose intended new direction was stopped in its tracks, described this as 'a complete bolt from the blue'. The story of the far-reaching closure decision is discussed in detail in Chapter 9.

From 'Sustainability' to 'Competitive Industry'

From the moment that Culture Secretary Lord (Chris) Smith decided to set up the Film Council, it was clear that the intention was to found an organisation focused on bringing 'sustainability' to the British film industry (Doyle 2014a). The Film Council's first chairman, Alan Parker, was an able proponent of the merits of building industry sustainability. The establishment of the Premiere and Development Funds – schemes that favoured projects with a strong market appeal and with appeal for distributors – created suitable mechanisms for the Council to foster the more market-led approach to new production that it wanted to see. But the general approach of using public money to support film projects that were commercial, and of wooing inward investment from Hollywood, was not popular with everyone. As is discussed in more detail in the next chapter, some in the industry disagreed with Parker's characterisation of indigenous independent production as an inherently uncommercial activity while others thought the whole idea of seeking to emulate the Hollywood studios was futile in the context of the UK. Beyond the industry, a number of academic critics argued that the emphasis placed on sustainability was somehow missing the point and there ought to have been a stronger commitment to bona fide local independent British film-making (Dickenson and Harvey 2005; Wayne 2006).

Even so, promoting a more distribution-led and business-minded approach was at the heart of the Film Council's sense of mission throughout the first phase of its lifetime. However, after its first three to four years in operation, the Council started to drift away from focusing purely on sustainability. Over time there was a gradual widening out of its funding and policy priorities as is evident from the new strategic plans drawn up at regular junctures throughout its lifetime. New priorities that were added related to, for example, support for regional production, skills training, archiving and investment in digitisation both in 2004 and again in 2007. In short, the Film Council gradually took ownership of, and committed resources to, an ever-widening range of priorities. In addition, from Phase 2 onwards an earlier sense that the Film Council's primary role was to promote industry interests gave way to the understanding that the main job was, in fact, to help the government come up with sensible policies to advance the wider public interest surrounding film support.

Accompanying these developments, a strategic repositioning over time on the part of the Council was signalled by a gradual but unmistakable retreat from the term 'sustainability'. That phrase was completely absent from the 2007 strategic plan, which instead spoke of fostering a globally 'competitive' industry – a small but important change in emphasis.

One of the key forces that determined how the priorities of the Film Council were reweighting over time was its leadership. Evidence from a range of interviewees confirms that the means by which the UKFC's sense of direction was determined and recalibrated was largely through an ongoing process of dialogue and negotiation between, on the one hand, the organisation's executive management – of which

John Woodward was unquestionably the key figure – and, on the other, its board. As is typical of arrangements for the monitoring of quasi-autonomous non-governmental organisations (quangos), or arm's length bodies in the UK, the Council was overseen by a board appointed by the government (in this case the DCMS) in accordance with Nolan principles.[1] The board of fifteen members met monthly to discuss and provide strategic oversight of the activities of the UKFC. It served both as a source of new ideas about the interventions and policy direction that the Council should take and as the body that moderated ideas emanating from within the organisation.

While monthly meetings of the board provided a forum for open discussion of strategy, former participants agree that the individuals who wielded greatest influence over decision making were the chairmen of the board and the organisation's CEO. A wide consensus exists that John Woodward was an effective CEO. But his energetic and decisive style of leadership was unpopular with a few critics in the independent production community, who question whether the extent to which he personally shaped the Council's agenda, and held sway over the strategic and operational direction of the organisation, was excessive. However, in a contrary vein, many former members of the board share the conviction that it was they – the board – rather than the CEO who were primarily responsible for directing the policy and (at a strategic level) the activities of the UKFC. Stewart Till, who was on the board for nine years, including five as chairman, said:

> We had a very, very strong relationship between the board and the chief executive and the way it worked, the board absolutely set the strategy with John's input and particularly common sense ... Perhaps in other organisations the chief executive sets the strategy and the board check it, but in this case I think the board set the strategy with John's absolute consensus and agreement. And then we gave him complete freedom to execute the strategy. (Stewart Till, Interview, London, April 2013)

Evidence of the influence of successive chairmen, all of whom were filmmakers and film industry executives of exceptional international stature, can be discerned through changes in the central focus of the Council's mission, from initially promoting commercial sustainability and a distribution-led approach towards, eventually, more support for independent production and innovation. The background of the first chairman, Alan Parker (1999–2004) involved working closely with the major US studios in creating a number of globally acclaimed and popular films.

Likewise, the second chairman, Stewart Till (2004–9), had worked as a senior executive within international distribution. The third and final chairman of the UKFC, Tim Bevan (2009–11) started his professional life as an independent producer and was seen by many as a champion of the creative community. It is notable that during Bevan's term as chairman, a decisive reweighting of priorities occurred, with much more emphasis on digital technology and innovation – issues not mentioned, for example, in Alan Parker's landmark speech in November 2002 – and with a more generous line adopted on sharing returns from successful projects with independent producers.

So, to some extent, the way that the Council's agenda shifted and broadened over its lifetime reflected changes at the helm and in the composition of its governing board whereby the 'Atlanticist' orientation, which had exerted significant influence in the organisation's early days, gradually became more diluted. A reweighting of priorities also reflected ongoing processes of negotiation between many differing sets of interests and concerns, as acknowledged by Woodward:

> What the Film Council did was sit down with its board of directors and decide which parts of the film industry needed greatest attention and it allocated its resources, its time, its money and its influence proportionately. It was done in a logical, coherent way and every three years we made a new plan ... modified the options after listening to the industry and then we put the plan into process. And at the end of the three-year process we'd report back on the plan. We'd generate a new one. It was very, very transparent. It didn't mean everyone got what they wanted because there are always a plethora of voices and opinions. There are certainly sectoral interests in the film industries ... and all the different interest groups have to be weighed in the balance. But that was the job. It wasn't impossible. (John Woodward, Interview, London, April 2013)

Some critics argue that the Film Council's gradual retreat from 'sustainability' and the elevation of other priorities was motivated by a dawning realisation and acceptance that sustainability was an unfeasible objective. The strategy of trying to mimic the Hollywood approach was doomed and, therefore, the UKFC had no choice other than to reposition itself, reweight its priorities, broaden the mission and repossess aspects of the cultural remit. According to Peter Watson of HanWay Films:

> Initially [the UKFC] was very ideologically driven. They had to pull back from [the concept of distribution-driven industrial development]

about half-way through ... but that set them off on the wrong course from the very beginning ... It was set up on the idea that basically the market is the way to build up an industry. I think John Woodward realised about 5 or 6 years into it that actually that was nonsense. There was no way you could do that. That is why there is intervention and tax credits and subsidy in [almost] every single country around the world. Otherwise, there would be no film industry because of structural issues that not even a quango with a lot of money can change. And so they change[d] direction to a certain extent, 5–6 years out. And certainly they changed their rhetoric ... They had to retreat from sustainability because, even flanked by their instruments of spin ... they failed absolutely to strengthen the production side ... So they had to change their game plan. (Peter Watson, Interview, London, March 2013)

Watson's argument that building a commercially sustainable industry was never a realistic ambition seems well-founded. It is widely recognised that the inherent structural weaknesses facing the production sector in the UK, as other European countries, are not readily subject to transformation using levers such as modest levels of public subsidy. That 'sustainability' as the primary mission may excite unrealistic expectations had not gone unnoticed at the Film Council. According to John Woodward, no-one at the Film Council welcomed a terminology that promoted the view that the UKFC's core objective was to bring about a self-sustaining industry that eventually would no longer require any public investment (Interview, London, February 2013). Sustainability was 'an unhelpful word' but, as Woodward acknowledges, 'it was Chris Smith who hung that around our neck' (ibid.).

For Stewart Till, chairman of the board of the UKFC from 2004 to 2009, sustainability was never an objective intended to be interpreted literally, but rather the use of this rhetoric was about investing a much-needed emphasis on industrial development (Interview, London, March 2013). 'Sustainability' was a term that helped set the tone and general sense of direction for policy interventions under the Film Council. To the extent that this terminology was merely shorthand for the strategy of promoting the more professional and business-minded approach to film-making that ministers wanted to see, it may be argued that no clear benchmark was being established to which the Council could or should later be held accountable or from which it therefore needed to retreat.

Even so, that sustainability was dropped in favour of a more rounded set of strategic priorities is evident not only from changes in how the

UKFC articulated its sense of mission but also how it allocated its time and resources. However, it may be argued that, rather than trying to disassociate itself from an organisational goal that proved unattainable, a broadening and reinvention of the Council's remit represented the positive evolutionary course of a body that was learning through experience and adapting to a new and improved understanding of how to perform its role more effectively. This was certainly how Deputy Chief Executive Tim Cagney saw it. For him, in this rather upbeat take, the UKFC's trajectory involved a gradual widening over time in its priorities, partly reflecting how the achievement of aims in one area enabled a focus on new priorities as well as 'a natural evolution' stemming from the Council's improved understanding of which priorities a film support body ought to pursue and how best to use the tools at its disposal:

> I think [the UKFC] got a better grip ... It understood the drivers behind the film sector ... and how to pull those levers and strings. There was a mixture of things ... It was trying to develop its plans, policies, goals and aims to support various areas of the film sector. And I think that's why you see its remit expanded. (Tim Cagney, Interview, London, February 2013)

The survival of any organisation is contingent on adaptation through learning – a form of collective sense-making and interpretation in which leadership plays an important role (Greiner and Schein 1988). Survival is also dependent on the ability to innovate and reconfigure in the face of changing environmental conditions and evolving stakeholder expectations (Johnson, Scholes and Whittington 2011; Teece, Pisano and Shuen 1997). The UKFC presided over film support at a time of shifting dynamics and when industry circumstances were in transition, not least because of the development of digital technologies and online distribution (Street 2012). John Woodward believed that although in 2010 there were 'still a lot of things to be done', so far as he was concerned the organisation had already played a decisive role as a 'change agent' and was well placed to achieve more:

> Did [we] get the proportion of time and money that was spent on each component part right? My own view is that the Film Council got it far more right than wrong ... It's like any activity. The more you do it the better you get at it. Was the Film Council a better organisation in year nine than in year one? Of course it was. And that's partly about practice, partly about repetition, partly about

having tried things and found areas where the remedies work or you can do more if you can refine the remedies; [or] you find that, with the best will in the world, what was asked for simply didn't deliver anything, so you had to stop. (John Woodward, Interview, London, April 2013)

It would be surprising if the UKFC's leadership did not believe in how it had learned from experience and, therefore, largely accomplished its mission. In the next section we examine a number of different aspects of the UKFC's operations to consider to what extent it succeeded in its mission.

Part III
Impact

CHAPTER 5

Flying Too Close to the Sun?

Introduction

The objectives pursued by the Film Council and the way in which it understood and articulated its mission gradually shifted and broadened over time. In this chapter, we investigate how well the Council's evolutionary development served in enabling it to satisfy the differing constituencies of interest that form part of the landscape of film provision. How did it address the various tensions between regional, national, European and international interests in an increasingly transnational film industry? To what extent were the concerns and interests of independent producers influential in shaping the Council's approach? How effective was the UKFC in negotiating and promoting competing economic and cultural objectives? Bearing in mind how the UKFC's agenda shifted over the organisation's lifetime, this chapter considers its performance in handling the main interest groups, concerns and expectations that it needed to take into account in setting out its policy agenda.

Unified Body versus 'Monolith'

As discussed in earlier chapters, when the idea of setting up a new film support body first surfaced in the FPRG Report, the case put forward for reviewing and possibly rationalising 'the machinery for providing Government support to film' centred on how a new unified organisation could 'provide strategic leadership', 'achieve greater coherence' and help eliminate 'gaps and areas of overlap in provision' (FPRG 1998: 50). So, although the ambition that impressed itself most firmly on the organisation's initial *raison d'être* was that of boosting the sustainability of the UK film industry, the Council was also founded on hopes that a single body with a remit straddling both industry and culture would provide a more effective platform for delivery of public support for film.

The Council managed to take charge of an all-encompassing programme of responsibilities by devolving delivery of various aspects of its remit to partner agencies. As Tim Cagney, the UKFC's head of partnerships from 2005 to 2010, noted, these included the BFI, which covered cultural aspects of the film remit, Skillset, which provided industry training, and the English Regional Screen Agencies, which dealt with film-related development objectives at a more local level (Interview, London, February 2013). Drawing on partnerships is a strategy that had grown more popular as a feature of public policy delivery in the UK in the 1980s and 1990s and had become 'particularly pronounced during New Labour's administration' (Dickinson, 2010: 3). While reliance on partnerships placed particular emphasis on the need for good relations between the Council and other agencies, given the differing sectoral interests each particular body represented, tensions and strains were at times an inevitable corollary (Interview 18, 2013). According to Tim Cagney,

> When you've got a public organisation that's the lead agency, there are huge expectations [that it can] fix any problems ... There [needs to be a] balance between demonstrating leadership – demonstrating how you are trying to develop support for various parts of the film industry – whilst at the same time not owning *all* of the problems. Because, at the end of the day, this is a commercial sector and a cultural sector, as well. So ... [the] ... role of brokerage is vitally important. (Tim Cagney, Interview, London, February 2013; emphasis in the original)

A concentration of industry expertise and of funding within the Film Council enabled the organisation, from the outset, to move forward with enacting its key goal of boosting industry sustainability. Consistent with this aim, both inward investment in film and the share of the UK box office accounted for by British independent films were on an upward trend during the organisation's life (Perkins 2012: 315). The UKFC's most famous success, *The King's Speech* (2010; dir. Tom Hooper) – a film that attracted critical acclaim and earned exceptionally high returns at the box office – came at the end of its lifetime. Thus, it may be argued that the coherence and strategic leadership brought by the Film Council, as a single body, helped facilitate successful pursuit of its industry-focused agenda.

But being a single, lead body also involved drawbacks. As the locus for film support, this inevitably meant that some perceived the Council as monolithic. The style of leadership projected by the organisation was very energetic and decisive and many acknowledged that this was effective. However, some critics felt that the Council was too arrogant and not sufficiently receptive to the views of all its stakeholders. For John Woodward, being charged with overall responsibility for all aspects of film support meant that the UKFC faced image problems and criticism from those who regarded it as too centralised and controlling:

[T]he strength of the Film Council came through the fact it was unified and all of the power and influence and money … all that brain power was in one place. That made it very, very strong. The flip side of that relates to the stakeholders themselves. That can make the organisation look very monolithic and it also means that, regardless of how many funds you have and how you disperse the money into executive agencies or different departments, the organisation is seen as a 'one stop shop' and that … works against you. (John Woodward, Interview, London, April 2013)

The UKFC's status as a single entity with overall control of public support for film was not self-determined but, rather, as we have shown in Chapter 3, this arrangement reflected and fulfilled the wishes of the Culture Secretary, Chris Smith. As Woodward recollected (Interview, London, February 2013), 'Chris was quite keen … to get away from this kind of situation where everyone would turn up from these different organisations each year and lobby for their bit of the pie' and what he wanted instead was a coherent body led by industry experts (ibid.). But investing all the resource for film support in one agency left open the risk that such an all-powerful body could abuse its status by pursuing an agenda contrary to what was required of it.

What is termed a 'principal–agent problem' or 'agency dilemma' may occur when the structure of institutional arrangements is such that one entity (the 'agent') – in this case, the UKFC – is required to make decisions and carry out actions on behalf of another (the 'principal') – in this case the DCMS. The dilemma exists because the agency may sometimes be motivated to act in its own best interests rather than those of the principal (Eisenhardt 1989). A common danger in organisations exhibiting principal–agent problems and/or invested with excessive centralised or monopoly power is that, rather than pursuing the remit that they are supposed to follow, they may instead expend too much energy and too many resources maintaining their own predominant status and survival.

Despite the status accorded the UK Film Council as lead support body for film, there is abundant evidence, not least through the strategic plans that it published at regular intervals (FC 2000b; UKFC 2004b; UKFC 2007a; UKFC 2010a), that far from straying from the task at hand the Council remained focused in pursuit of its mission as a public support body for film throughout its lifetime. How that mission was understood and put into operation was shaped and recalibrated by the CEO and board through processes that were, according to John Woodward, 'very, very transparent' (Interview, London, April 2013).

Although the UKFC's executive management, led by Woodward, was influential in setting the agenda and shaping the ideas put before the board for consideration at monthly meetings, according to Woodward a 'constructive tension' existed in the relationship between management and board (ibid.). Woodward recollects that, rather than being in any way passive in discussions, members of the board were 'like big strong gorillas, male and female, who had very, very strong opinions'. Several former members of the board, including all of its chairmen, agree that UKFC monthly board meetings were characterised by vigorous and productive discussion and debate. However, others take a differing view, suggesting that meetings were 'filled with reportage' and 'the board were never really asked what their ideas were' so it 'had incredibly little influence on anything' (Interview 16, 2013). One filmmaker said that independent producers, once appointed to the board, wanted to be 'good team players' and so 'you get semi-captured, you get silenced' and become more reluctant to make public criticism of the UKFC (ibid.).

Although agreement on this is not universal, most former members of the board that we have interviewed support the view that it was they – the board – rather than the CEO who were primarily responsible for directing the policy and, at a strategic level, the activities of the UKFC. As argued in Chapter 4, evidence of the influence wielded by the board can be found by examining key shifts in the central focus of the Council's mission (from, at first, promoting a distribution-led approach towards eventually providing greater support for independent production and innovation), which correlate with and reflect changes in the chairmen of the board.

Professional versus Hubristic

That the Film Council was too centralised, controlling and 'arrogant' was a recurrent theme in evidence from independent producers. Those independent film-makers who are critical about excessive centralisation of power within the organisation also tend to be fundamentally dissatisfied with the overall strategic approach adopted by the UKFC.

Some critics take the view that, within the Council, power was too tightly controlled in the hands of just a few key figures on the board and within the senior executive management team, especially John Woodward. According to one film-maker, Woodward's ability to influence UK film policy was excessive and stemmed from how politically well-connected he was:

The Film Council was completely the brainchild of John Woodward who at [inception] was an extremely unpopular CEO of the BFI … The idea of everything being distribution-led … was his mantra … [He managed] … to create this quango, that somehow usurped the BFI and British Screen … through being … an organ of the New Labour/Cool Britannia propaganda machine, and understanding the political game brilliantly, and being a very, very effective operator, John Woodward managed to ingratiate himself and sold the whole concept of the UKFC. (Interview 30, 2013)

Contrary to what is suggested above, most of the evidence we gathered indicates that it was the wishes of Chris Smith that were key to the establishment of the Film Council and its original *raison d'être*. That said, as we have shown in Chapter 3, John Woodward was certainly centrally involved in some discussions about the new organisation's formation. In the view of some independent producers, this enabled Woodward to create organisational structures and processes at the Council that concentrated strategic decision-making power at the top end and largely in his own hands. One leading independent film-maker (Interview 16, 2013) suggested that the set-up adopted by the Film Council conformed with an 'hour-glass' model – typically, a three-layer structure with a strategic elite at the top, a constricted span of management at the middle level and functional departments beneath (Kreitner 2009). An hour-glass structure locates power in, as well as pressure upon, the pivotal intersection point between top and bottom, where middle managers are accountable to the strategic visionaries above and responsible for overall coordination of activities at group level below (Buchanan *et al.* 2003).

As Henry Mintzberg (1983: 1) has remarked: '[A]nyone interested in understanding organisations and how they end up doing what they do' cannot ignore the importance of power. Where this is located depends largely on organisational structure and where decision making is located (Pfeffer 1981). The broad structure adopted by the Film Council (see Figure 5.1) – with strategic decisions passed from board of directors to the CEO, from the CEO to the senior management team and then from executive management to functional departments – is typical of public sector organisations. This simple departmental structure provided clarity in relation to the chain of command, decision-making processes, areas of responsibility and accountability.

Within this structure, the chief executive's office was unquestionably a central presence acting as the primary vector via which ideas and decisions about what the organisation should be doing were transmitted

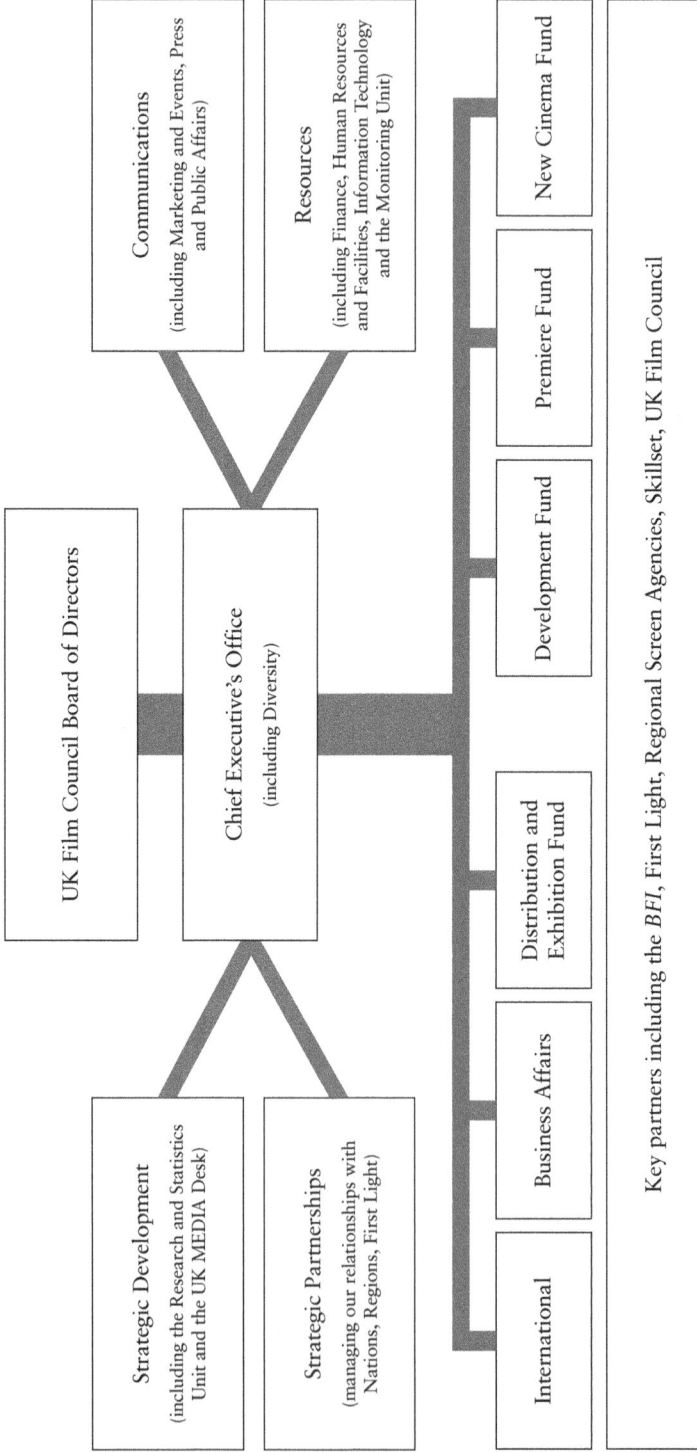

Figure 5.1 UKFC organisational structure.

Source: FC (2003: 33).

UK Film Council Board of Directors

Chief Executive's Office
(including Diversity)

Communications
(including Marketing and Events, Press and Public Affairs)

Resources
(including Finance, Human Resources and Facilities, Information Technology and the Monitoring Unit)

Strategic Development
(including the Research and Statistics Unit and the UK MEDIA Desk)

Strategic Partnerships
(managing our relationships with Nations, Regions, First Light)

International

Business Affairs

Distribution and Exhibition Fund

Development Fund

Premiere Fund

New Cinema Fund

Key partners including the *BFI,* First Light, Regional Screen Agencies, Skillset, UK Film Council between the board and the management. For some, this 'all-powerful' role for the CEO inevitably placed an unhealthy constraint on criticism from independent producers and, in turn, on accountability. According to one independent producer:

> [Woodward] was ten years in post. He was unchallengeable ... Nobody was prepared to speak out publicly. There was no dissent. No-one would say anything because, you know what, their livelihoods depended on this. (Interview 30, 2013)

Woodward played a leading role in the command chain but, as he points out, 'that's the job of the chief executive' and maintaining tight leadership control was appropriate 'because the chief executive in the end is responsible for it all' (Interview, London, April 2013). Interviewees we spoke to from across the film sector and including several former UKFC insiders generally agreed that the style of leadership provided by Woodward as CEO was energetic, decisive and highly effective. Woodward points out that, while offering strong leadership, he also oversaw processes for initiation and implementation of strategy, which were 'iterative' and enabled the UKFC's policies to benefit from the expertise of relevant individual members of the board and executive management (ibid.).

The level of power wielded by individuals within organisations may stem not only from organisational structures but also from a variety of factors including personal reputations, differential levels of access to information flows, participation in networks and political knowledge (Kilduff and Krackhardt 2008). Success and achievement in the role of leader of public sector or arm's length bodies has in recent years arguably become less dependent on sector-specific expertise than on possession of a set of more generalised qualities and competencies, including 'good interpersonal skills' and 'the ability to fashion and communicate options for the future' and, most crucially of all, 'political skills' (Dickinson 2012). Thus, the prevailing sense of the UKFC's CEO as a powerful leader may reflect not only the conspicuous experience and expertise that qualified Woodward for this role, being a former chief executive both of PACT and of the BFI, but also Woodward's own endowment of personal qualities and competencies conducive to accretion of power in the context of contemporary public sector leadership in the UK.

Critics who felt that that power within the organisation was excessively centralised also complained of arrogance on the part of its senior executives and too much 'spin'. As Peter Watson of HanWay Films put it, the Film Council was 'an organisation drowning in hubris' (Interview, London, March 2013). According to Watson:

> It strutted the stage of film and media very confidently. There is no doubt about that. And it was extremely good at publicizing itself ... at describing the successes of the film industry and British cinema in a way many of us didn't recognise. It was very good at claiming responsibility for the good news and for associating itself with the highlights during the decade it was in power, as it were. But it wasn't very good at actually looking at some of the failures ... that continued to beset the industry. Most of them are structural and it didn't really do anything to try and address that. (Peter Watson, Interview, London, March 2013)

The extent to which the Council devoted itself to sustaining positive publicity about its strategic approach and performance was reflected even in the layout of its premises. In Peter Watson's disenchanted view:

> If you looked at the physical geography of Little Portland Street where they had their HQ, John Woodward's office ... was flanked on the one side by the press office and on the other side the statistics office ... And they were his two most important instruments of spin. (Peter Watson, Interview, London, March 2013)

One Film Council insider conceded some validity to criticisms that the organisation sometimes focused excessively on 'spinning of the evidence' (Interview 18, 2013). On the other hand, all publicly funded bodies are under pressure to demonstrate to their political paymasters and the wider public the ways in which they are successfully fulfilling their remit and providing value for money (Knell and Taylor 2011). It is notable that, for example, Arts Council England, which is similarly required to justify the way in which it uses public funds to support the arts, regularly commissions impact studies and reports that confirm the value of its interventions.

Another area of perceived excess concerned high salaries for senior executives. Disquiet had been triggered right from the start when, in 2000, the inaugural head of the Premiere Fund was appointed at a salary of some £180,000 per annum. The Council justified high payments on the basis that, to attract talented professional film executives, it needed to pay something approaching market rates. Woodward pointed out that the UKFC was 'utterly transparent' about salaries and expenses and since appropriate procedures were followed for oversight by 'DCMS, who approved all the senior salary packages through to the Board of Directors who looked after the annual budget ... [There was] nothing to be ashamed about' (Interview, London, April 2013).

Even so, payment of high salaries in a public sector context where problems including 'multiple principals, the difficulty of defining and measuring output, and the issue of the intrinsic motivation' call into question the appropriateness of such incentives is problematic (Ratto and Burgess 2003: 23; Van Thiel and Leeuw 2002). Moreover, in the words of one industry expert, high salaries created the wrong perception among independent producers who often have to live a 'hand to mouth' existence (Interview 14, 2013). According to one producer (Interview 12, 2013) the pay that senior executives in the UKFC were awarded was set at 'probably 30 per cent more than the market rate'. High salaries contributed to an abiding perception, particularly among independent producers, of an organisation that was fatally prone to arrogance and hubris. As one interviewee put it:

> One signal failure at board level was allowing the executives within the Film Council structure to behave towards the constituency without the necessary level of consensual respect ... There was an extremely arrogant assumption that the executives knew better than the constituents they were serving – which was ironic because that's where they were all recruited from. (Interview 12, 2013)

Only towards the end of the Council's life were steps beginning to be taken to address levels of executive pay. By this stage, the perception had taken hold of an agency in which top personnel were overpaid – a pattern commonly to be found among quangos and that contributed to a view that, as a class, these bodies lacked appropriate governance and were a suitable target for government cost-cutting campaigns (Gash and Rutter 2011).

Satisfying Complex and Disparate Constituencies

The core mission for the Film Council at inception was to promote the commercial sustainability of the UK film industry. A dominant concern around that time was how 'difficult it is for smaller countries to try and compete with the Americans' (Middleton 1996: 2.2). So, to ensure that the new body was suitably configured to address the long-standing problem of under-performance on the part of British-made as compared with Hollywood films, much of the responsibility for initial development and oversight of the Film Council was vested in the hands of two film executives – Stewart Till and Alan Parker – who had achieved very considerable success within the Hollywood model and could bring this expertise to bear. Not surprisingly then, diagnosis of the problems facing the UK film industry by the Council was inflected by a keen appreciation of strategies seen as conducive to the commercial success to the US major studios. Written evidence from the Film Council to the House of Common's Media, Culture and Sport Select Committee during Phase 1 of the Council's life pointed to a number of lessons to be drawn from the Hollywood experience:

> As the commercial success of the US film industry demonstrates, a winning film industry is distribution-led ... Distribution 'pulls' production and the combined efforts create a significant profit-centre. Unfortunately, the indigenous commercial UK film industry remains resolutely production-led ... In the UK, films are not 'pulled' into production by a single distributor or sales agent with a global reach, but 'pushed' into production by highly entrepreneurial producers ... As a consequence, the linkage between the production base and the cycle of market exploitation (cinema, DVD/video, pay/free TV, secondary markets) is structurally weak ... This industrial structure also fails to deliver a consistent flow of films such that risk can be spread across a slate of projects ... Obviously, this approach also does nothing to build the significant corporate structures which are essential to achieve a sustainable industry. (HC CMSC 2003: 18–19)

The approach of seeking to learn lessons from the Hollywood studios, although broadly regarded as a sensible way of promoting the commercial acumen of the UK industry, was not universally accepted as being the most appropriate strategy for public support of film in the UK. Some independent film-makers thought that attempting to copy the Hollywood studio model – in which both the scale and the corporate structure of vertically integrated film companies with multi-national distribution subsidiaries and sufficient resources to produce large portfolios of films every year are significant success factors – was futile in the UK context, not least because of the small scale of resources available to support UK film-making (McVay, Interview, London, March 2013). As far as international trade in audio-visual products and services is concerned, it is widely accepted that, realistically, 'there is little prospect that the unique circumstances that have given rise to the predominance currently enjoyed by United States exporters will be repeated elsewhere' (Doyle 2014b: 325). Yet, particularly during Phase 1 of its existence (2000–4), the Film Council placed a strong emphasis on emulating the distribution-led approach of the Hollywood studios as a means of enabling UK films to compete more effectively in the global marketplace.

Emphasis was also placed on promoting inward investment in UK film production activity, particularly from the US majors, as a means of strengthening the skills base and infrastructure of film-making in Britain. More collaboration with the Hollywood majors was intended to improve the competitive positioning of UK film producers in an increasingly transnational film industry. However, not least since attempting to turn the UK into the 'Hollywood of Europe' (Mulgan and Paterson 1993) may prove an elusive goal, some took the view that a more culturally driven agenda for film, in line with the interventionist approach of European public support bodies such as the CNC, would amount to a better and more appropriate use of limited public funds (Dickinson and Harvey 2005). According to John Hill (Interview, Glasgow, March 2013), who served on the board from 1999 to 2004, although some weighting was given to the need to address cultural issues, there was little or no sense of affinity with European approaches to film support. For example, most board members were against the UK rejoining the Council of Europe's European Cinema Support Fund scheme, Eurimages, and the 'pro-Hollywood position' of key figures such as Stewart Till exerted a strong influence. As Hill put it: 'I think British film industry leaders sit uneasily within the European film industry – they identify themselves with Hollywood.'

In 2002, Alan Parker argued in his landmark speech to film-makers that 'the evidence from too many years is clear that our producers are never going to build the companies which will form the basis of a successful film industry' (Parker 2002: 9). In Parker's view, the industry needed to reinvent itself by getting away from having too many small companies 'delivering parochial British films' and instead it should adopt a much more demand-led distribution-focused approach to film production (Parker 2002: 6, 9). The inherent logic of the argument that making films with popular appeal is the first step to commercial success is difficult to fault. Nonetheless, the implication of Parker's speech was that too often film-making in the UK was driven by the self-indulgent vision of producers, rather than by concerns about likely market demand. This caused upset and concern in some quarters. According to one prominent film-maker:

> [I]n my view [Parker's speech] was completely wrong headed ... He
> and John Woodward got it completely wrong ... And many of the
> initiatives that were taken thereafter were trying to follow through
> on that policy and it was all going in the wrong direction ... [There
> was] a sort of a prejudice against producers and the production
> companies ... He said, 'I think it's time everybody realised that pro-
> duction companies can never make viable businesses.' Now there
> were a lot of quite viable production companies sitting in the audi-
> ence thinking, 'Hang on a minute!' ... A lot of people were appalled.
> (Interview 16, 2013)

The fact is that promoting a more distribution-led approach as seen
as part of the core ideology of the Film Council created an inevitable
tension between the organisation and one of its core constituencies –
independent producers. The designation of independent production as
an inherently uncommercial activity was regarded by some producers
not only as inaccurate but also, in practical terms, as unhelpful to the
image of a sector that, as the Middleton Report (1996) had confirmed,
already suffered from a range of difficulties that impeded its efforts to
attract private sector investment.

Alan Parker acknowledged in his speech that British producers were
good at making culturally significant films and he argued that it was not
a case of supporting either commercial or cultural film-making because
both are part of the ecology of the film industry. However, the main
thrust of his argument was that production activity in the UK needed
to be much more closely based on making work that appealed to distributors and international markets. His rationale as to why change was
needed was blunt:

> We need to abandon forever the 'little England' vision of a UK indus-
> try comprised of small British film companies delivering parochial
> British films. That, I suspect, is what many people think of when they
> talk of a 'sustainable' British film industry. Well, it's time for a reality
> check. That 'British' film industry never existed, and in the brutal age
> of global capitalism, it never will. (Parker 2002: 9)

Many independent producers disagreed with this prognosis and,
more fundamentally, they regarded the direction being taken by the
Film Council as ideologically ill founded. Some, such as John McVay

(Interview, London, March 2013), were concerned by an apparent lack of sympathy towards the cultural aspects of supporting film and believed that the main purpose of public support for film ought to be to promote creative and culturally relevant local film-making rather than 'looking to emulate the Americans'. Others were sceptical about trying to ape the US approach but without any of the key advantages of structure and scale enjoyed by the Hollywood majors. According to Peter Watson of HanWay Films:

> John Woodward and Alan Parker came up with this whole concept of distribution-driven industrial development, which became sort of like an article of faith ... That set them off on the wrong course from the very beginning ... Alan Parker despised the whole culture of film-makers being supported by the state [...] and believed the only thing would be to operate as a commercial film-maker ... He helped make the UKFC face away from Europe where so many of our film-makers had developed long-standing relationships and a support network... and told everyone that the only way for us to compete was to follow the [Hollywood] studio model. But without any real understanding of what it involved to be a studio which is a globally integrated distribution entity with billions of dollars of capitalisation. (Peter Watson, Interview, London, March 2013)

Moreover, the notion that intervention should be targeted at supporting distribution rather than production and that funding should be channelled towards commercially promising film activities rather than at production of culturally worthy content, where prospects were comparatively poor, raised fundamental questions about the rationale and purpose underlying public support for film. As one prominent film-maker argued:

> [W]hat is the point of an intervention in the film industry if it's not the *making* of the films? ... Actually, when it really comes down to it, it has to be seen, in part, as a *cultural* intervention, otherwise why are we bothering? There are other industries that you could subsidise with less money and that would probably employ more people. We don't employ that many people. It's quite expensive. So actually, why are we doing it? [I]t is ... economic ... but it's *also* a cultural issue. (Interview 16, 2013; emphasis in the original)

One of the difficulties facing the Council in managing its relationship with independent film producers was that, given its widely publicised remit of promoting 'industry sustainability', it was commonly understood that the primary *raison d'être* of the organisation was to support the interests of industry. But the film industry does not consist of film-makers alone. 'Industry' is a term that encompasses a number of different sectors from production to distribution to exhibition and the concerns and interests of these sectors are not identical. According to one well-informed insider, many in the distribution and exhibition sectors felt that the UKFC was too 'supplier led' and concerned with the interests of producers (Interview 18, 2013). But the latter are not a single unified constituency and so, even were the Council's efforts confined to supporting production, it still faced a complex array of competing pressures in relation to how best to direct its support. For example, whereas some producers were calling for tax breaks to be framed in such a way that cultural stipulations would not deter inward investment, others were less convinced about the merits of directing public support towards major international players and wanted to see more emphasis on support for genuine local British film-making (Dickinson and Harvey 2005; Wayne 2006).

The strain faced by the Council in managing its relationship with industry and in juggling its allegiance to industry versus other key stakeholders – in particular, the government – was exemplified by a dispute that broke out in 2004 about reform of tax breaks. In the face of a threatened withdrawal of generous tax incentives for investment in UK film, many UK film-makers made public their view that the Film Council really ought to be 'standing up to government' to prevent any potential cuts in tax breaks. However, John Woodward took the view that the UKFC, as a publicly funded body, had no business trying to defend discredited tax breaks and, in a conference speech to industry in 2005, he made clear that the Council's main job was, in fact, to help the government come up with sensible policies to advance the wider public interest surrounding film support.

Although, from Phase 2 onwards, the Council sought to project itself as a neutral and independent body whose purpose was to champion the public interest, this self-image is somewhat contradicted by the agency's close identification with the need for a much more business-minded and market-driven approach to film-making. A recurrent source of friction between the Film Council and independent producers was the recoupment terms surrounding grants that it awarded. Many complained that, although part of a publicly funded body, the Business Affairs Department of the UKFC behaved as though it was a commercial studio, setting itself high targets for rates of return from Lottery-funded films that made a profit and refusing to allow producers any share in the Council's recoupments. According to independent producer, Peter Watson:

> [A]ll the terminology they used ... and the way they comported themselves was more like studio executives than people who were there with a public service ethos ... They were extremely tough with producers on terms of trade ... They demanded aggressive positions when it came to credits on films ... They fought producers tooth and nail to get the best recoupment position for their money ... In squeezing the producer that way they weakened the producer ... They were obsessed about the recoupment targets. (Peter Watson, Interview, London, March 2013)

The criticism that senior executives comported themselves more like Hollywood executives rather than public servants was symptomatic of a more fundamental aspect of the model of support model embodied by the UKFC that many regarded as problematic – that is, its evident devotion to economic and commercial priorities over and above cultural ones, notwithstanding acknowledgement of film's cultural importance within the rhetoric of its strategy statements. The Council's funding schemes included the New Cinema Fund, which provided some opportunities for radical and culturally significant film-making, but most resources were channelled into the Premiere and Development funds whose purpose was to support distribution-led work and encourage a more market-driven approach to production.

By and large, the cultural aspects of the film support agenda were devolved by the UKFC to another agency – the British Film Institute (BFI) that, for decades, had been the main support body for British film and was historically well regarded as a cultural institution. But this 'divvying up' of responsibilities and the relegation of the BFI to the position of a sort of 'junior partner' of the UKFC meant that, from the outset, there was tension inscribed within the institutional architecture of the Film Council – a tension epitomised by what many interviewees described as 'a very awkward and very difficult relationship between the BFI and UKFC' – a tension that was to remain as 'a fault line' throughout the life of the UKFC (Interview 18, 2013).

Film Support: A Challenging Mission

Support bodies for film must juggle the interests of several differing constituencies of stakeholders. But this challenge is a typical feature of public sector bodies who generally, as agents, 'have to serve many masters'

(Ratto and Burgess 2003: 6). Film support bodies that are 'unified' also face the challenge of 'an expedient but unhelpful bifurcation of film policy and a tendency for it to be conceived as either/or: either industrial and charged with economics and sustainability, or cultural and concerned with public value and audience engagement' (Mansfield 2009: 5). Reflecting the differing and sometimes competing priorities associated with cultural industries, prevailing models of support for film often attract criticism for placing too much emphasis on commercial as opposed to cultural aims, or vice versa (Bintliff 2011). While the use of public funds to support films that fail to generate large audiences is criticised by some, others argue that support should be directed solely towards films of artistic and social merit rather than in pursuit of commercial and industrial goals (Goodridge 2010). Reconciliation of the inherent tensions between industrial and economic versus cultural goals is a persistent and knotty challenge for film support bodies.

Trying to satisfy all stakeholders with an interest in public support for film is difficult, not least because of the complexity of the film industry and the numerous differing sectors and constituencies of interest, all of which expect to be prioritised and respected (Mansfield 2009). As Alan Parker has remarked, it was problematic for the UKFC to be stretched across numerous facets of supporting film support and to have a 'finger in every single pie' (Interview, London, March 2013). A related challenge is that of managing relationships with key stakeholders. Friction concerning a threatened discontinuation of tax reliefs in 2004 showed how some were critical of the UKFC for not being strongly enough on the side of industry and its commercial interests. Others, however, argue that the Film Council was 'in its upper echelons populated by industry people with a strong Atlanticist orientation' and the agency ought to have had stronger commitment to independent film-makers (Wayne 2006: 63).

For bodies involved in dispensing public funds, some level of disaffection, particularly among applicants whose funding requests have been rejected, is to be expected (Marquis and Marquis 1995: 171). Even so, as one close to the action concedes, the 'style' in which relationships with independent film-makers was handled was problematic. According to Tim Cagney, CEO of the UKFC from 2010 to 2011 and subsequently appointed deputy-director of the BFI:

> Definitely one of the lessons the BFI has taken on board is to constantly engage, constantly ensure that we are really listening to what people have to say ... [A]t times the Film Council was probably accused ... of slightly operating in a vacuum. Was that the intention

of the board and the senior managers? Definitely not! But I think as things start to get much harder and more thinly spread, those questions come up. (Tim Cagney, Interview, London, February 2013)

Challenges encountered by the Council in managing relations with key stakeholders were to some extent indicative of the disparate nature of its client industry. A reweighting in the priorities it pursued over time reflected ongoing processes of negotiation between differing industrial concerns and cultural aspects of film support that were also integral to its official remit. Not only did the Council need to juggle its dual priorities, it also needed to foster good working relationships with other organisations with whom it operated in partnership to deliver its objectives. A key partner for the UKFC was the BFI, which, as we have noted, was primarily responsibility for delivering on cultural aspects of the film remit. As we shall explore further in Chapter 9, that relationship played a key role in the UKFC's demise.

Given the multi-faceted and complex nature of the agenda associated with promoting film, another challenge facing public support bodies is to manage expectations carefully. Aspirations on the part of the New Labour Government of growing the UK's creative industries meant that, for the Film Council, economic and industrial priorities were naturally going to be uppermost and there were high hopes that, tasked with promoting sustainability, the new body would transform the UK film industry's commercial prospects. However, as discussed in Chapter 8, despite some successes, such ambitions proved to be excessive and the UKFC's general approach to film support was subject to criticism for failing to address concerns and complexities surrounding excessive reliance on inward investment from Hollywood (Dickinson and Harvey 2005).

The following chapters analyse more closely the performance of the Council across a number of specific parameters. Chapter 6 homes in on the UKFC's production funding schemes and asks how effective these were in enabling the organisation to fulfil its remit. Chapter 7 considers the role played by the Council in helping the UK film industry adjust to a digital environment. Did it do enough to encourage successful adaptation towards, and exploitation of, the major changes in technology affecting film production and distribution that have taken place in recent years? Chapter 8 completes our analysis by drawing on data from a number of secondary sources to assess how effective the schemes and interventions used by the Council were in terms of achieving its objectives.

CHAPTER 6

The Production Funds

Introduction

Whereas several aspects of the Film Council's remit were delegated to partner agencies, one core aspect of its mission over which it retained in-house control throughout its lifetime, and which provided an essential and ongoing expression of its general approach to film support, was the allocation of public funds for film production. This chapter examines how, after taking over the administration of Lottery funding from the Arts Council of England and also incorporating film investment bodies (British Screen Finance and the BFI's Production Department), the Film Council managed and organised the allocation of public funding for film.

The Council separated the public funds available for film into three separate streams. Emphasis was placed on hiring expert professionals from industry to head each individual fund. In this way, the UKFC worked to position itself, as Tanya Seghatchian (head of Development Fund (2007–10); Head of Film Fund (2010–11)) argued, as a 'vanguard organisation' seeking to professionalise an independent sector that had seemingly become reliant on state handouts (Interview, London, January 2014). However, as suggested by the differing perspectives examined in this chapter, this strategy for the invigoration of the independent sector, although distinctive and in some respects effective, was by no means universally well received at all times.

Here, we trace how the Film Council's funding schemes took shape and developed over time and consider how effective these funds were in enabling the agency to satisfy its remit. This chapter examines how the wider objectives of the Film Council were translated into each funding scheme and the role that was played by the key individuals appointed to head each scheme. It reflects on how relations between the fund heads and the independent film sector developed over time. It also considers why, from an initial strategy of dividing the funding into separate streams, the Film Council eventually switched to a merged or single production fund – a model that, following the demise of the UKFC, has continued to find favour with the successor body now responsible for overseeing allocation of funds for film production, the BFI.

UKFC Funding Streams: Phase 1

On opening its doors in April 2000 as the lead agency for film in the UK, the Film Council assumed responsibility for the British Film Commission (BFC), established in 1991 to promote inward investment, plus three other existing bodies investing in film production. The most established of these was the BFI's Production Department (previously Production Board), which had become a stand-alone department in the 1970s and 'specialised in experimental and low budget material' (Wickham 2003: 9). The BFI had been involved in film funding and production as a 'minor and rather unofficial activity' since the 1950s (Dupin 2012: 197). British Screen Finance (BSF), on the other hand, was set up by the Thatcher Government in 1985 to replace the National Film Finance Corporation (NFFC), created by a Labour Government, and resulted in what Simon Perry (Macnab 2013), CEO of the organisation from 1991 to 2000, describes as 'an accidentally interesting model of private/public partnership'. With Rank, EMI Group Ltd, Channel 4 and ITV Granada as investors, the company received a direct government grant of £2 million per year over its lifetime for its main production fund, and a further £2 million annually to administer the European Co-Production Fund (Fowler 2002: 220). This relatively small amount was invested in producing films considered to be additional to what the market may support and in building alliances with Europe (Simon Perry, Telephone interview, September 2014). In contrast, the Arts Council of England's Lottery Film Department had only been in operation since 1995, when Conservative Prime Minister John Major introduced Lottery funding for film and gave responsibility for distributing it to the Arts Councils of England, Wales, Scotland and Northern Ireland.[1] In addition to investing in individual film projects, the Arts Council of England (ACE) set up the film production franchises scheme in 1997, which allocated £92 million of funding to three franchises over six years (Caterer 2011). The UKFC became responsible for administering the second half of the scheme from 2000 onwards.

In terms of the reorganisation and reallocation of Lottery funds, the model adopted by the UKFC can be considered distinctive on two levels. First, it separated Lottery funds into three different streams in the form of the Development, New Cinema and Premiere Funds and then, second, hired industry professionals to head each one. By delegating decision making for investment to qualified professionals (FC 2000b: 14), the organisation distanced itself from its predecessors in a number of ways. For example, ACE had lacked expertise in film-making and thus outsourced decision making to a committee. As explained by one such member, Fiona Clarke-Hackston (Interview, London, February 2013) of the British Screen Advisory Council (BSAC), the committee met once a month having spent all weekend reading paperwork for no remuneration but felt bound by Lottery constraints as to the types of project they could approve. This led to some questionable decisions that, as outlined by Petley (2002), were seized on by the media.

British Screen Finance, on the other hand, had less money at its disposal than the Lottery proceeds distributed by ACE. Yet Fowler (2002: 220) argues that BSF nevertheless made 'good returns on its investments by European "subsidy" standards' as its production loans were not 'soft' and it only invested the minimum amount required for a film to be made. According to Perry (Telephone interview, September 2014), this approach resulted in a consistent 50 per cent recoupment rate that was then reinvested in production while its development funding also performed well, with about 30 per cent being paid back in contrast to the normally expected rate of 10 per cent. Over the years, however, British Screen's success became synonymous with Simon Perry's leadership, a situation that, according to Jenny Borgars (Interview, London, December 2013), who worked for both BSF and the UKFC, was 'both the joy but also the problem with [the organisation]' because decision making appeared to lie in the hands of just one individual. This is despite the fact that before the creation of the UKFC, it could be argued that a number of gatekeepers existed within Britain's film funding landscape due to the variety of investment bodies in operation.

The BFI's Film Production Department had a long history of supporting cultural films and had gained particular success at certain points over the years (Dupin 2012). However, it lacked experience of investing in commercial film-making and, as indicated by Alan Parker (Interview, London, March 2013) who was chairman successively of the BFI and the UKFC, there was a feeling that as a large organisation it was too big to affect change quickly. Set up as a smaller body bringing in industry expertise and with a decidedly commercial outlook, the UKFC sought to usher in a new era of public support for film. From the outset, however, this attracted criticism, with the supposedly 'lean' structure of the nascent body questioned. In a House of Commons debate following its first year of operation, Conservative MP Peter Ainsworth (Hansard 2001a) raised a question regarding the number of staff employed by the UKFC and how this compared to the total staff of the bodies it had subsumed. Culture Secretary, Chris Smith, stated that the Film Council employed seventy-three staff, fifty of whom had transferred from previous bodies on 1 April 2000 (see Table 6.1). This meant that the UKFC employed an additional twenty-three staff, although it was noted that these included 'finance, business affairs, policy and industry training

Table 6.1 Number of staff employed by existing UK film bodies in 1999 and 2000.

	April 1999	April 2000
British Film Commission	11	11
Arts Council of England's Lottery Film Department	11	13
British Film Institute's Production Department	9	11
British Screen Finance	17	15
British Film Institute*	445	403
BFI externally funded staff*	48	71
Total	541	524

Source: Hansard – Written Answers (2001a: Column 202W).

*In respect of all but British Film Institute figures, these relate to the numbers of staff transferring into the Film Council on 1 April 2000.

functions which previously either did or did not exist as activities or were functions undertaken by external lawyers and accountants or by other departments within the Arts Council or the British Film Institute' (ibid.).[2]

Ainsworth (Hansard 2001b) again raised a question later in the year asking 'how many representatives of the Film Council attended the latest Cannes Film Festival; at what costs to public funds; and how many new British films were screened at the festival'? On this occasion, the new Culture Secretary, Tessa Jowell, stated that twenty-eight UKFC and BFC staff had attended the Cannes *Marché*, the commercial film market that runs parallel to the main film Festival, at a cost of £66,500, while 100 British films were shown or promoted. The suggestion of profligacy on the part of the Council will be further examined in Chapter 8, when staffing and efficiency are considered. However, at the time, it was reported that some UKFC staff felt the criticism of overstaffing was unfair because 'the level of submissions for project funding far outweighs supposedly equivalent posts under the old structure, possibly due to the Council's higher profile' (Minns 2001). Moreover, the recruitment of dedicated finance and business affairs staff, as outlined above, was also a key element of the administration of the Lottery funding streams, as the Film Council sought to pursue a relatively aggressive recoupment strategy in an attempt to return substantial net profits. With this in mind, we next examine the UKFC's introduction of three high-profile funding schemes in the form of the Development, New Cinema and Premiere Funds.

Development Fund

In the first instance, the decision to create a fund purely for film development was particularly welcomed by industry stakeholders. In 1998, the Film Policy Review Group identified a lack of support in this area as a major weakness within the UK film industry. With an allocation of £5 million per year (reduced to £4 million from 2004 onwards), the Development Fund became one of the largest of its type in Europe and was headed by Jenny Borgars, previously a development executive for British Screen Finance. While this suggests a degree of continuity with what had gone before, BSF had a much smaller budget and only developed material with a view to investing in the production itself (Finney 1996: 23). In contrast, the Development Fund 'was not set up to be an exclusive conduit of material to the Production Funds, but rather to engage with as broad a spectrum of the industry as possible' (UKFC 2005b: 5).

Through its slate funding initiative, the Development Fund invested not only in individual projects but also a range of production companies. This was an attempt to create more 'sustainable' production companies and thus satisfy the UKFC's wider objective. As producers within the UK independent sector tended to work on a project-by-project basis, slate funding offered production companies a larger sum of investment (from £50,000 to £0.5 million over the years in which it operated), which could be used to hire staff, create a culture of development and essentially build a slate of projects to work across at any given time. For Borgars (Interview, London, December 2013), the slate funding initiative occurred in two distinct cycles, with the initial approach simply being to back a range of producers, leaving it 'entirely in the producers' hands' as to how best to utilise the money available to them. The second cycle, however, launched in 2004 with an investment of £2.5 million per year for three years, 'centred on seven experienced, robust companies' with the capabilities and expertise in-house to achieve the following:

- Manage an increased level of development spend (averaging £0.8 million per year);
- Bring in matching finance from the industry;
- Bring in collaborative relationships with distributors and sales agents;
- Offer a series of new doors for a diverse range of producers and talent to access development funding;
- Rise to the challenge of converting projects regularly. (UKFC 2005b: 2)

The difficulty with the Development Fund, however, both in terms of slate funding and individual projects, was that the development process occurs too early in the lifecycle of a film to judge effectively whether the investment had been a success. As Borgars (Interview, London, December 2013) noted in relation to slate funding in particular, 'If you really want to build a company that can work, you give them funding over ten years. You let them fail miserably for a while and then they will start to get it.' However, even the Lottery film franchises that occurred during ACE's tenure were only funded for six years with success usually coming during the latter stages of the agreement or, indeed, once the funding had been concluded (Caterer 2011).

Examples of films that the Development Fund invested in during Borgars's tenure and that went on to be successful include the critically acclaimed *The Magdalene Sisters* (2002; dir. Peter Mullan), winner of the Golden Lion at the Venice International Film Festival, and *Kidulthood* (2006), which performed particularly well at the box office with young audiences, a traditionally elusive demographic when it comes to UK film. While *The Magdalene Sisters* went on to secure production funding from the New Cinema Fund, *Kidulthood* attracted investment from outside the UKFC. Notably, Jonathan Glazer's 2014 film, *Under the Skin*, featuring Scarlett Johansson, was in development for such a lengthy period that it first received UKFC funding from Borgars in 2005. Again, this demonstrates the time it can take before being able to judge whether an investment has been successful although, as demonstrated by the objectives above, the conversion of projects was not the sole aim of the fund, which also included developing talent, skills and production companies.

New Cinema Fund

The New Cinema Fund was allocated £5 million a year to support new talent and encourage innovative film-making through the use of digital technology for low-budget features and short films (FC 2000b). It also had a strong commitment to 'working with filmmakers and funding bodies in the regions and Nations' and those who have been traditionally marginalised or under-represented within the industry (UKFC 2005a: 7). This type of fund was more of a continuation of the work carried out by the BFI, BSF and ACE, with its focus on low-budget features (that rarely went above £3 million), innovative film-making and working with talent outside the mainstream. Producer Paul Trijbits (Telephone interview, December 2013) was selected to head the fund, having built a reputation for producing films of this kind, in the form of Richard Stanley's *Hardware* (1990) and Danny Cannon's *The Young Americans* (1993), which he described as 'quite commercially minded [and] aiming at a wider, younger audience', thus differentiating them from 'the movies people were generally making in Britain [at the time]'.

The original Film Council Board set up the three funds. However, they lacked a detailed brief so that each fund head was able to determine how best to utilise the money available in accordance with the wider aims of the organisation. Trijbits (Telephone interview, December 2013) took the view that the New Cinema Fund should create 'multiple points of entry for talent; new talent, existing talent ... talent we know, talent we didn't know' and while producing single features was always a key aim, he also set out to create a broader talent base through a number of short film schemes. This included a nationwide Digital Shorts programme run by the nine newly established Regional Screen Agencies as well as the more bespoke Cinema Extreme for advanced film-makers.

By way of response to digital developments, the New Cinema Fund supported low- and micro-budget projects, such as Bille Eltringham's experimental *This is Not a Love Song* (2002), which was majority funded by the UKFC and was the first UK film to receive a 'simultaneous Internet and in cinema premiere' (UKFC 2005a: 6). This was in addition to introducing a pilot scheme enabling both first-time and more established directors a space in which to experiment with the film-making process, and the Moving Image Initiative, a partnership with ACE aimed at creating opportunities for 'innovative work by film and video artists for cinema and new distribution platforms' (UKFC 2005a: 7).

The New Cinema Fund had a number of successes in developing feature film talent during Trijbits's tenure. For example, he invested in *Bloody Sunday* (2002) by Paul Greengrass, who went on to direct two films in the *Bourne* film franchise, and *Red Road* (2006) by Andrea Arnold, who was awarded the Jury Prize at Cannes for this, her first feature, and also her follow-up film, *Fish Tank* (2009). The groundbreaking documentary, *Touching the Void* (2003), directed by Kevin MacDonald, was an example of the type of experimental film-making encouraged by the fund, while the award-winning *A Way of Life* (2004), the debut film by Ghanaian-British director Amma Asante, demonstrated its commitment to diversity, with Asante going on to direct the acclaimed period drama *Belle* (2014), dealing with race and class in eighteenth-century Britain.

More than the Film Council's other funding schemes, the New Cinema Fund built on the work of predecessor bodies to the Film Council in engaging with European film-making. By 2005, seventeen of the thirty-three films supported had been co-productions while the Fund also co-sponsored the Rotterdam International Film Festival Lab, CineMart and the Berlinale Talent Campus (UKFC 2005a: 4). The latter, as the world's biggest training event, was particularly important in terms of developing and supporting talent, with the New Cinema Fund being a major contributor together with Creative Skillset.

Premiere Fund

The Premiere Fund had a larger allocation of £10 million a year (reduced to £8 million from 2004 onwards) to facilitate the production of popular mainstream British films and 'attract significant audiences at home and abroad' (FC 2000b: 14). This was perceived as a relatively new approach, which sought to encourage the production of profitable films, a difficult thing to achieve even for Hollywood studios, which are able to spread risk and generate revenue through various streams. It was particularly tricky in the UK context, given the strict guidelines in Lottery funding. For example, as outlined by Caterer, ACE and BSF had attempted something similar in the mid-1990s through the experimental scheme the Greenlight Fund:

> The idea behind this fund was to attract directors of 'international repute' into the industry through larger awards made to films between £3 million and £10 million ... However, the Greenlight Fund was difficult to reconcile with British Screen's policy of 'additionality', the idea that 'Money could only be granted if the film would otherwise not be made.' (Caterer 2011: 22)

If a film was supposedly commercial with a relatively high budget and key talent attached, then the market was expected to oblige with funding.

Simon Perry (Telephone interview, September 2014) views this slightly differently, however, stressing that by encouraging the production of 'high-profile, culturally British films by experienced directors', the aim of British Screen Finance's Greenlight Fund was to 'stem the talent drain to Hollywood'. For Perry (ibid.), this 'clear cultural objective' differed from the Premiere Fund, which instead sought to support 'mainstream commercial films'. As Caterer (2011: 113) goes on to suggest, the UKFC was able to adopt such an approach just five years later as the concept of 'additionality' had become 'less politically charged', while the solicitation of projects, 'once considered a dangerous step towards "croney-ism"', was now regarded as strategically vital to the success of Lottery funding for film. Nevertheless, in contrast to the Development and New Cinema Funds, the rationale behind the Premiere Fund was trickier to defend with regard to the distribution of public money, therefore the focus was as much on 'attracting audiences' as on generating profits (FC 2000b: 14).

The Premiere Fund's head was Robert Jones, who had been the executive producer of *Sirens* (1993), *The Usual Suspects* (1995) and *Hard Eight* (1996). He also had experience of film distribution, acquisition and financing. With an original investment ceiling of £1 million per film, the aim was to invest in eight to ten films per year, ranging in budget from £1 million to £8 million. However, one of the first awards made by Jones was of £2 million to the costume drama *Gosford Park* (2001) by Hollywood director Robert Altman, a decision that proved prudent as the film not only went on to win an Oscar, a Golden Globe and a British Academy of Film and Television Arts (BAFTA) award but had also fully recouped its UKFC investment by 2003. This early success was crucial as it gave the new body the hit film it needed and began to generate more positive media coverage for Lottery funding for film. Yet it raised questions as to whether this was the kind of film a national public body should be funding.

This was followed by further awards that broke the original investment ceiling of £1 million, most notably the animation *Valiant* (2005; dir. Gary Chapman) (£2.5 million), family film *Five Children and It* (2004; dir. John Stephenson) (£2.1 million), *The Constant Gardener* (2005) (£1.9 million) by Fernando Meirelles and Mike Leigh's *Vera Drake* (2004) (£1.2 million). Of these, the latter two performed best, attracting numerous awards and critical acclaim while also recouping part of their investment. Other films were not as well received, however, such as the controversial *Sex Lives of the Potato Men* (2004; dir. Andy Humphries), which was awarded more than £1.5 million from the Premiere Fund and was dubbed 'one of the worst films ever made' (Humphries 2004). Hill (2012: 339) explains that although it was defended by the Film Council 'on the grounds that it would appeal to young working-class males rather than middle-aged, middle-class critics (and the film did, it seems, eventually turn a profit on the back of video and DVD sales)', it also demonstrated 'how the funding of a film on an apparently "commercial" basis could nonetheless attract considerable hostility from the very same newspapers that had previously lamented the lack of commercial success of Lottery-funded films'.

Criticisms

A number of criticisms were made in the independent film sector with regard to the administration of the Premiere and New Cinema Funds in particular. One such criticism was the fact that both Trijbits and Jones were given executive producer credits for the films they had chosen to invest in despite dispensing public money. In our interviews with each of them, they took the view that, as practitioners, they had been hired for their production expertise and were actively involved in making the films happen by helping raise the necessary finance. Being able to do this, rather than simply 'ticking boxes', as phrased by Jones (Telephone interview, December 2013), was what made the role attractive but it nevertheless attracted controversy within the independent sector.

Exception was taken by some to the UKFC's ' "commercially aggressive" attitude to British producers in fixing recoupment on the Premiere and New Cinema Fund at 50 per cent and 25 per cent respectively' (Mansfield 2009: 20). Not only did this lead to difficulties with commercial financiers who 'refuse to subordinate their recoupment positions to "soft" money (i.e. subsidy)' (ibid.), but there was also a developing argument that producers should be incentivised by being able to 'share' in recoupment through either a producer corridor or 'locked box' system (Olsberg SPI 2010). It is important to highlight, however, that although this recoupment strategy differed from that of ACE and the BFI's Production Department, British Screen Finance's production loans were also not offered on 'soft' terms and subsequently led to a good return on investment (ROI).

A third point of criticism concerned limiting tenure periods for the fund heads to allow for a diversity of gatekeepers. While the importance of this was recognised by CEO John Woodward (Interview, London, November 2008), he similarly acknowledged that a fixed period was never really 'formalised' from the outset, leading to Borgars, Trijbits and Jones being in post for between five and seven years before changes were eventually made. These points of criticism had a significant impact on relations between the fund heads and the independent film-makers they were there to support, something that we will consider before going on to examine Phase 2 of the funding streams in more detail.

The Rhetoric of the UKFC: Insider and Outsider Perspectives

In the course of almost fifty interviews with UKFC board members, senior executives, policy-makers and film industry stakeholders, contrasting perspectives emerged. There was a sharp contrast between how those inside the organisation viewed the UKFC and the opinions of the wider film community. While seemingly obvious, these diverse perceptions were important because as a leading policy body the UKFC performed a dual role: it provided strategic leadership for the industry while also acting as a Lottery distributor, investing in particular projects, schemes and initiatives. Yet, the organisation often struggled to articulate its position to the various constituencies that make up the wider UK film industry, a difficulty highlighted by the DCMS in its 2007 Peer Review (cited in Olsberg SPI and Barratt 2010: 93): 'Should [the UKFC] promote film production generally or protect British film? It should do both, whilst improving relations with smaller, indie producers.' It was the relationship with the independent sector, which was largely reliant on public funding for production, which proved the most difficult, with independent producers being particularly vocal in their criticism of the organisation.

Producer Tanya Seghatchian, head of the Development Fund from 2007 to 2010, perhaps best summed up how the UKFC sought to see itself when she described it as a 'vanguard organisation':

> It was the first and only time, really, that there was a cohesive group of people who were going to act as change agents for the benefit of the industry as a whole, and to take on board all the interested parties and all the vested interests and enable us to create a viable cross-sector industry. (Tanya Seghatchian, Interview, London, January 2014)

Jenny Borgars, who preceded Seghatchian in the same role, similarly explained how, from its inception, the UKFC

> deliberately took a stance to say, 'We are a shining new beacon for how public money is going to be invested in film', and a very aggressive stance in effectively saying, 'These are the flaws that we judge in the industry as it stands [and] there are things we are seeking to change and address.' (Jenny Borgars, Interview, London, December 2013)

These views were echoed by Robert Jones (Telephone interview, December 2013), head of the Premiere Fund from 2000 to 2005, who said, 'From an internal point of view, I think, at the beginning, there was a real crusading sense amongst many of us because it felt like there was a ship that needed turning round in the way things were approached in the industry.'

This discourse, which highlights the need for 'change' within the industry and for particular 'flaws' to be addressed (in addition to Jones's nautical metaphor), is also encapsulated in Parker's (FC 2000b: 1) foreword to the agency's first public statement in which he declared, 'Sometimes within the UK film industry it's hard to know if we're waving or drowning.' While many saw this rhetoric as 'brave' or 'bold', in that it was explicit about shaking up the industry, others felt it tipped over into 'arrogance' or 'hubris', with these being the most frequent terms to come up in interviews with UK independent producers, some of whom had also served on the UKFC board at one time or another. According to one such producer and board member:

> There was the feeling that the UKFC arrived and they were the professionals, because they were largely people who had come from the studio system where money is never an issue, everything is well capitalised, decisions can be made quickly. (Interview 16, 2013).

For those working in the UK film sector then, an under-capitalised industry relying on public subsidy, what resulted was to a certain extent an 'us and them' situation, making it difficult to work collaboratively with producers, as explained by another producer and board member (Interview 12, 2013). John McVay (Interview, London, March 2013), CEO of PACT, supported this view, explaining how, in his opinion, UKFC executives were essentially saying to the indigenous production sector, 'We will give you money but you're not making the sort of films we think you should be making' and that this, to him, 'is hubris of the worst sort in any kind of public agency'.

It was important, therefore, to establish carefully policed tenure periods for the funds so that they did not become associated with particular individuals or be seen to promote certain types of projects. The introduction of new fund heads between 2005 and 2007 offered an opportunity to re-evaluate the rationale behind each one and deliberately pursue new strategies. In doing so, Phase 2 saw the end of executive producer credits and the recruitment of fund heads with different backgrounds and skill sets from their predecessors. In 2007, the UKFC also agreed along with the BBC and Film4 that the new tax credit 'should accrue to UK film production companies in order to help achieve the Government's policy of creating sustainability in the UK film production sector' (Mitchell 2007). However, the 'locked box' system, or rather the pool of money recouped from a successful investment that 'the producer can draw down for the development of future projects' was only introduced after responsibility for film in the

UK had passed to the BFI (Mitchell 2013). As outlined below, these changes resulted in a slight shift in the rhetoric proclaiming industry expertise, which had been the defining characteristic of the UKFC's distribution of public funds, to a clearer acknowledgement of the public service element of the role, as well as an attempt to create a more supportive environment for the independent sector by providing smaller investment across a wider range of projects. It also demonstrates the importance of key individuals to the direction and style of the funds as, after the new wave of fund heads had been installed, relationships with the independent film sector appeared to strengthen over time.

UKFC Funding Streams: Phase 2

At the Development Fund, Jenny Borgars was succeeded by Tanya Seghatchian. As producer and director of the award-winning British film *My Summer of Love* (2004), she had also been instrumental in bringing the *Harry Potter* franchise to the big screen. A practitioner with first-hand experience of the development process, her appointment demonstrated the UKFC's desire to delegate decision making to qualified professionals. However, discussing her reasons for joining the agency after being involved in one of the most successful franchises in film history, Seghatchian (Interview, London, January 2014) underlined the 'public service' nature of the role, viewing the UKFC as 'absolutely the environment in which I'd be able to give back to my industry'. Seghatchian was largely welcomed by the independent sector due to her attempts to provide more autonomy for those film-makers securing investment from the Development Fund:

> My primary objective was to create a distinction between the first-timers and newcomers who I felt needed more support ... and the more experienced individuals who I felt could probably manage things very effectively on their own ... So I put in a distinction between first-time screenwriters and filmmakers, and experienced practitioners, which hadn't existed before. (Tanya Seghatchian, Interview, London, January 2014)

This approach arose from having been involved in the process from the 'other side' as a producer, when she would have appreciated further intervention from funders or indeed felt more experienced than those providing investment. Applications from emerging talent were assessed quarterly while those from more established practitioners were reviewed on a rolling basis. Furthermore, rather than work primarily with producers, there was also an attempt to allow writers and directors to generate their own material independently (Mitchell 2007).

During her tenure, Seghatchian also revised the Development Fund's approach to slate funding, replacing it with the Vision Awards scheme. The original slate funding initiative was in some ways reminiscent of ACE's film franchise scheme, albeit on a much smaller scale, and over two cycles it exchanged an initial 'hands-off' style for a more 'market-driven approach', highlighting specific objectives. Seghatchian (Interview, London, January 2014) still thought that while the initiative had been 'useful for the period it had been in place ... [awards] were essentially favouring the bigger companies with relationships with distributors and sales companies built in'. In an attempt, therefore, to use public money to create more diversity in the independent sector, the Vision Awards sought to invest less funds across more production companies if they could 'demonstrate strong talent relationships and a [particular] vision [that filled] strategic gaps in the industry' (ibid.). It is difficult to ascertain the overall success of the Vision Awards under Seghatchian, given that they were only introduced in 2008, but the BFI has continued with the scheme since assuming responsibility for Lottery funding in 2011.

The practice of less investment across a wider range of projects and companies was to characterise Phase 2 of the UKFC's funding streams. For example, at the New Cinema Fund producer Trijbits was replaced in 2006 by Lenny Crooks, who came from a public sector background, having run the Glasgow Film Office (GFO) and established the Glasgow Film Fund (GFF) that successfully leveraged public and private investment for film production. In contrast, perhaps, to his predecessor, Crooks (Telephone interview, January 2014) not only saw himself as a public servant but was explicit about the fact that those employed by the UKFC should be aware of their public service role: 'My view, coming in, was that the funds had begun to overlook the public service element, becoming a little bit studio-like.' In part, he felt this had diminished the distinction between Premiere and New Cinema Fund films, as the latter had begun to move towards the 'centre ground'.

In an attempt to reconnect with the original objectives laid out for the fund in 2000, namely to discover new talent, utilise digital technology and work outside the mainstream, Crooks said that he sought to invest in a wider range of lower budget films:

Before handover, the average budget for a New Cinema Fund film was £2.7 million and [the UKFC] put over £550,000 into each film. After I came in, the average budget was £1.1 million and we put in but nothing substantive had yet been developed. For example, the Digital Cinema Initiative (DCI) was a consortium of the major US studios that attempted to set an agreed standard for digital film, allowing ease of screening of digital content. Although set up in 2002, it would be 2005 before they issued their DCI Specification version 1.0 that set out technological requirements for screening digital cinema. Being DCI compliant was viewed as important in the scheme. An early intervention into digital cinema in Sweden, for example, suffered as a result of equipment not being DCI compatible and being thus unable to show Hollywood films.

Significantly, neither Buckingham nor Perrin was an expert in digital cinema; rather both, by their own admission, were industry strategists and not technologists. Perrin notes that having decided on digital cinema

[w]e set about learning about it. We went to manufacturers, we went to conferences, we spoke to technical experts to try and learn a bit about it. This was in the pre-DCI days. There were good, solid, high-definition projectors in those days, but they were 1.3k, not the 2k or 4k you see today ... We spent a considerable time figuring out how could we harness the potential value of digital cinema to achieve our objectives ... We came up with the concept of the digital screen project, which was, basically a way of spreading digital geographically, so that there was a representation of digital in most places around the country. (Steve Perrin, Interview, Sheffield, November 2013)

Access, rather than digital development, was initially a key driver in the development of the Digital Screen Network. As Steve Perrin argues:

A lot of people, I don't think deliberately but perhaps understandably, misinterpreted our objectives. Our objective was not to promote the concept of digital. We saw digital cinema as a tool to achieve our aims and objectives. However, one of the spin-offs was that the UK got this taste of digital, began to think about it, and started to accommodate their thinking to it. So, that was one of the spin-offs. But we did not set out to convert the world to digital. We said, here's a technology, we can use it as a means to an end. (Steve Perrin, Interview, Sheffield, November 2013)

The original conception was simple, but in reality masked a myriad of complex logistical and technological challenges. At its core was the economic calculation that it was cheaper to make and distribute a digital film than a 35 mm print film. John Woodward reflected:

£350,000 ... that gives the numerical sense of us pulling away from the centre ground, and that gave us a greater space in terms of perception between what the New Cinema Fund and the Premiere Fund was. (Lenny Crooks, Telephone interview, January 2014)

As we will demonstrate in Chapter 8, there was a sharp increase in low- and micro-budget film-making over the decade in which the UKFC was in operation, partly due to the rise in digital technology and a challenging financial market (Northern Alliance 2008). In collaboration with Film4, the New Cinema Fund selected Warp X to set up a low-budget film studio, which launched in 2006 and closed in 2013. During this period, Warp X produced a slate of ten low-budget features, including the critically acclaimed *Tyrannosaur* (2011; dir. Paddy Considine), *Berberian Sound Studio* (2012; dir. Peter Strickland) and *For Those in Peril* (2013; dir. Paul Wright).

Applicants to the New Cinema Fund were required to present a clear festival strategy, as this was considered the best way for non-mainstream films to gain critical attention and reach an international market (UKFC 2009b). During Crooks's tenure at the New Cinema Fund, this approach achieved considerable success, most notably with James Marsh's documentary *Man on Wire* (2008), which was awarded both the Grand Jury Prize and the Audience Award at the Sundance Film Festival before securing US distribution. With successful box office returns, *Man on Wire* not only went on to fully recoup its UKFC investment but also won an Oscar and a BAFTA. Other examples of the range of films invested in by the New Cinema Fund include *Adulthood* (2008), Noel Clarke's successful follow-up to *Kidulthood*, the political comedy *In the Loop* (2009; dir. Armando Iannucci), a spin-off from the BBC television series *The Thick of It* (2005–12) and Andrea Arnold's award-winning second feature *Fish Tank* (2009; dir. Andrea Arnold), with the latter two also receiving development funding from the UKFC before successfully moving into production.

A similar shift had also occurred at the Premiere Fund where producer Jones was replaced in 2005 by Sally Caplan (Interview, London, November 2007), who came from a distribution and acquisitions background and saw her role as investing in films that would 'connect more with audiences'. Her primary concern was generating high box office figures and international sales for cinema, DVD and television rather than securing critical acclaim, festival selection or awards success. In contrast to the £2 million given to the award-winning *Gosford Park*, which would have represented a quarter of Caplan's £8 million budget, her approach was closer to that of Seghatchian's and Crook's, as she felt it more appropriate to invest less money into a higher number of films.

The wider economic landscape had changed during this period, with the second set of fund heads experiencing a more pressured environment as the recession and subsequent global financial crisis made it harder to find financing for films. Thus, although the Film Council's Business Affairs department had always been involved in approving the investments made by each individual fund, it was particularly vital that those films at the commercial rather than cultural end of the spectrum had in Sally Caplan's words, a 'plausible financial plan' in place before the UKFC committed money (Interview, London, November 2007).

In a Premiere Fund update to the board shortly before the closure of the Film Council, it was highlighted that achievement of the 50 per cent recoupment target was becoming more difficult due to adverse market conditions and, consequently, the fund may only be able to invest in the 'most obviously commercially films, which obviously creates a conflict with the requirements of additionality' (UKFC 2009e: 10). This suggests that, internally at least, the UKFC still sought to adhere to the concept of funding films that were additional to those provided by the market, even if this was not necessarily how the Premiere Fund was interpreted by outside stakeholders in the industry.

Examples of the type of commercial films in which the Premiere Fund invested about £1 million during Caplan's tenure include the 2007 reboot of the *St Trinian*'s franchise, the alien invasion movie *Attack the Block* (2011; dir. Joe Cornish) and *StreetDance 3D* (2010; dirs. Dania Pasquini and Max Giwa), which was not only credited with 'discovering and nurturing new creative talent in the UK' but also enjoyed 'the most successful opening weekend of any film [that the UKFC] has supported in its 10-year history' (BBC News 2010). These films differed from the decision to invest in *Gosford Park*, however, as they were all produced and directed by emerging or established British-based film-makers with content that could also be understood to be culturally British. Nevertheless, each of these examples may be interpreted as equating commercial film-making with what appeals to young, cinema-going audiences. Yet the UKFC's greatest success on an international scale was the multiple Oscar-winning *The King's Speech* (2010; dir. Tom Hooper), a period drama that received initial investment from the Development Fund, followed by £1 million from the Premiere Fund. In a similar manner to *Man on Wire*, the success of *The King's Speech* demonstrates the difficulty of pursuing an 'obviously' commercial approach, as it is relatively difficult to know in advance which films will translate into international box office success.

At the same time as the UKFC was receiving plaudits for being the only public funder to recognise the potential of *The King's Speech*, its funding schemes and then the organisation itself came to an abrupt end in the wake of the financial crisis and the arrival of the Conservative-led Coalition Government. Against the background of the financial crisis and concerns about its impact on funding for public bodies, a decision was taken at the Film Council in 2010 to merge the three schemes into one unified Film Fund headed by Seghatchian with £15 million a year to invest. As explained by Seghatchian (Interview, London, January 2014), the serious cuts imposed on arts organisations by the DCMS meant that the UKFC had to find a way of managing a reduction in funding with 'minimal impact on the industry, so that the brunt of that had to be dealt with by the staff rather than by the film-makers'. A board paper outlining the strategy of the Film Fund (UKFC 2010a) suggests that although money would still be available for development, short films and emerging and established film-makers, it was no longer regarded as necessary to publicly separate these via different schemes. The decision to merge the production funds may well have been driven by the need to cut costs. However, the merger of the three funds into a single strand – a unified model that has been retained by the successor body to the UK Film Council – does call into question the fundamental rationale of the previous strategy of explicitly differentiating between the development and production process and between mainstream and more innovative film-making.

Conclusions

One of the endemic pitfalls of evaluating funding schemes such as the Film Council's Production and Developments Funds is the tendency to focus excessively on just a handful of high-profile successes or notorious failures. This approach had been reproduced over the years by the Film Council itself in its promotional material and indeed by the media in their reports on the use of Lottery funding for film (Dawtrey 2011; Petley 2002). In our analysis, we have cited many examples but also have retained a focus on the wider objectives underlying the Film Council's funds in relation to supporting talent, training, skills and production companies. Examination of the funding schemes and how they developed over time once again demonstrates the strong emphasis placed by the UK Film Council on embedding industry expertise at the core of its activities and, through this, on cultivating a more strategic and business-minded approach to film-making in Britain. The aspiration of making the production sector more sustainable clearly influenced the

Council's approach to film support as it evolved and executed an action plan to 'professionalise' the independent sector.

The means to achieving this involved separating Lottery funding for film into three distinct streams to invest in development, support new talent and encourage more commercial modes of film-making. Thanks to a number of well-chosen investments in the latter category, the UK Film Council managed to turn around earlier negative media perceptions of the way that Lottery funding for film had been distributed. The restoration of public confidence in how Lottery funding was being administered counts as a significant achievement for the UKFC. As acknowledged by John Woodward (Interview, London, February 2013), media criticism of the unsatisfactory manner in which Lottery support for film had previously been distributed in the late 1990s was sufficiently voluble and sustained to threaten the very continuation of such funding. Addressing this 'was the first part of the Film Council's mission because I knew if we didn't turn [media] perception around [the government] was going to take the Lottery money away' (ibid.).

Despite an important success on this front, the rhetoric and methods employed by the Film Council were not always welcomed by independent film producers and at times the organisation struggled to articulate its position and allay perceptions that its schemes tended to privilege commercial expertise over the public service aspect of distributing public funding. A shift to redress this imbalance that took place in the second phase of the funding schemes is acknowledged by independent producers including, for example, Peter Watson of HanWay Films, who noted that in the latter years of the UKFC, 'there was an attempt to engage in a more supportive way' (Interview, London, February 2013). Even so, and underlining how contradictory are views about what the primary aims underlying public investment in film should be, the success of the Film Council's funding schemes in fostering reinvigoration and professionalism resulted in mixed feelings on the part of independent film-makers.

Another contentious issue that would face the UKFC throughout its lifetime would be both understanding and shaping the role that digital technologies were playing across the film industry. The next chapter focuses specifically on this area of the UKFC's strategy and practice.

CHAPTER 7

Digital – A Missed Opportunity?

The UKFC Digital Screen Network [DSN] strategy is designed to diversify the range of films available at cinemas around the UK, with special emphasis on provision of greater geographical equality in diverse programming offers. It will do this via the wider distribution of films that will become possible via digital technology. At heart, the scheme is audience focused and clearly aimed at growing and developing audience appetite for viewing a wider range of films. It is designed to be effective over the medium to long term. The strategy will encompass all types of cinemas, from existing specialised cinemas (art houses), independently owned cinemas, smaller circuit cinemas and multiplexes.

(UKFC 2005c)

Introduction

In retrospect, it is easy to identify digital technology and the disruptive nature of the Internet as two key factors shaping the broader screen landscape over the last decade or so. Debates about 'piracy', the role of intellectual property (IP) and the impact of digital technology on the screen industries have recognised the importance of the shift to digital (Balio 2013; Iordanova and Cunningham 2012; Ulin 2014). This chapter examines the role played by digitisation and its wider ramifications in both the strategic thinking and operational practice of the UKFC for the UK film industry's patterns of production, distribution and exhibition.

This chapter explores the extent to which strategic thinking regarding the impact of digital technology informed the direction and role taken by the UKFC in engaging with what, in retrospect, were industry-changing processes. Was the organisation too slow to identify the transformative impact that digitisation would have on all areas of the film industry? To what extent were its interventions concerning production and distribution and exhibition successful in achieving what they initially set out to deliver? Did the UKFC, during its lifetime, enable the UK film industry to fully address both the challenges and opportunities that the transformation to a digital environment posed?

We initially examine the UKFC's strategic engagement with digital from 2000 to 2003. The chapter then examines and evaluates one of the Council's key interventions that directly addressed digital change, the development and implementation of the Digital Screen Network (DSN), before finally we account for the strategic shifts in the organisation's thinking around digital over its lifetime.

Early Thinking: 2000–3

In his overview of how public policy gets implemented within organisations, Peters (2014) identifies the growing complexity of that process. He argues that the network style of implementation will often result with policies being 'made at the same time as they are being implemented' (Peters 2014: 135). This suggests the policy implementation is often less linear or top-down than may officially appear and that such a network process is often identified in studies of institutions. In this study of the UKFC, there are a number of factors that shaped the backdrop against which we need to place its early thinking regarding the impact of digital technology and the Internet. It is worth noting that by the late 1990s and early 2000s it was still unclear how digitisation was going to play across the media industries more generally. There was a considerable degree of strategic uncertainty about how, or even in some quarters, whether, the Internet and digitisation would be the 'game-changers' that they subsequently turned out to be. Commercial newspapers, for example, were busy setting up websites and giving away their journalism for free at this time, a model that in retrospect proved to be damaging to the industry (Brock 2013).

Across the UK, television industry commercial free-to-air (FTA) broadcasters were slow to recognise the impact of digitisation during the 1990s. The BBC, in contrast, would lead the field on digital strategic thinking during the 1990s, with Director-General John Birt widely credited with driving through strategic shifts in the ways in which the BBC thought about digital both during and after his tenure. He recalls:

> The BBC ended up better positioned for the new century, for the new digital era, than any other established broadcaster in the world. But this was not a smooth and easy experience: it was a voyage into the unknown, propelled by curiosity, instinct, enterprise and luck. It was a journey marked by disasters narrowly averted, by intrigue, and by bad decisions as well as good ones. (Birt 2002: 452)

Thus, even at the often lauded, digitally orientated BBC, John Birt acknowledged the uncertainty that characterised the transition to digital across the creative industries and the process of trial and error that was part of that process. It was amid such uncertainties that the UKFC came into being in 2000.

Paul Webster worked across the film production sector, including as head of production at Miramax Films (now Miramax) in the mid-1990s, before then leaving to create Film4 at Channel 4. He was on the UKFC board (2000–4) and notes: 'The thinking about digital at the start of the decade was, I think, very basically that this was the future, but nobody [across the industry] quite knew what the future would look like – I am not sure they do now' (Interview, London, March 2013). As we argued earlier in the book, the task of creating a 'sustainable' film industry (without this ever being clearly articulated in terms of achievable goals) was one that to some extent both dominated and distorted the strategic focus of the UKFC in its initial three-year planning cycle (2000–). In this context, digital, beyond some concern about issues of DVD 'piracy', was not at the forefront of the Council's thinking during the period. It is notable that in Chairman Alan Parker's 2002 speech on the state of the UK film industry, and the role the Film Council should play in shaping its future direction, digital technology and the Internet barely merited a mention (Parker 2002). Within the production community there was growing discussion about the impact of digital technology, through digital video (DV), on the ability to make low-budget films but little sign of awareness that within a decade digital film would become the industry mainstream (James 2001).

One well-placed figure at the UKFC acknowledged that in its start-up mode the Film Council was not strategically focused on the impact that digital technology and the Internet were having on the UK industry, noting:

When people were talking about sustainability ... the initial discussions ... were all framed in terms of quite an analogue vision of building film companies that worked across the value chain of cinema, trying to bring films into cinemas, into DVD and television, etc. No one was really talking about what impact the Internet had at that point, because we were still grappling with it – and to the extent that we were talking about it no one was really talking about digital. (Interview 18, 2013)

Indeed, within more traditional sections of the film production sector of the industry there was a degree of hostility to digital, and a view that

35 mm film-making was not going to disappear quickly and would thus remain at the centre of mainstream commercial film-making for some time. The production focus of the UKFC board in its first iteration also, to some extent, helped to reinforce the perception that digital was some way from directly impacting on the industry in a significant manner during the early 2000s. Among the exhibitor wing of the industry, often viewed as one of the most conservative sectors of the industry, there was also resistance in addressing, or even seriously contemplating, the possible seismic changes and disruption that both digital technology and the Internet may bring.

The combination of an initial politically framed strategic agenda focused on building a sustainable film industry, an in-built board orientation towards the production sector and wider resistance in acknowledging the impact that digital technology may have across the industry, resulted in less attention being focused on long-term thinking about the implications of the shift to digital. BSAC Chief Executive Fiona Clarke-Hackston suggests that criticism of the UKFC's failure to address digital with sufficient attention during this 2000 to 2003 period is unfair, and needs to be placed within the context of the approaches to digital in other areas of the screen industries at that time. She argues:

> I don't blame the UKFC; you play the political cards you have got. But I do think that this in some ways held them back, so I don't think they realised [regarding digital] what was going on, but I don't think they were alone in that either. Some of the broadcasters, such as ITV, were really slow to realise that. Sky got it years ago, and that is why Sky is worth more than ITV on the stock market ... A lot of people ... didn't get [digital]. (Fiona Clarke-Hackston, Interview, London, March 2013)

This, of course, is not to suggest that debates or discussion around digital were absent in the UKFC. For example, as we noted in the previous chapter, the New Cinema Fund (NCF) under Paul Trijbits was explicitly set up to recognise digital and the changing ways in which people were making films. It could be argued that the UKFC saw the NCF, with its focus on low-budget digital production, as the core focus of its digital intervention. Producer Paul Webster suggests:

> You know, one of Paul's early initiatives and kind of think-tank idea was called 'Digital or Die', and the idea was that digital would revolutionise means of production, that budgets would come down, that people would be able to make films very simply and share them,

much of which has come true. In the Film Council, as a whole, I think, the attitude was very positive towards the idea of the digitalisation of the industry and therefore the democratisation of the business. (Paul Webster, Interview, London, March 2013)

From a strategic perspective, while it was accepted that the UKFC was not as quick to focus on digital as it should have been, it was also argued that:

[t]here were bits and pieces going on, but there wasn't a coherent focused approach to digital. I don't think we really talked to the technology companies and that kind of dialogue wasn't going on … You have actually got all these incumbent stakeholders who want you to stem the tide against digital at one point instead of embracing it. So that became a tension that you have to manage, and we got better at bracing the opportunities rather than just thinking about the challenges as we went on. (Interview 18, 2013)

Given the strong producer representation on the board during the early years of the Council, it would appear that little sustained thought was focused on the impact of digital on the distribution and exhibition aspects of the industry. To some extent this reflected much of the dominant thinking across the sector that viewed the UK industry as basically a cottage industry largely focused on production, which was one of the things that the UKFC wanted to alter. The arrival at the UKFC of Pete Buckingham as the new head of Distribution and Exhibition in 2002 significantly altered this situation, although ironically digital strategy would only emerge as a by-product of apparently more pressing strategic objectives for the UKFC regarding audiences' access to film.

Into Tomorrow

Pete Buckingham is widely viewed as the key architect of many of the UKFC's most important interventions in developing a strategic vision that placed digital at its core. A key move was the creation by Buckingham of the UK Digital Screen Network that became a central aspect of the UKFC's intervention in the digital arena. In this project he worked closely with Steve Perrin who had moved from the post of head of Research and Statistics.

However, the digital transformation of the industry was not part of their brief. Steve Perrin recalls, 'Our broad task was to develop strategies, using public funds, Lottery money, to widen the range of films on offer to the cinema-going public. Basically we were tasked to do that ... How we did it was up to us' (Interview, Sheffield, November 2013). Both Buckingham and Perrin had wide experience of the commercial distribution and exhibition aspects of the industry, and both were clear that if they were to build wider audiences for film and have a wider range of films being watched by audiences then UKFC attention needed to broaden from its dominant supply side intervention.

By 2003, the UKFC's Digital Technology Strategy Group (the internal forum for debate on digital issues) had produced an interim position paper. This document (UKFC 2003a: 2) reflected the relative uncertainty across the film industry about the perceived impact that digitisation would have across production, distribution and exhibition and noted that sections of the industry felt that 'claims about the predicted diffusion of technology are overstated'. This was far from the consensual view of the industry and the report also noted that many took 'the opposite view, that current technological change represents a major paradigm shift' (UKFC 2003a: 3). The document in discussing UKFC digital strategy finally concluded with a rather anodyne strategic objective: 'To contribute to the exploration, development and adoption in Europe and beyond of new technologies especially in production, distribution and exhibition' (UKFC 2003a: 4). It advocates both a 'watching brief' for the organisation while suggesting it also acts as 'a catalyst for bold and imaginative strategic thinking' around digital strategy (UKFC 2003a: 6). It noted that three Digital Futures Seminars would take place with the industry in 2003–4, to help focus, enable and develop future scenario building about the role of digital across the industry.

In the end only two such seminars took place, the first in June 2003 and the second in January 2004. They were important in that they crystallised some of the divergent thinking about the role and impact of digitisation across different sectors of the industry. The seminars saw senior UKFC executives meet with screen industry managers, including the BBC and Channel 4, to discuss digital's ability to reshape the sector. The term 'technology' was dropped from the second seminar, which focused on the exhibition and distribution challenges faced by the industry, whereas the first seminar had been more concerned with the way that technology was changing skills and training needs, although this had also ranged widely across the impact of digital on the industry (UKFC 2003b, 2004a). One area of difference that emerged in the second seminar was around the extent to which digital strategy merited becoming a dedicated and specific strategic priority of the UKFC. The record of the seminar notes:

Neil Watson [UKFC] argued that digital should be viewed as a means to an end, as a facilitator; this meant that there shouldn't have to be a digital strategy for the FC; instead digital should be part of the means to a variety of FC ends rather an end in itself. [CEO] Terry Ilott [Hammer Films] presented the opposite view that digital technology was far more than a means to an end, it was changing how everything in the film sector was done – he argued that the FC must do more than simply mainstream digital across its existing range of strategies. (UKFC 2004a: 8)

In many ways this debate would continue both within the UKFC and the industry more generally and would remain unresolved until 2007, when the UKFC would explicitly identify the transformative impact of digital on the industry in its policy (UKFC 2007a).

By the time of the 2004 seminar, the Digital Screen Network was already being talked about as a key initiative by the UKFC (although it would not be formally launched until later that year). In retrospect, it would be this initiative that would prove both to be the single largest investment by the UKFC in a digital programme and to mark a move to engage with the distribution and exhibition sectors of the industry. Although, as we noted above, what became a digital flagship initiative of the UKFC, had emerged not from any specific shift in its thinking about digital strategy, but rather a more prosaic concern with its priority of extending access to film and engaging the widest possible audience for non-specialist film.

Becoming Digital: The Digital Screen Network

Peter Buckingham's challenge was how best to utilise capital funds to realise the goal of extending the range of films available to the public. For Buckingham it would be about starting with the audience, rather than focusing on the production sector and also moving away from the traditional thinking around promoting exhibition. The UKFC had abot £15 million worth of capital funds from the Arts Council that they had used for supporting exhibition as well as a prints and advertising support fund that was about £1 million a year for 'specialised' films, £1 million a year for 'British' films and a further £1 million a year for educational support.

Working with Perrin, and drawing on market research they had commissioned, both came up with digital cinema as the strategic way forward to enhance wider audience engagement with film. In 2003, digital cinema exhibition was being discussed in parts of the industry

The digital screen work is not just for exhibition … The economic value of the digital screen work is probably more important to the distribution sector because it changes their business model for everybody when that happens. They had to stop making prints. They didn't need to spend £700 on a print; they could spend £40 on a digital file. So digitisation has very serious implications for audiences and the diversity of films and the product that you could put in front of audiences, but, in business terms, it's as important for the distribution sector, and was always intended that way. (John Woodward, Interview, London, April 2013)

Thus, more copies of the film being made available offered the potential for wider dissemination of the content to cinemas. These required digital projectors to screen the content. Exhibitors had to agree that as part of the process of having substantial (but not all) their costs covered by the scheme of projection installation, they would show an increased amount of specialised film.

This was allied with changes in the Prints and Advertising (P&A) Fund that involved an increased budget and a greater focus given to which specialised films the UKFC would choose to promote, in the hope that this would bring them to a wider audience. The tender to secure the delivery of the DSN through the installation of digital projectors was issued in March 2004, and the organisation tasked to deliver the introduction of digital exhibition was Arts Alliance Media (AAM) led by Thomas Hoegh. AAM had been involved in digital aspects of film distribution and exhibition through its Love Film arm and its own attempts to begin digitising cinemas. The tender was won against larger and more established companies because, according to Hoegh:

We provided a very simple and more or less foolproof system, whereas the nearest competitor who was the finalist with us, provided something which required a lot of extra costs and was complex to run. (Thomas Hoegh, Interview, London, March 2013)

The scheme was launched on 9 August 2004, with a call to cinema owners wishing to secure the installation of digital screens. By the close of this process at the end of 2004, 280 eligible applications were received with a broad geographical spread (although with under-representation in Northern Ireland, parts of Wales, rural East Midlands, Cornwall and Scotland) and with 153 multiplex applications, 76 from specialised cinemas and 45 from commercial independent cinemas (UKFC 2005c). The scheme would lead to the installation of digital projectors in 212 cinemas across the UK and create 240 digital screens. Of these, 79 per cent of the cinemas were outside London, with almost £12 million spent on the project.

Two aspects of the scheme proved to be particularly controversial, one was the positioning of the projectors in the main screen, thus allowing easy access to screen Hollywood, as opposed to specialist film, and the other was the Virtual Print Fee (VPF), which critics argued added a disproportionate cost to distributors attempting to gain screen time for small independent films. It is also clear that given that the DSN scheme was committed to engaging with the main commercial cinema exhibitors in the UK, as well as the independent cinema chains, some form of commercial consideration was going to be part of the wider arrangement for these major exhibitors. John Woodward accepted that by positioning the digital projectors in the main auditorium it to some extent benefited the Hollywood studios. He argued:

> I am not denying that the reality of where the projectors were sited ... if you look at the screening patterns, what you'll find is that overall the number of independent and niche films that were shown in cinemas during that period shot up, and that was as a result of digital projection. Does that mean that every film that the independent distributors and film makers wanted to get shown got shown? No, of course it didn't, but compared to what was going on when they had 35 mm projectors in those screens, the change was enormous. (John Woodward, Interview, London, April 2013)

Steve Perrin also acknowledges the criticism that the DSN attracted from parts of the industry as it gave money to the commercial sector. He argued that through the scheme:

> [w]e were agnostic as to the type of cinema, but we were very clear that we wanted geographical spread. One of the debates that took place was ... why would someone like the Film Council want to give what was in those days, £60,000 worth of equipment to Odeon? They've got enough money of their own, whereas there were cinemas that could do with that sort of money ... If certain cinemas in certain locations had made certain contractual commitments to us, that fitted with our strategy and they were big, multiplex companies, then so be it. This was a commercially based strategy. This was not 'Let's help the cinemas.' ... We're not giving money to Odeon. We're saying to Odeon, you show a wider range of films for your local audience and what we would do was support the audience. (Steve Perrin, Interview, Sheffield, November, 2013)

He notes that a similar criticism came their way when the revamped P&A fund selected particular films that it wished to promote. He recalls:

> Some of those films came from big studio-based companies. People say, 'Why are you giving money to Warner Brothers? They can afford to do it themselves.' But the answer being, yes, they can afford to do it themselves, but they aren't going to do it. If they're going to go out in the 35 mm cinema, with thirty copies, because that's what they think is right, there's no way in the world they're going to go out with fifty. But if we go to them and say, 'Look, this is what you've got. We think there's a market here, here and here, we'll support you if you go into those markets.' Which they did, then we gave them money. So, no, they don't need our money; it's the local population for whom the film now becomes available that we're supporting, not Warner Brothers. [It was] a difficult concept to argue. (Steve Perrin, Interview, Sheffield, November 2013)

From 2003 to 2009, specialised films released in the UK as a percentage of total releases increased by 18 per cent. Within this broad category, documentary film releases increased from ten in 2000 to fifty-six in 2009, while foreign language releases also increased from 131 in 2002 to 161 by 2009, with year-on-year dips and spikes (UKFC 2010b). Films such as *Lust* (2007; dir. Ang Lee), *The Diving Bell and the Butterfly* (2007; dir. Julian Schnabel), *Che Part One* (2008; dir. Steven Soderbergh) and *Broken Embraces* (2009; dir. Pedro Almodóvar) all received UKFC support through the P&A fund to bring these to wider audiences. For others within the industry there was a perception that extending the film audience could have been achieved by means other than the DSN, such as targeting funds towards community-based organisations committed to bringing cinema to new audiences. However, it was felt that the ability of Hollywood to benefit from the transformation was also achieved in more subtle ways. Heather Stewart, the BFI's Creative Director of Programming, has suggested:

> The definition of specialist cinema, I think, was a bit too lax and so, you know, big American indie pictures start to come into the category of specialist cinema and so in terms of the kind of tick-boxing that those mainstream halls might have to do to prove that they were showing a wider range of films, it didn't really do much. It was just business as usual. (Heather Stewart, Interview, London, March 2013)

However, perhaps the biggest issue that dampened some of the industry enthusiasm for the DSN was centred on the Virtual Print Fee (VPF).

The Virtual Print Fee

The VPF is a subsidy set by the film companies and paid by distributors to exhibitors to offset the costs of transforming cinemas into digital spaces. The savings on creating and distributing 35 mm prints that digital clearly allows is to all intents and purposes not enjoyed by the distributors within the film industry chain. As a result, there is an additional cost to independent films being distributed digitally that the technology has in reality made obsolete. A European Digital Cinema Forum (EDCF) held in London in April 2008 brought together many of the then seventy-three distributors in the digital cinema industry to discuss this issue. Of these, only five operated with a market share above 10 per cent, so smaller distributors in reality had about 1 per cent of the market. The VPF was widely viewed by this sector as an imposition on them, orchestrated by the major film companies. At the EDCF conference in 2008, Jim Slater noted how Pete Buckingham acknowledged the issue:

> [Buckingham] accepted that the VPF concept actually means that the industry is effectively duplicating the old analogue model of the cinema business for at least the next seven years, and although he saw that this meant that they couldn't make full use of the opportunities that digital can provide, he felt that most exhibitors would need funding via a VPF. (Slater 2008: 37)

Thomas Hoegh, CEO of AAM, accepted that, in hindsight, this aspect of the business model related to the DSN project was, and remains, problematic.

> Yes, there's one thing that I would have done differently, and that would have been to try to negotiate with the studios exceptions to the VPFs for the most marginal film: independent film. So some kind of scale would exist that if something went out on less than X prints, then that could be exempt from VPF. This is to make sure that there's growth in the film culture, that there was diversity in product, but it wouldn't have any meaningful economic impact in a detrimental sense from the studios' perspective because we are talking about something here that would be less than a per cent of box office annually anyway. That's the one thing I would like to have negotiated. (Thomas Hoegh, Interview, London, March 2013)

Hoegh suggested that while the VPF did not block independent films from being distributed, it did impact on the original goals of the scheme. He observed:

> I think films that needed to get out there got out there anyway. But I think we could have seen a lot more creative use of such an exemption to get really experimental stuff out. So the experimental stuff has not had access. It's easier to get a short film because they are exempt. So it's easier to get a short film out there than [it] is now to get a feature film at the very marginal end. (Thomas Hoegh, Interview, London, March 2013)

For some observers, such as Heather Stewart, creative director at the BFI, the VPF became part of a number of issues related to the UKFC's focus on the DSN as a means of delivering on its widening access to film priority. For Stewart, the rolling costs of digital technology renewal and upgrading were always going to be a challenge and the VPF simply militated against access to the range of independent films envisaged. She argued:

> The UKFC's thinking was, 'If people in Britain want to have more access to a wider range of films including UK films, then the way to kind of democratise the access is to make it easier to show films.' What I'm saying to you is that [the DSN] wasn't the right strategic decision because actually what you've done is made it very difficult for small distributors to get the digital prints in cinemas because it actually can work out more expensive than buying a 35 mm film … We've got 35 mm projectors that are sixty years old that are fine. While digital projectors need upgrading after four years, where's your capital budget? Now this isn't the Film Council's fault, but strategi-cally I never quite understood why that was the number one thing you'd want to do because it didn't achieve the goals. You wound up making it hard for distributors and not achieving the kind of depth of choice that you might think it was going to achieve. (Heather Stewart, Interview, London, March 2013)

The VPF remains an issue in the distribution sector and was identified as such in the 2012 *Film Policy Review*, which noted:

> [T]he Panel recognises that the Virtual Print Fee (VPF) mechanism, which has enabled the industry to finance digitisation across a large

part of the UK's cinema estate will, if unchecked, have a continuing and detrimental impact on independent distributors and smaller exhibition venues. It is already having a negative impact on their capacity to make available British and specialised films to audiences across the UK. (DCMS 2012: 31)

Phil Clapp, CEO of the Cinema Exhibitors' Association (CEA), writing in the trade journal *Cinema Technology* in 2014, also acknowledged that the VPF still inhibits some aspects of the sector's functioning:

This is particularly the case when it comes to flexibility of programming, where the influence of VPF payments on behaviour will continue to be felt for some time to come, resulting in less immediate freedom when it comes to booking and programming than many had hoped would be the case in the digital age. (Clapp 2014: 18)

Clearly the impact of digitisation across the distribution and exhibition sectors will continue to reshape the business models and the nature of these sectors for some time to come. The transformation from the dominance of 35 mm film prints to digital across the UK industry in the space of just over ten years is striking and the ramifications of this transformation are being continually worked through.

The DSN was not envisaged originally as a showcase for the UKFC's strategic thinking on digital and while the audience-led drive to expand choice has happened it has also been uneven. For some industry figures, such as UKFC head of UK Partnerships Chris Chandler, while the Digital Screen Network was originally supposed to extend the range of film available, it achieved mixed results. It did, however, in his opinion play a key role in shifting the exhibitor sector to digital (Interview, London, February 2013). In his analysis of the UK film industry between 2001 and 2010, Sean Perkins (2012: 322) noted that these years saw a rise in the specialised films released as a percentage of overall releases from 53 per cent in 2003 to 69 per cent in 2009. In addition, the market share for these films also grew from 5 to 15 per cent and then dipped in 2010 to 6.3 per cent. He argues that

[w]hile the overall market share for all specialised film categories remains low, interventions such as the National Lottery Prints and Advertising Fund have increased the release width of many specialised titles, enabling these titles to reach audiences outside London and the major cities. (Perkins 2012: 323)

The more specific use of the P&A Fund to back European films such as *The Lives of Others* (2006; dir. Florian Henckel von Donnersmarck) and *Broken Embraces* (2009) increased the number of prints available and helped establish the possibility of wider access for such films beyond the art house circuit.

The DSN project had unintended consequences, being less successful in its original aims, but also facilitating a wider industry shift in structure and also strategic thinking about how digital was going to change all aspects of the film business. In this sense, it echoes aspects of Hanson's (2007) suggestion that what we are seeing is technological consolidation, digital replacing celluloid, rather than major cultural and social shifts in film culture. For Phil Clapp, who worked in the early 2000s in the DCMS before becoming chief executive of the CEA, the lack of robust policing of the scheme, once digital projectors were in place, had shaped the inability of the DSN to deliver across all of its original objectives. He maintained:

> The Digital Screen Network was a pioneering initiative; there was nothing like it even in countries which were quite fond of public intervention, like France. And while it certainly wasn't the publicly stated objective of the DSN, in terms of a beginning of an understanding of what the potential of digitalisation might be, in terms of programming and other aspects, I think it gave us [the UK] a significant headstart. All pioneers suffer the same kind of fate and undoubtedly in hindsight the Film Council may have approached how it distributed the 238 projectors slightly differently. It probably should have, and I'll probably get shot by some of my members for saying this, been tougher with cinemas in terms of the objectives of the DSN around specialized film ... The Film Council got tough too late.

> Even if cinemas signed up to show a certain proportion of specialised film, the Film Council weren't really that serious about it. So people took the projectors, and said, well, actually, it's going to be too much hassle for them to remove the projectors, so I don't really need to worry about that. And it was only in the latter stages [2008–9] that the Film Council started to get tough [but by then] that ship had already sailed. (Phil Clapp, Interview, London, October 2013)

However, some critics of the UKFC recognise that whatever its original aims and objectives the DSN was important for the film industry in the UK. Philip Knatchbull, CEO of the film content and distribution and exhibition company Curzon, notes that whatever the original aims of the DSN project it was a UKFC success story:

> I think that was really helpful actually; you see I think that demonstrates how, if you kick-start something, it can really generate further progress in encouraging other people to look at it. So they kick-started an amazing revolution ... If they hadn't put the money in when they did, the UK probably wouldn't have been as early adopter of digital projection as it now is; practically every single major screen is being converted to digital. That isn't the case in Europe. I am convinced that actually that policy and strategy was a good one. There was a lot of criticism at the time when a lot of multiplex cinemas were accessing this public money, but again it's seed money; you put a little bit in and they can see what they can do with it, and then they go, 'Actually, this really makes sense; we are going to invest a lot of money in transforming all our estate.' My viewpoint is that worked and if they were to apply the same principle to production and distribution and exhibition as a joined-up sort of approach, then I think you can reintroduce this idea of funding a number of different integrated companies. (Philip Knatchbull, Interview, London, June 2013)

As the DSN scheme came to its conclusion, by the end of the decade digital was moving into the mainstream of UKFC thinking.

Digital Moves Mainstream

It is worth reflecting on Street's (2012) argument that understanding the impact of technologies on innovative practices is always challenging, not least as they often co-exist with previous forms. She notes how debates about digital in the UK are often linked with notions of innovation, however spurious they may eventually turn out to be. There is little doubt that, by 2007, within film policy rhetoric the UKFC had finally moved digital to the mainstream of its strategic thinking. Following industry consultation from November 2006 to February 2007 around the challenges faced by the film industry in the digital age, the organisation's three-year plan acknowledged that

> [t]here is a pressing need for all of the UK Film Council's funding priorities to be regularly reviewed in relation to the impact digital technology is having on film. There is no monopoly of wisdom on the practical consequences of the changes being driven by digital

technology, but it is clear that public policy for film and the moving image must be supple and flexible if it is to maximise the opportunities which are likely to arise over the next few years. (UKFC 2007a: 8)

Of course, digital technology issues, initially around the production context, had been on the UKFC policy radar more or less since its inception, without ever having moved to the core of its strategic thinking. By 2004, for example, 'digital technology' was number six of seven areas identified as being in need of strategic development (UKFC 2004b). Yet with the exception of the DSN and the New Cinema Fund, while the rhetoric of digital was articulated, the specific policy focus on what exactly the role of the UKFC should be in this area was less clearly defined.

The 2007 three-year plan marks a broader recognition of the transformative impact of digital on the screen industries, although the only new policy initiatives explicitly digital in focus included 'a Film Digitisation and Marketing Fund (an enhanced Prints and Advertising Fund)' with a new budget of £4 million and 'a UK-wide Digital Film Archives Fund of £1 million per year' (UKFC 2007a: 2). It was also noted that future expansion of the Digital Screen Network, although it was widely acknowledged as innovative, would be rejected on the grounds that there was 'limited support and strong views that the market will deliver [further expansion]' (UKFC 2007a: 15).

Yet when Tim Bevan became chairman of the UKFC in 2009, he felt that a major strategic rethink of the position of digital within the organisation's thinking and practice was needed. He argued:

The whole Film Council needed to have a re-evaluation, if you like, a look at what its function was and how it sat within the media landscape at that point. I felt that the production side of it was in pretty good shape ... [R]eally, what needed looking at was how the new world of distribution was going to sit and what effect that was going to have on the film industry basically, and that we needed to have our wits about it in terms of looking forwards ... Thinking of the profound effect that the Internet might have on our industry ... whether the traditional models and the traditional windows of distribution could work, the coalition between television and theatrical distribution, video distribution, television distribution, all the rest of it – and just look at all of that very carefully indeed. So that was one of the things that we wanted to do. And then secondly, that we should set a proper sum of money aside for ... I think it was going to be called an 'Innovation Fund', where in terms of the new technologies and all the rest of it, where people were working in areas where they would have a substantial impact on our industry, be it in production, be it in distribution, be it in whatever basically – that people could make an application for funding to support that. Now that never actually came to fruition, that fund, because by the time we had just elected to proceed with it, is when we got shut down. (Tim Bevan, Interview, London, April 2014)

The 2010 three-year plan (UKFC 2010a) indicated that £5 million was to be dedicated to the Innovation Fund, in part looking at new business models for film in the digital age. Perhaps not surprisingly, given the media landscape of 2010, this final unrealised three-year plan gives a clear indication of the direction of strategic travel for the UKFC between 2010 and 13, with a greater central focus on digital and its significant impact across the industry than is evident in any of its predecessors. Given the sudden demise of the UKFC, which we discuss in Chapter 9, it would of course remain a plan unrealised.

Conclusion

In a discussion of film policy, Jack Newsinger (2012: 141) notes the high degree to which writing about the UK film industry treats it as a 'single entity' and, as a result, fails to understand its differing sectors. This chapter has been particularly interested in the distribution and exhibition elements of the industry and their interface with UKFC policy with regards to digital. Peters (2014) has noted that how policy gets implemented in organisations is increasingly driven by the range of networks within which they are located. The UKFC was a highly networked organisation, often trying to reconcile the competing demands of a complex industry. It is argued here that, almost initially by default, the DSN became the most high-profile intervention in the digital arena during the UKFC's lifetime. It is ironic that, given this, its origins came out of a drive to extend access to specialised film, rather than help transform the distribution and exhibition industry for the digital age. As the DSN rolled out and evolved it also had significant unintended consequences. For Thomas Hoegh, CEO of AAM, it

gave the independent sector a head start, and not just cinema, but also the distributors. It gave them a head start to figure this [digital] out. So I think they were in a much better position than anywhere else in the world to think about what the practical realities of the digital film future would look like. I think it enabled many cinema owners to think radically different[ly] about how they run their cinemas. The whole aspect of alternative content has become now a serious business and, most importantly, a risk mitigator in the release calendar, so a programmer can now sit and say, 'Oh, there's weakness in October; let's see if we can find some alternative programmes we can put in there, so that we don't have a deep dip in the worst week.' That's the biggest contribution for alternative content and it's becoming more of a core element [for cinemas]. (Thomas Hoegh, Interview, London, March 2013)

Other professionals located across differing parts of the industry, such as producer Paul Webster, echo the view that

without doubt on the exhibition side of thing, the Digital Screen Network really helped oil the wheels. It would have happened anyway – it has happened all over the world, but they [the DSN] sped up the process. Now if they hadn't existed at all where would we be today? Probably, you know, probably more or less the same kind of landscape, but I think in getting here the journey was eased by the Film Council – I think it was a very, very potent enabler in that area and kind of successfully bridged the gap between public policy and private innovation. (Paul Webster, Interview, London, March 2013)

Others are more critical of the general manner in which the UKFC never, in their view, got to grips with the role and impact of digital across the sector. For example, UKFC head of UK Partnerships and consultant to the BFI Chris Chandler argues:

The Film Council happened to exist over the decade – the rough decade – when digital film making became a real thing ... I think that arguably more interest could have been shown in digital experiments rather than the use of digital to do things. [Yet] their support for the shift to digital exhibition I think was very good. (Chris Chandler, Interview, London, February 2013)

In one sense, the UKFC was unclear of how digital would impact and play out and in this they reflected the uncertainty that existed across differing sectors of the film industry in the UK in the first decade of the new century. The organisation initially saw digital and its role though a production lens, and not until after Pete Buckingham arrived in late 2002 and energised, with Steve Perrin, the distribution and exhibition arms of the UKFC did it develop a digital core through the DSN that, although never intended to be so, became its leading digital legacy. What emerges in this chapter is the extent to which digital strategy at the UKFC developed progressively over the years and then often played out with unintended consequences. It also demonstrates the real policy challenge of addressing and understanding changes taking place across a connected but also highly disparate industry such as film.

By 2007, the tide was turning and at a rhetorical level at least digital was moving up the strategic agenda, although whether it should be embedded in all UKFC activity or become a dedicated priority was still unresolved in UKFC thinking. By 2009, the root and branch reevaluation by the last chairman of the UKFC, Tim Bevan, changed this and the focus from then until the organisation's demise was in helping the transformation of the industry to engage fully with the mainstream digital environment. The focus in this chapter has been on digital, but measuring the performance of the organisation against other objectives that were set during its lifetime is worth further scrutiny and is examined in the next chapter.

CHAPTER 8

Performance against Objectives

Introduction

This chapter provides an analysis of the UK Film Council's performance over its lifetime in relation to some of its key stated policy objectives and funding schemes and initiatives. It is well recognised that cultural industries, including film, produce economic and non-economic impacts but measuring these impacts can prove challenging (Bakhshi *et al.* 2008; Throsby 2004). Similarly, measuring the performance of public bodies whose job it is to support cultural industries is fraught with difficulty, not least because such bodies are accountable to diverse stakeholder groups and the objectives that they are, or ought to be, pursuing can be a matter for divided opinions. The conditions surrounding the inception and development of the UK Film Council made this a distinct organisation with few obvious comparators around the globe. Therefore, assessing the Film Council's performance, when we are discussing a support body with a wide remit whose sense of mission shifted over its lifetime, is by no means an easy task.

Our analysis draws extensively on secondary source statistical data and, where possible, we have used data for the years starting in 2000, when the Film Council began operating, up until 2011, when responsibility for film in the UK passed to the BFI. Mindful of the fact that historical data is subject to revision, we have relied heavily on the most up-to-date published sources in the *BFI Statistical Yearbook 2014*. Where comparative data over the lifetime of the UKFC is not available, we refer to the statistical yearbooks published by the UKFC from 2002 to 2010 and the BFI thereafter. Where substantive variances in methods of data collection occur, we have sought to ensure reliability by narrowing the focus to more limited periods within the 2000–11 time frame. In addition, bearing in mind that time lags may occur between the instigation of schemes and interventions and the achievement of desired impacts, some of the data used in our analysis relates to surrounding periods before the creation, and after the closure, of the Film Council.

Sources of data drawn upon include the UKFC's *Group and Lottery Annual Report* and *Financial Statements* (2000–10) and its Annual Review (2000–6). We also focus on an internal Scenario Planning discussion paper (UKFC 2009b) produced towards the end of the Council's lifetime, which is of particular relevance since it assesses the effectiveness of policies and interventions to date from the Council's own perspective. In addition, attention is paid to an independent assessment carried out by external analysts Olsberg SPI and Jim Barratt (Olsberg SPI and Barratt 2010), which was commissioned by the UKFC's Monitoring Unit and delivered in September 2010, two months after the DCMS announced that the organisation was to be closed down.

A number of aspects of the Council's broad remit were devolved to partner agencies, such as the BFI, Regional Screen Agencies, Creative Skillset and First Light – see Appendix 1 – and detailed analysis of these activities is outside of the scope of this study. The UKFC's dual role of providing strategic leadership for the industry while also acting as a Lottery distributor and investing in particular projects, schemes and initiatives was dealt with in the performance assessment conducted by Olsberg SPI and Barratt (2010) by separating the 'direct' from the 'strategic' impact of the UKFC, a convention also adopted within our analysis.

In a milestone planning document produced by the Film Council in 2009, the central question the organisation posed for itself was 'how effective have our policies and interventions been to date?' (UKFC 2009b: 1). Performance assessment was based on four objectives that, from the Council's perspective, summarised its mission. These were to:

1) help build a competitive film industry with the creativity and skills to succeed
2) stimulate greater choice for film audiences
3) promote UK film in the wider world
4) widen opportunities to learn about film and encourage participation.

In the analysis that follows in this chapter, we focus on the first three of these aims (in the next three sections respectively) but exclude the fourth since this relates to an aspect of the UKFC's agenda that was largely delegated to the BFI. In addition to analysing the Film Council's efforts to build a competitive industry, widen choice and promote exports, we also (in the section on Value for Money/Efficiency) consider the UKFC's performance in delivering value for money, looking at indicators including operating expenses, staffing levels and recoupment rates. Efficiency indicators are important because cost savings were the stated reason for closing down the Film Council.

By way of introduction, it is worth noting that in the period in which the Film Council acted as lead support body for film in Britain, the UK film industry experienced significant positive change. For example, between 2000 and 2011 cinema admissions rose by 20 per cent from 142.5 million to 171.6 million while box office gross income increased by 78 per cent from £583 million to £1040 million (BFI 2012b: 9, 11; UKFC 2010b). In addition to this rise in cinema exhibition, the number of feature films produced in the UK during the same period rose from 80 in the year 2000 to 345 in 2011 (with films with budgets less than £500,000 included from 2003 onwards) while the value of UK production also increased by more than 125 per cent during the same period (BFI 2014: 180, 182).

Prior to the creation of the UKFC, the DCMS's *Creative Industries Mapping Document* (CITF 1998: 51) showed that for the year 1996, overseas revenue for films made in the UK was £522 million, more than double the 1986 figure. With imports amounting to £431 million, this resulted in a trade surplus of £91 million. By 2006, this had risen to an estimated trade surplus of £128 million (UKFC 2008: 152). Oxford Economics (2012: 1) calculated that, in 2009, the 'core UK film industry', including multiplier impacts, was contributing more than £4.5 billion to UK gross domestic product (GDP) and more than £1.2 billion to the Exchequer through gross of tax relief and other fiscal incentives. The 'core' industry was defined as all companies and individuals involved in film production and, in the distribution and exhibition sectors, all activities associated with 'UK-made films' (UKFC 2008: iii).

This positive assessment cloaks some ambiguities and unfavourable trends. For instance, although since the 1980s the number of attendances at cinema screens throughout the UK has increased, US-made films rather than domestic productions dominate overwhelmingly at the UK box office. In addition, insofar as levels of film production activity in the UK have increased in the twenty-first century, it is questionable to what extent this is attributable specifically to the activities and interventions of the Film Council. That the film industry is subject to developments at an international level, which are often outside the control of national public agencies, is a difficulty acknowledged by the UKFC from the outset:

The industry is much larger than it was in the 1990s, but its fortunes fluctuate from year to year in response to changes in the international filmmaking climate, cost competitiveness, currency value, fiscal and other forms of public financial support (e.g. Lottery funding), developments in private sector film financing, as well as the degree of commercial and creative success achieved by films made with UK participation. (UKFC 2002: 66)

Having acknowledged the limitations and challenges that inevitably beset efforts to assess the Film Council's performance, the next three sections below examine changes that took place within the film industry during the tenure of the Film Council in the context of the organisation's key stated objectives.

Building a Competitive Film Industry with Creativity and Skills

Value of UK Film

The total value of film production activity is an important indicator of the state of health of any national film industry. During the period when the UKFC was lead support body for film, the value of UK production rose by more than 125 per cent from £579 million in 2000 to £1,321 million in 2011, as shown in Table 8.1. Following a relative low of £598 million in 2005 as a result of changes to the UK's tax incentive schemes, production spend steadily increased to more than £1 billion from 2009 onwards with the 2011 figure representing the highest sum of production budgets on record. These figures include domestic UK features, international co-productions and inward investment, and it should be noted that this rise is largely a result of the UK's success in attracting the latter in the form of large-budget productions backed by US studios but qualifying for UK tax breaks. This is discussed further in the section on Promoting UK Film in the Wider World.

The proportion of expenditure on film production in the UK accounted for by domestic feature films has therefore been on a notable downward trend, amounting to 37 per cent of overall UK spend in 2000 and falling to only 15 per cent by 2011. This can be attributed in part to the impact of the global financial crisis on film financing and indeed the rise of low- and micro-budget film-making as a result of the proliferation of digital technology. Yet it also calls into question the UKFC's success in fulfilling what was regarded as a primary objective – that of developing a sustainable indigenous film industry. Olsberg SPI and Barratt (2010: 23) note how the UKFC financed a proportionally greater number of domestic features over time as the market became more challenging. In other words, reliance on public subsidy grew during the Council's tenure.

Table 8.1 Expenditure on film production in the UK, 2000–11.

	Inward investment (£m)	Domestic UK (£m)	Co-production (£m)	Total (£m)
2000	367	212	—	579
2001	199	180	—	379
2002	266	156	128	550
2003	733	236	158	1,127
2004	584	126	169	879
2005	307	192	99	598
2006	559	167	111	837
2007	604	168	79	851
2008	434	236	52	722
2009	835	242	39	1,116
2010	1,012	201	76	1,289
2011	1,071	198	52	1,321

Source: BFI (2014: 180).

Volume of UK Film

Looking at how the volume of UK independent films produced has changed over time, Table 8.2 reveals a marked increase from only 33 domestic features produced in 1994 to 167 in 2013. In part, this reflects the effect of Lottery funding support for film, which was introduced in the mid-1990s. These figures are also complicated by a sharp rise in low- and micro-budget film-making since the turn of the new century and indeed prior to 2003 no data on domestic features with budgets below £500,000 was collected. If low-budget features are stripped out and the focus is purely on UK independent films with budgets of more than £500,000, levels of film-making almost doubled from thirty-three in 1994 to sixty-three in 2013. However, the number of productions in this category remained steady during the tenure of the UK Film Council at about sixty-two per year and so the significant factor that contributed to an uplift was Lottery funding, which was introduced ahead of the setting up of the new film body.

With regard to the objective of developing a sustainable UK film industry, it is notable that production activity in the UK, rather than being concentrated in the hands of a few players, has remained dispersed among a very large number of companies. For example, in 2002 there were 160 production companies associated with UK domestic features

Table 8.2 Number of feature films produced in the UK, 2000–10.

	Inward investment	Domestic UK	of which budget > £0.5m	of which budget < £0.5m	Co-productions	Total
1994	13	33	—	—	—	46
1995	14	34	—	—	—	48
1996	25	73	—	—	—	98
1997	20	84	—	—	—	104
1998	16	67	—	—	—	83
1999	22	70	—	—	—	92
2000	28	52	—	—	—	80
2001	23	51	—	—	—	74
2002	16	37	—	—	66	119
2003	46	62	48	14	106	214
2004	28	63	40	23	105	196
2005	51	101	55	46	68	220
2006	29	125	57	68	53	207
2007	33	175	72	103	33	241
2008	32	231	83	148	30	293
2009	37	258	89	169	38	333
2010	30	303	78	225	36	369
2011	36	264	86	178	45	345
2012	39	242	65	177	45	326
2013	37	167	63	104	37	241

Source: BFI (2014: 182).

and co-productions. Of these, only one UK production company was involved in seven features, followed by four companies with three each and sixteen companies with two. This means that the other 139 production companies were associated with only a single feature (UKFC 2002: 71). No significant changes to the landscape were evident following a decade of intervention by the Film Council. In 2010, of the 232 production companies recorded, 218 were involved with a single feature followed by eleven with two films each and three companies with three. In other words, no improvement was achieved in relation to the problem that few, if any, UK independent film production companies are in a position to spread risk across a portfolio of film projects, as is a requirement for commercially successful and sustainable film-making.

Budget Trends

Film is a highly risky business and, although large budgets do not guarantee the success of any film project, production budget levels nonetheless offer a potentially useful yardstick as to the likely market appeal of a film. Figure 8.1 traces median[1] budgets for films made in the UK from 2003 to 2010 – a substantial portion of the UKFC's lifetime. It demonstrates that while co-production budgets remained relatively stable and while budgets for inward investment features experienced a massive increase from £11.5 million to £17.5 million between 2003 and 2010, budgets for UK domestic features more than £500,000 fell from an already modest figure of £2.9 million to just £1.2 million over the same period. Effectively, domestic film production has remained a low-budget business while the overall value of UK production has been inflated by the presence of large-budget inward investment films shooting in Britain.

Release Rates

Budgets are especially significant when analysing the proportion of independent domestic UK films securing theatrical release, as 'released films tend to have higher budgets than unreleased films' (BFI 2011: 66). For example, with considerably more low- and micro-budget films being produced between 2003 and 2010, Table 8.3 shows how almost 90 per cent of

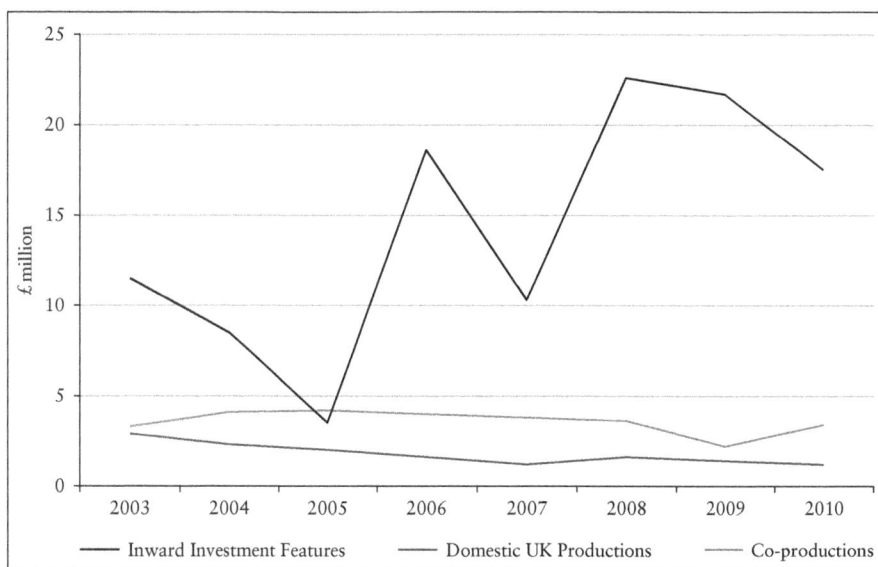

Figure 8.1 Median feature film budgets, 2003–10, £ million.

Source: Chart based on data about median film budgets published in BFI (2011: 150).

Table 8.3 Release rates of independent domestic UK films by budget, 2003–11.

Budget band (£m)	No. of films produced	% released in the UK and Republic of Ireland*	% released internationally*	Median budgets of released films (£m)
<0.5	973	11.6	12.5	0.2
0.5–2	348	37.9	40.8	1.0
2–5	157	59.2	66.2	2.7
5–10	56	71.4	76.8	6.5
10+	12	83.3	91.7	12.0
Total	1,546	25.1	27.3	1.1

Source: BFI (2014: 85).

*Within two years of principal photography.

those with budgets under £500,000 fail to secure theatrical release within two years of principal photography, either within the UK and Republic of Ireland or internationally. Release rates rise steadily as budgets increase, with those costing more than £10 million securing a domestic release rate of 83 per cent and 92 per cent internationally. Those films that achieve a release rate of more than 50 per cent tend to cost in the region of £2 million to £5 million, yet, as noted, the median budget for UK domestic features is only £1.2 million. So, despite efforts on the part of the Film Council to help professionalise the UK independent production sector, it remains that most UK domestic films are low-budget features that achieve only very limited releases.

Market Share

For the minority of UK films that do achieve theatrical release, it is worth examining their subsequent share of the UK theatrical market. Between 2001 and 2013, the average share of the UK box office accounted for by all UK films was 25 per cent. However, of this 25 per cent share, studio-backed UK films accounted for 18.5 per cent with independent films comprising only 6.5 per cent. On a positive note, the share of the UK box office accounted for by UK independent films rose from 3.8 per cent in 2001 to 6.6 per cent by 2013 (BFI 2014: 18).

When the country of origin of all films released in the UK and Republic of Ireland is analysed from one year to the next, the dominance and overwhelming success of US-made features is clear. In 2002, solo and co-productions originating in the USA (excluding US/UK productions) accounted for 43 per cent of all film releases but achieved a 73 per cent share of the box office (UKFC 2002: 15). By 2013, US productions had dropped slightly to 35 per cent of all film releases but continued to attain a 73 per cent share of the box office (BFI 2014: 17). In comparison, UK productions accounted for 21 per cent of all film releases and 24.4 per cent of the box office in 2002. Yet, when broken down into UK independent films and UK/US productions, the latter still clearly dominates, accounting for only 6 per cent of releases but 18.2 per cent of the box office. Despite UK studio-backed films dropping considerably to 2.3 per cent in 2013, they still accounted for a 15.5 per cent share of the box office while UK independents experienced only a slight increase.

The most striking feature emerging from analysis of the UK box office over time is the continued and unbroken dominance of the US major studios that typically have tended to account for more than 70 per cent of proceeds, a pattern undisturbed by the efforts and interventions of the UKFC from 2000 to 2011.

Wider Choice for Film Audiences

Country of Origin

While USA solo and co-productions dominate at the UK box office, there has nevertheless been a modest increase in releases and market share for films from other countries. In 2002, films from outside the UK and US, for example, those classified as Other Europe, India and Rest of the World, accounted for 36 per cent of all releases but only 2 per cent of the UK box office (UKFC 2002: 15). By 2013, these figures had risen to 45 per cent and 5 per cent, respectively, and, perhaps most significantly, box office gross for such films increased to £59 million, compared with only £18 million back in 2002 (BFI 2014: 17). While this forms part of wider international trends, such as growth in the popularity and success of Bollywood films, it also reflects initiatives taken by the UKFC, as discussed in previous chapters, in the form of the Prints and Advertising Fund and the Digital Screen Network, and their success in bringing a wider range of what is described as 'specialised' films to UK audiences.

Digital Screens and Subtitling and Audio Description Facilities

By the end of 2013, just over 98 per cent of all screens in the UK were equipped for digital projection, an extraordinary rise given that in 2005 no less than 99 per cent of screens were analogue (BFI 2014: 114). As detailed in Chapter 7, the origins of this rapid rise can be traced to the UKFC's Digital Screen Network initiative, which created 240 digital screens across 212 UK cinemas between 2005 and 2007, of which 79 per cent were cinemas outside of London. However, the industry has since taken up the conversion to digital with 3,868 digital screens installed across the country by 2013, 43 per cent of which are 3D capable. Moreover, all of the UK's digitally equipped cinemas have English language subtitle and audio description facilities, meaning that from 2008 onwards the number of subtitled screenings have increased by 120 per cent to about 1,000 weekly (BFI 2014: 115).

UK Films on Terrestrial Television

In 2002, of the total number of films broadcast across the UK's five terrestrial channels, 20 per cent were considered to be UK films but only 0.2 per cent of these were less than eight years old (UKFC 2002: 58). By 2011, the broadcast of UK films had fallen to 10 per cent, yet, despite this decrease, 2.9 per cent were now recent films (BFI 2012b: 125). Average audiences for all films shown on peak time network television dropped significantly over the same period, however, due to the proliferation of cable, satellite and digital channels and competition from Internet services. Films broadcast on ITV1 attracted audiences of 4.7 million in 2002, with BBC One not far behind with 4.2 million. By 2011, the audience for films broadcast on BBC One had decreased to 3 million while ITV1 experienced a more dramatic fall to only 1.2 million. This drop was also replicated at the lower end of the scale with Five (now Channel 5) audiences decreasing from 1.6 million to 1 million (BFI 2012b: 127).

Throughout its tenure as lead support body for film, the UKFC sought to 'work with broadcasters and other platform operators to improve public access to British and specialised films' (UKFC 2009b: 9). This involved encouraging broadcaster support for UK film through efforts to grow audiences and investment in film production. Some success was achieved: in 2006 a Memorandum of Understanding (MoU) was established with the BBC that agreed a small increase of £2 million per annum in film investment, despite it being a time of constrained programming budgets. However, as the figures outlined above suggest, little progress was made in improving access to British and specialised films for terrestrial audiences and, in addition, there was a failure to establish similar agreements with either Channel 4 or the satellite operator Sky.

Promoting UK Film in the Wider World

Inward Investment and Co-production

As noted in Table 8.2, the number of inward investment films rose from thirteen in 1994 to thirty-seven in 2013 with an annual average of thirty-two during the UKFC's tenure. These numbers have fluctuated over the years due to a number of factors, many of which lie outside the control of national public agencies, such as exchange rates and the impact of the global financial crisis on film financing. A spike in 2005 stemmed from a large number of mainly Indian inward investment features. Yet, as outlined earlier, since the introduction of a new tax incentive scheme in 2006, the UK has been successful in attracting large-budget productions backed by US studios but qualifying for UK tax breaks. A sharp upward trend is therefore noticeable, with inward investment rising from 63 per cent of the total value of UK production in 2000 to 81 per cent by 2011. Co-production levels, on the other hand, dropped from sixty-six in 2002 (prior to which the number of UK co-productions were not made available by shoot) to only thirty-seven in 2013, while their value has decreased from a high of £169 million in 2004 to £52 million in 2011 (BFI 2014: 182, 180). This can be attributed to changes in the regulatory environment whereby co-production qualification rules were tightened up and, moreover, the new film tax relief (introduced in 2006) applied to UK expenditure only rather than to the total budget of a film.

The Film Council readily acknowledged, in the 2010 *Statistical Yearbook*, that a surge in inward investment in UK film production at the end of the decade was largely down to 'the decline in the pound-dollar exchange, the bedding-in of the UK tax relief and the resolution of the writers' and actors' disputes in the USA' (UKFC 2010b: 133). However, in its internal scenario planning document assessing the effectiveness of its own policies and interventions to date as at 2009, the organisation also highlighted the strategic role it played in the negotiation of the new tax relief system in 2006 following the government's withdrawal of sections 42 and 48, describing the outcome in the following terms: 'UK Film Council intervention over tax breaks "saved" the British film industry' (UKFC 2009b: 8). But the same paper also acknowledges that 'the structure of the existing UK Film Tax Credit actively militates against co-productions', meaning that the organisation's efforts in devising Co-Production Treaties become 'largely irrelevant' without a change to the new system (UKFC 2009b: 16, 13) – something the UKFC was not able to achieve during its lifetime.

It is significant that the UKFC directed more funds towards encouraging inward investment than to support for co-production. For example, the Office of the British Film Commissioner (OBFC) received £900,000 per annum to help maximise inward investment through film production while the UK Film Council US Office cost £350,000 annually and sought to strengthen European, US and international relationships to create opportunities for UK film (UKFC 2009b: 13–14). In contrast, co-production support received just £45,000 per annum to help achieve the following goal: 'To work with the UK Government to modernise the UK's film co-production agreements and to assist the UK industry to benefit fully from them' (UKFC 2009b: 16).

Film Exports and International Box Office Performance

Between 2000 and 2011, the total value of UK film industry exports rose substantially from £0.7 billion to £1.7 billion. The £1.7 billion earned in 2011 is comprised of royalties (£1.2 billion) plus film production services (£0.5 billion) (BFI 2014: 228). The primary destination of UK film exports has tended to be the US, which took 48 per cent of total exports in 2001 (UKFC 2002: 48). For the period between 2008 and 2012, however, this dropped to 41 per cent while the EU market became just as significant, also at 41 per cent. Asia, Other Europe and the Rest of the World accounted for 6 to 7 per cent during the same period.

As demonstrated in Table 8.3, a strong association is evident between budgets and international release rates and, similarly, higher budgets are generally associated with greater box office receipts. Table 8.4 shows how for those films with budgets of more than £5 million released in at least one of nineteen territories, average international box office takings are more than $43 million. This contrasts sharply with a mean box office of about $4 million for films that achieve a release in the £2 million to £5 million budget band, a category within which UK domestic features will much more typically belong.

Table 8.4 Box office (US$) for independent domestic UK films released in at least one of nineteen territories by budget, production years 2003–11.

Budget band (£m)	No. of films released	Median box office (US$ 000)	Mean box office (US$ 000)
<0.5	122	12	91
0.5–2	142	120	733
2–5	104	917	4,072
5+	54	5,322	43,151
Total	422	150	4,299

Source: BFI (2014: 85).

Awards and Talent Support

Table 8.5 is drawn from data in the *UK Statistical Yearbook 2014* (BFI 2014: 79) that traces the number of awards won by UK films and British talent at major festivals and at the BAFTA Film Awards and Academy Awards over time. The number and share of major awards won by UK films has remained relatively consistent between 2001 and 2013 with an average of twenty-six prizes per year and a 14 per cent share of total available awards.

Data regarding award wins for UKFC-funded feature films was only recorded between 2007 and 2009 and is thus too limited to draw any reliable conclusions. It also fails to take into account the different types of awards on offer in terms of critical prestige, audience feedback or industry sales. For example, the most high profile are the Academy Awards, Golden Globes Awards, BAFTAs or the highest honours presented at A List international film festivals, such as the Palme D'Or (Golden Palm) at the Cannes Film Festival, the Goldener Bär (Golden Bear) at the Berlin International Film Festival and the Leone d'Oro (Golden Lion) at the Venice Film Festival. However, given the range of films funded by the New Cinema Fund in particular, representation at the British Independent Film

Table 8.5 Number and percentage of awards for UK talent, 2001–13.

Year	Number of UK award winners	UK share %
2001	25	14
2002	24	15
2003	22	13
2004	22	13
2005	23	14
2006	25	14
2007	32	15
2008	32	15
2009	36	17
2010	24	12
2011	30	15
2012	23	14
2013	26	15

Source: BFI (2014: 79).

Awards (BIFA) and festivals such as Sundance and Toronto are perhaps of equal importance in terms of generating industry interest and securing audience awards, with the latter often better indicators of commercial success than the critical acclaim bestowed by juries.

In its Annual Reviews published between 2000 and 2006, the UKFC documented selected awards and nominations for films supported by both the Premiere and New Cinema Funds. By its final review (UKFC 2005/6: 17–21), the list included thirty-nine productions spanning fiction and documentary features, short films and international co-productions and it specified the different types of award nominations and wins secured. As highlighted by Olsberg SPI and Barratt, however, the international appeal and recognition of UK talent is not well-quantified and indeed contains subjective elements:

> To merely quantify results as an absolute number of films would be to perhaps overlook individual successes such as ... the New Cinema-funded Andrea Arnold's *Fish Tank*, for which she won the Best Director award at BIFA 2009. The film also won the prestigious Jury Prize at Cannes and the BAFTA in 2010. (Olsberg SPI and Barratt 2010: 27)

This lack of quantifiable data and indeed an over-reliance on the reporting of particular high-profile successes, such as Oscar winners *Gosford Park* (2001), *Man on Wire* (2008) and *The King's Speech* (2010), for example, works to obscure the exact nature of the UKFC's role in talent support and development.

Value for Money/Efficiency

As we discuss in detail in the next chapter, the UK Film Council was closed down by the Coalition Government as part of a 'raft of DCMS cost-cutting measures' that involved the 'merger, abolition or streamlining of 16 public bodies' in an attempt to deal with the effects of the global financial crisis (Shoard 2010). A subsequent report by the National Audit Office (2011: 7) found that, actually, the abolition was 'not informed by a financial analysis of the costs and benefits of the decision'. Nonetheless, the Film Council had attracted controversy from its inception with many suggesting that it was relatively profligate in terms of its overheads. In this section we analyse a range of indicators that bear upon the organisation's efficiency. These include levels of operating expenditure, staffing levels and salaries and recruitment rates.

Turnover and Operating Expenses

One useful means of examining the efficiency of the UK Film Council is to analyse operating expenses and how these changed over the lifetime of the organisation. Table 8.6 demonstrates that while the Council's operating expenses as a percentage of its group turnover were especially low in its first year at 7 per cent (a figure that can be attributed to the high level of delegation income received by the nascent agency as a result of the transfer of film rights from the Arts Council of England), on average administration costs generally accounted for 13 per cent of its overall annual income. A 13 per cent average is significantly lower than the peak of 16.6 per cent in 2004 in which operating expenses totalled almost £9.3 million. Reductions in costs towards the end of the organisation's life reflected the fact that the Council was actively taking steps to slim down its overheads in its last three years of operation, primarily due to funding cuts and in view of threats posed by a possible change in government. By 2010, operating costs had been reduced to 11.4 per cent of group turnover.

Table 8.6 UKFC group turnover and operating expenses, 2001–10.

Year ending March	Group turnover (£m)*	Operating expenses (£m)	Operating expenses as % of turnover
2001	99.1	7.0	7.0
2002	59.9	7.8	13.1
2003	58.1	7.9	13.7
2004	55.9	9.3	16.6
2005	57.7	9.1	15.7
2006	71.2	8.6	12.0
2007	58.0	8.6	14.8
2008	57.6	8.8	15.3
2009	63.2	8.4	13.3
2010	72.6	8.3	11.4

Source: Data compiled from UKFC Group and Lottery Annual Reports 2001–10.

*Turnover consists of funding received from National Lottery (share of proceeds, investment returns and recoupment from both ACE and UKFC projects), Grant-in-Aid funding and British Screen Finance Group income.

These reforms occurred too late to save the Council from closure. In 2010, the DCMS was seeking to 'reduce the administrative costs of UK-wide and England Lottery distributors to 5 per cent of their total Lottery income', and a National Audit Office report (NAO 2010: 15) showed that of thirteen eligible bodies, all but two had administration costs higher than the new government target of 5 per cent. Prime among these was the UKFC with costs standing at about 27 per cent of income. The NAO's calculations were based solely on Lottery income rather than total group turnover, which explains why the figure is above the 11 per cent recorded in Table 8.6. Despite clear evidence that the Film Council was taking steps to curb its overheads, its cause was not helped by the fact that the NAO (2010) found the UKFC to have proportionately the highest administrative costs among thirteen Lottery fund distributors.

Salary Costs

A major item within the Council's costs was staff. The overall number of employees rose significantly over the organisation's lifetime from fifty-four in 2001 to ninety-two in 2010, which partly reflects a widening of the Council's remit over time, albeit that many functions were devolved to partner agencies. Expansion in staff numbers contributed to a doubling of the Council's wage bill from £2.9 million in 2001 to £5.7 million in 2010. Average salary costs across all staff rose by a relatively modest amount annually over the period, from £54,000 to £62,000 (see Table 8.7). But this overall trend masks the fact that levels of remuneration for some senior staff were, for a public sector organisation, exceptionally high and they rose very significantly over the Council's lifetime.

For example, between 2001 and 2010, the chief executive's salary rose from £118,500 to £208,500. In 2010, some seven senior staff members, including the heads of funding schemes, were in receipt of salaries above £100,000 with the highest salary band being £165,000 to £170,000. CEO John Woodward (Interview, London, February 2013) argues that salary levels reflected the skills of those industry professionals holding key executive positions and indeed staff were 'quite often being employed at less than their market rate but they chose to come to the Film Council as it was an interesting place to be'. However, others take the view that payment of such high salaries to public sector employees was excessive and, as discussed in Chapter 6, this fuelled perceptions of an organisation that was prone to 'hubris' and where costs were not controlled as tightly as they ought to have been.

Table 8.7 UKFC staff numbers and salary costs, 2001–10.

Year ending March	Average monthly number of permanent staff (FTE*)	Annual staff costs (£m)	Average salary cost per staff member (£ 000)
2001	54	2.9	54
2002	80	3.9	49
2003	84	4.2	50
2004	90	5.0	55
2005	90	5.3	59
2006	90	5.5	61
2007	90	5.8	65
2008	90	5.6	62
2009	92	5.9	64
2010	92	5.7	62

Source: Data compiled from UKFC Group and Lottery Annual Reports 2001–10.

*FTE: Full-time equivalent.

Recoupment

The UKFC had a direct impact on the UK film industry through its distribution of Lottery funds to domestic features between 2000 and 2011. As detailed in Chapter 6, some £17 to £20 million was distributed annually (reduced to £15 million in 2011) via the Development, New Cinema and Premiere Funds. The organisation also pursued a relatively aggressive recoupment strategy, setting targets of 25 per cent and 50 per cent, respectively, for its two production funds while one in ten development awards were expected to be converted into production and thus recoup their investment.[2]

Whereas critics argue that salary and administrative costs at the UKFC were too high, one key measure by which the organisation was able to demonstrate high levels of efficiency was in terms of the levels of recoupment achieved. As explained in Chapter 5, the Film Council tended to take an aggressive stance on 'recoupments' or expected repayments against original investments or grants awarded once a film project achieves success and starts to earn income. Table 8.8 shows how the UKFC was successful in recouping a relatively high proportion of its original investments with an overall average of 49 per cent achieved between 2003 and 2010. This rate of recoupment probably understates

Table 8.8 UKFC film recoupment income, 2003–10.

Year ending March	Total investment via funds (£m)	Recouped income (1) (£m)	Surplus (2) (£m)	Total recoupment (£m)	Recoupment as total investment (%)
2003	20	6.8	0.2	7.0	35
2004	17	3.3	0.6	3.8	22
2005	17	7.3	0.4	8.1	48
2006	17	13.8	2.4	16.2	95
2007	17	5.7	0.8	6.5	38
2008	17	9.4	1.2	10.6	62
2009	17	8.3	2.0	10.2	60
2010	17	4.2	0.6	4.9	29

Source: Data compiled from UKFC Group and Lottery Annual Reports 2003–10.

1 Income received from a film right is offset against the value of the right on the balance sheet.

2 Income in excess of the original value of the right is taken to the income and expenditure account as film recoupment income.

the success of the Council, as its biggest international success, *The King's Speech*, was released in 2010 and the high returns that followed accrued to the successor body, the BFI. In instances such as this, an astonishingly high level of recovery can be attained, as occurred in 2006 when receipts from *The Constant Gardener* led to a recoupment level of 95 per cent of the UKFC's total investment for the year.

The performance of the UKFC's recoupment strategy was not well managed in respect of the press, however, with media reports tending to focus on the success or failure of individual projects. Following the publication of recoupment data from 2006 to 2010 by Minister for Culture, Communications and Creative Industries Ed Vaizey, Dawtrey's (2011) examination adopts this same approach by highlighting the success or otherwise of particular film-makers in receipt of Lottery funding, with documentary director James Marsh who made *Man on Wire* (2008) considered to be the most commercially successful while both *Chéri* (2009) and *Tamara Drewe* (2010) by Stephen Frears had failed to pay back any of their investment. However, Dawtrey (2011) goes on to suggest that the aggressive strategy adopted by the agency is perhaps one reason 'why the UKFC execs were paid so well. Getting money back from tricksy distributors isn't a job for amateurs' before also acknowledging how, by international standards, the Film Council performed admirably as 'outside the UK, it's increasingly rare for any subsidised film to recoup 100%'.

Conclusions

In his statistical analysis of film in the UK between 2001 and 2010, Perkins (2012: 330–1) highlights how during the period in which the UKFC acted as lead support body for film there was a 'major shift in the production and consumption of feature films' with audiences now faced with a complex multi-platform world and producers and distributors experiencing significant challenges as 'traditional business models come under pressure'. The UKFC's operations and activities became increasingly dispersed and multifaceted during this period, resulting in a 'family' of numerous partner organisations pursuing various priorities (UKFC 2009c). Our analysis underscores the complex array of activities, both strategic and direct, for which the Film Council took responsibility over its lifetime and the diverse range of associated impacts across production, distribution and audience access.

The Film Council was particularly successful in encouraging inward investment in the form of large-budget productions backed by US studios that qualified for UK tax breaks, and indeed the organisation was instrumental in successfully negotiating a new tax relief system in 2006. These achievements led to a significant increase in the value of UK film from 2000 onwards with production spend rising to well over £1 billion by the end of the decade.

The Council also performed exceptionally well in terms of recoupment thanks to an aggressive strategy for recovery of investment that utilised the skills and expertise of industry professionals within its Business Affairs department. While it attracted criticism for its corresponding high salaries and overheads, it nevertheless exceeded international benchmarks and expectations by averaging almost 50 per cent recoupment on original investments.

Through its Digital Screen Network initiative, the UKFC set in motion the conversion from analogue to digital cinema with just over 98 per cent of all screens in the UK now equipped for digital projection. Releases of films from countries other than the UK and the US and the market share achieved by such films increased modestly during the UKFC's lifetime. In addition, a number of UKFC-funded films were successful in securing large audiences and prestigious international awards, with high-profile examples including the Oscar winners *Gosford Park* (2001), *Man on Wire* (2008) and *The King's Speech* (2010).

One notable area of shortcoming was performance in respect of the UKFC's original objective of creating a sustainable UK film industry. One independent producer (Interview 11, 2013) noted, 'If the Film Council works, then it should be getting smaller every year.' Yet, as we have demonstrated, the organisation became larger over its lifetime as its remit expanded and it took on more staff.

Reliance on public subsidy among UK independent producers actually increased during the UKFC's tenure and UK productions continued to struggle for domestic and international release. Despite a decade of determined reinvigoration and professionalisation of the UK independent production sector, the UK film industry was no closer in 2011 than it had been back in 2000 to becoming commercially self-sustaining. And US-made films continued in their unbroken dominance of the UK box office. However, whether it is fair to criticise the Film Council in respect of this unsurprising state of affairs is questionable since, in truth, creating a sustainable UK film industry was never an objective that a public support body of limited means could have achieved.

Part IV
Strategic Lessons

CHAPTER 9

The Last Days of the UK Film Council

I think the last Government – and this is not a criticism of the last Government – had struggled to bring this merger together, potentially because of some of the personalities involved. It might reassure members of this Select Committee who, as Members of Parliament, are used to being criticised for tribal politics and artificial rows, that the film industry makes Westminster look like a village tea party in terms of some of the rivalries that go on in it.

(Ed Vaizey cited in HC CMSC (2011))

Intimations of Mortality

In this chapter, we shift from a tale of creation to one of destruction, preceded by an uncertain interim phase. From the summer of 2009 merger talks between the UKFC and the BFI were in train. The key question during that period, in the run-up to the general election of May 2010, was which body would survive. In the end, it was the BFI. Here, we detail the background to the UKFC's sudden demise, which was totally unexpected by its leadership, and, indeed, much of the wider film industry, policy community and commentariat.

The full detail of the merger discussions in 2009–10 remains shrouded by prudence and discretion, with relatively little documentation presently on the record and considerable unwillingness on the part of key players whom we approached to speak about it. Geoffrey Nowell-Smith's (2012b: 306–7) useful brief account has been the best available to date. He notes the 'increasingly strained' relations between the two bodies early in 2009 and that in evidence to the House of Lords Communications Committee early in that year 'Eric Fellner, Vice-Chairman of the BFI, floated the idea that it might be time for the BFI to regain its independence'.

On the UKFC's side, the desire to change relations with the troublesome BFI was unequivocally stated at its May 2009 board meeting. Noting that the fourth set of new Ministers in its lifetime had been appointed at the DCMS, the CEO's report noted:

[G]iven the state of UK public finances, closer working at an operational level between the UK Film Council and the BFI would be requested including the option of a full merger.

In a detailed discussion the board discussed the pros and cons of a full merger with BFI and agreed this would finally resolve the structural overlaps and stakeholder confusion over film cultural policy/activity which had existed since the creation of the UK Film Council. Further discussions were obviously required to explore all aspects of this issue. (UKFC board minutes, 30 June 2009, minute 8)

With this 'final resolution' firmly in mind, it is not surprising that, in May 2009, John Woodward had 'commissioned a document setting out the legal and financial options for a possible merger between the two organisations':

Two possible models emerged. Either the BFI might be absorbed into the UKFC through the creation of a BFI Trust of which the UKFC would be sole trustee, or the UKFC could be folded into the BFI. The former model, which was the preferred one, would leave the UKFC in control; the BFI would retain its charitable status but probably have to lose its Royal Charter. The latter would make the UKFC the trading arm of a still chartered BFI. Either way, savings of up to £500,000 per annum could be expected through a merger of the back-office of the two organisations and the removal of unproductive interfaces between them.[1] (Nowell-Smith 2012b: 307)

According to John Woodward, both he and Tim Bevan, the UKFC's incoming chairman, as successor to Stewart Till, had anticipated the coming cuts irrespective of whichever government would be elected in May 2010 (Interview, London, February 2013). Nowell-Smith (2012b: 307) reports that Dyke and Nevill were only told about the merger plan in July 2009. The issue finally surfaced in public when on 20 August 2009 the Minister for Culture, Tourism and the Creative Industries, Siôn Simon, announced that the BFI and UKFC were to be merged. Cost cutting was the rationale given in the DCMS's statement:

The proposal is for a streamlined organisation, which can spend more of its money on film and services and less on infrastructure, and in turn offer better support for Britain's film culture and promotion of its film industry. (DCMS cited in Pulver 2010: 1)

Not surprisingly, given that both he and Woodward had already read the runes and taken their own initiative, Tim Bevan, the UKFC's chairman, warmly endorsed the DCMS's line, in terms that implicitly suggested that his organisation would not be the loser and, indeed, that the BFI ought to have been absorbed earlier:

> We know that the climate for public funding is going to get much tougher, and it's therefore sensible that we ask ourselves why there are two publicly funded film organisations in the UK. We need to look at the scope for savings across the board, to push as much money as we can into new film activity. (Bevan cited in Pulver 2009: 1)

By contrast, the BFI's chairman, Greg Dyke, gave a much more luke-warm and highly conditional reception to the idea – indeed, his comment may be read as a qualified rejection of a merger and a stout defence of the status quo:

> The BFI is in good shape and having a very successful year, but we welcome this move if it enables us to further develop our potential to provide a better service to the public. The BFI is a much cherished organisation and has a vital and leading role to play in developing film culture and heritage in this country. (Dyke cited in Pulver 2009: 1–2)

The minister's announcement indicated that he was setting up a 'Working Group, chaired by the DCMS with equal representation from the two bodies ... to consider how a single body would be structured and how to improve its service by reducing gaps and overlapping' (Screen Daily 2009: 1). At that point, evidently a report to the DCMS was expected before the end of 2009 – although this did not eventuate – and it was anticipated that the still largely distinct cultural and economic remits would be brought together in a single organisation, overcoming the fault-line created when the UKFC was originally set up.

This ministerial intervention, which occurred during Ben Bradshaw's tenure as Secretary of State for Culture, Media and Sport,[2] initiated a complex series of negotiations, with the DCMS apparently determined to effect a merger before the next general election, but – in part, through delaying tactics and apparent loss of focus in the DCMS as the election approached – failing to bring this about. Siôn Simon resigned his ministerial post in February 2010 'leaving his secretary of state, Ben Bradshaw, to push the merger forward, in the hope that the plans would be finalised, at least in outline, by the end of the financial year and before the impending general election' (Nowell-Smith 2012b: 308). On the evidence available to us, prior to the general election of May 2010, both the BFI and the UKFC still had future plans that gave every indication of maintaining two separate existences and gave no indication of how a merger would actually be implemented (BFI 2010a; UKFC 2009b).

While inconclusive talks went on in private, views about the merger had been probed to some extent in public by the House of Lords Select Committee on Communications, which published a major report on the film and television industries at the start of 2010 (HL SCC 2010). The Committee expressed concern about how 'a merged organisation might meet the different objectives which the two bodies currently pursue and what its status might be, bearing in mind that the BFI has charitable status and a Royal Charter'. In response, Culture Secretary Ben Bradshaw said that care would need to be taken in retaining the charitable status of the BFI in a new organisation. He further remarked:

> We are very well aware of the sensitivities of the BFI in particular, but we hope that we will be able to come up with a model that can preserve the qualities of both organisations and at the same time release money ... If one speaks to people who work day-to-day in the film industry, they often do not quite understand why we need to have these two separate organisations. (HL SCC 2010: 34, par. 105)

Merger, then, was still on the cards.

In its recommendations, however, the Lords Communications Committee was extremely guarded about the advantages of a merger, and particularly solicitous of the future status of the BFI:

> 107. We do not consider that a small saving, which a merger of the UK Film Council and the BFI would be likely to achieve, would by itself justify an amalgamation.
>
> 108. If, however, the proposal for the merger of the UK Film Council and the BFI goes ahead, it will be important that any organisational changes neither prejudice nor deter private donations to the BFI's education and archival work. (HL SCC 2010: 35)

Merger Talks

Both organisations' boards and their CEOs were involved in the merger talks, as well as ministers and civil servants at the DCMS. To judge by comments made to us by informants on either side of the discussion, the negotiations were conducted in a wary and mutually mistrustful atmosphere. The UKFC's chairman Tim Bevan later remarked in public testimony that the talks were 'not what would be called a smooth road' (HC CMSC 2011: Examination of Witnesses, Response to Q150). For their part, senior figures inside the BFI believed that throughout the discussion their body's values were not being respected by the UKFC and that the aim was a take-over (Interview 25, 2013).

We have been unable to access the significant advisory documentation relating to the merger produced by consultants to, and lawyers for, both bodies. The UKFC's pro-merger stance, however, was indicated in a letter sent early in 2010 by the chairman, Tim Bevan, to Siôn Simon at the DCMS (copied to Greg Dyke). He wrote:

> I am writing to let you know the outcome of the UK Film Council Board Meeting on Tuesday 26 January, when we discussed at length the common resolution committing the UKFC in principle to a merger with the BFI.
>
> First, I can report that my Board unanimously voted in favour of the merger resolution, as drafted and agreed with the BFI setting out a commitment in principle to create a new film organisation which will benefit UK film audiences and the UK film industry.
>
> However, for the record I should also point out that we have no interest or intention of allowing the important and wide range of publicly-funded activities for the film industry and for film culture to be subsumed into the BFI as proposed in Greg Dyke's recent letter to you.[3] (Letter from Tim Bevan to Siôn Simon, 11 February 2011)

Bevan's letter is clear evidence of a divergence of views between the UKFC and the BFI. He received a reply from the minister (despite the fact that the letter was dated two days earlier than the one received):

> Thank you for securing support from your board for the joint resolution to merge the UKFC and BFI into a single new film organisation to support film in the UK. I am very pleased with the progress that has been made so far.
>
> Obviously, the 'conditions' attached by the BFI have not been agreed by the other parties. I believe it is important in which case [sic] that we focus on what *has* been agreed: the process for deciding the preferred constitutional structure and governance of the new body. The next step will be the completion by [the accountancy firm] Grant Thornton of their report, which the Department commissioned after the Project Board, to consider the issues we discussed then, including the structure and governance of the new organisation. We expect the report next week.

I am confident that with the high commitment shown by both organisations we will be able to reach agreement on all issues as part of this process. (Letter from Siôn Simon to Tim Bevan, 9 February 2010; emphasis in original)

The minister's confidence proved to be seriously misplaced. If we step back and examine the record over the period of negotiations, there is more evidence of parallelism than convergence in the two would-be merger partners' plans.

The BFI board's minutes allow us to reconstruct its approach and stance, as well as the process of assuming new functions that were required for its eventual displacement of the UKFC. At times these documents, which are accessible online,[4] bear the legend 'a number of points in this minute are confidential and have been removed', which limits the detail available and the inferences that can be drawn. What is quite clear, however, is that Greg Dyke's carefully worded and very lukewarm reaction to the announcement of Creative Industries Minister Siôn Simon reflected the BFI's adamant rejection of any take-over. The BFI board's minutes consistently put quotation marks around the term 'merger' as a distancing device.

On 16 September 2009, the first direct impact on the BFI of the Labour Government's decision to seek a merger was noted as taking the form of an 'instruction from DCMS to UKFC that no new appointments should be made to the Boards of either the UKFC or the BFI (this instruction was related to the ongoing "merger" discussion between the DCMS, UKFC and the BFI)' (BFI board Minutes, 16 September 2009, minute 4.2(d)). This was followed by a decision to retain legal counsel to advise further on the matter, and for the chairman, Greg Dyke, to seek a meeting of the two boards later in the year. The earliest inklings of the BFI's future negotiating stance emerged at this point, namely that it would seek to remain a charitable body and retain its 'cultural integrity' in line with its Royal Charter and charitable status. Furthermore, any 'new' BFI should be funded directly by the DCMS rather than the UKFC (BFI board minutes, 16 September, minute 7). At the November 2009 meeting of the BFI board, it was decided that Greg Dyke would request the Minister, Siôn Simon, to ensure 'that the BFI's vision for the proposed "merger" between the BFI and the UK Film Council be properly considered' (BFI board minutes, 16 November, minute 7).

By February 2010, along with its legal advice, the BFI had secured a report from the accountancy firm Grant Thornton (the details of which have remained confidential). Disingenuously, given its evident opposition, the board's minutes reaffirmed the BFI's commitment to 'the principle' of a merger while at the same time setting out its own conditions (BFI board minutes, 24 February 2010, minutes 4.1, 4.2). These were detailed and indicate just how much the BFI would have to bend with the prevailing wind in order to retain its institutional identity, while modifying its present status:

It was agreed that:

1) the Board of Governors was willing to offer DCMS the right of veto over the appointment of the BFI's Chair and Deputy Chair, and suggested that a DCMS official might be an observer to the recruitment process;
2) the Board of Governors was willing to offer DCMS the right of veto over the appointment of the BFI's Chief Executive, and suggested that a DCMS official might be an observer to the recruitment process;
3) while the Board was willing to accept the appointment of the National Audit Office as the BFI's auditors (subject to the consent of the Charity Commission), they reserved the right to check the market rate for audits from time to time. (BFI board minutes, 24 February 2010, minute 4.3)

Taken together, these concessions amounted to major changes in the BFI's governance. The 'willing' acceptance in the board's minutes reads more like necessary acquiescence to save the organisation's skin. In March 2010, now less than two months away from the general election, Greg Dyke was to have 'further meetings with both Ben Bradshaw, Secretary of State for Culture, Media and Sport, and Tim Bevan, Chair of the UK Film Council, to negotiate the terms of an agreement' (BFI board minutes, 17 March 2010, minute 3). By this stage, it was clear that the fate of any such agreement would depend on which government was elected in May. As Nowell-Smith recounts:

[A]n outline agreement was reached before the end of March [2010], leaving the BFI and its Charter formally intact but with crucial questions about the form the new organisation would take and the ends it would pursue still very much up in the air. (Nowell-Smith 2012b: 308)

We have not been able to access this agreement. However, the high degree to which matters were still unresolved was evident from the fact that just one day before the general election, on 5 May 2010, the BFI board decided that 'Greg Dyke and Amanda Nevill would draft a paper for the new Government setting out the Board of Governors' view on the proposed "merger" ' (BFI board minutes, 5 May, minute 4).

The BFI's continuing determination to pursue its desire to escape the grip of the UKFC was also evident when, in early July 2010, in response to the new Coalition Government's announcement of a ministerial review of film, its position was clearly stated as follows:

> After considerable discussion the Governors agreed that it would be in the interests of the BFI for the BFI to be funded directly by DCMS rather than via the UK Film Council ... Governors wished Government to treat film (from the BFI's perspective) as culture, as 'the 7th art', and to treat the BFI as it deserved – as both a museum and a contemporary art institute ('we are both Tate Britain and Tate Modern'). (BFI board minutes, 8 July 2010, minute 5)

This statement – formulated a mere fortnight or so before the axe finally fell on the UKFC – crystallised years of frustration and resentment at the BFI's subordinate position and a renewed demand for proper recognition of its role and status. As we shall see, the BFI did win the argument in some respects but not without complications.

The Lingering Death of the UKFC

The UKFC's sudden abolition followed the May 2010 general elections, which had resulted in the formation of a Conservative-Liberal Democrat Coalition Government. The Conservative wing of the Coalition came into power determined to axe at least some quangos strongly associated with Labour. When still in opposition, the new Conservative Prime Minister, David Cameron, had identified the communications regulator, Ofcom, as a possible target. After the general election that body experienced a deep cut and a firm rolling back of its policy-formation role rather than annihilation. The BBC had also been fingered, with apparently collusive attacks by the Murdoch media camp and the Tories. It too faced cuts and a substantially redefined use of the television licence fee that supports public service broadcasting (Schlesinger 2009). But well before those actions were taken, it was on the UKFC – never before publicly in the frame for closure – that the ultimate blow fell.

On 21 June 2010, the new government announced that the merger talks were on hold. In a written statement to Parliament, the new Minister for Culture, Communications and Creative Industries, Ed Vaizey, said: 'There are no current plans to merge the UK Film Council and the British Film Institute' (Macnab 2010). Privately, because he had seemingly considered the two bodies to be incompatible, Vaizey told John Woodward (Interview, London, February 2013) that he wanted the UKFC to concentrate on the film industry and develop the idea of a new 'Creative Industries Council', with the BFI continuing to support film culture. Both Woodward and the UKFC's chairman, film producer Tim Bevan, who had strongly favoured a merger, still would have preferred to move ahead on this.

There is no evidence that the Conservatives were especially committed to a merger. The previous year, when in opposition as Shadow Minister for Culture and the Creative Industries, Ed Vaizey had commissioned a wide-ranging consultant's report on the film industry written by Maud Mansfield, to which he had appended an appreciative note. While this document reflected criticisms by producers made about the UKFC (not least its tough-minded approach to recoupment), it was broadly in support of that body's continued existence. The problem of the division between the industrial and cultural remits and how this affected the UKFC and the BFI was remarked on, as was the likely benefit of a merger, not least in respect of potentially enhancing the exploitation of the BFI's audio-visual archive. But if the balance of negative judgement tipped anywhere in the Mansfield report, it was towards the perceived underperformance of the BFI and the obstacles presented to its future organisational development in the digital age, largely seen as due to the rigidity imposed by its charitable status:

> There is a strong public policy argument for freeing the BFI from the pressure to self-generate income, thus allowing it to focus attention on its core remit of supporting films that the market cannot sustain, facilitating access and opening up the NFTVA [National Film and Television Archive]. Merger with the UKFC, and the corresponding clarification in strategy, would serve this purpose. (Mansfield 2009: 36)

Contrary to some views, it is unlikely that, in the end, the report played a significant role when the Conservatives took over the DCMS, although plainly they had been alerted to the merger issue. Given that the government had rowed back from a decision just the previous month, the UKFC's reversal of fortunes came as a bitter blow. The coup de grâce was administered privately to the UKFC during the weekend before the public announcement was made in the House of Commons.

The BFI heard about the decision the following day. At that time there was no suggestion that the UKFC's functions would be transferred to the BFI, as the government really had no clear succession plans (Interview 25, 2013). Indeed, in her evidence to the Commons Culture, Media and Sport (CMS) Committee, the BFI's CEO, Amanda Nevill, said: 'The announcement was as big a surprise for us as it was for the Film Council' and that there had been no detail behind the statement (HC CMSC 2011: Reply to Q153).

The public statement to abolish the UKFC was made in the House of Commons on Monday 26 July 2010, by Jeremy Hunt, the new Secretary of State for Culture, Media and Sport (Hunt 2010a). The official reason given to the House of Commons was that

> abolishing the UK Film Council and establishing a direct and less bureaucratic relationship with the British Film Institute ... would support front-line services while ensuring greater value for money. Government and Lottery support for film will continue. (HC CMSC 2011: par. 114)

Hunt further said that the UKFC's £3 million overheads were 'money that could be better used to support film-makers' (Macnab 2010: 37).

But at that time, no decision had yet been taken as to which body or bodies would subsequently administer the UKFC's functions. Stung by the news of abolition, and angered by the lack of planning, the Film Council's chairman, Tim Bevan, responded thus:

> Abolishing the most successful film support organisation the UK has ever had is a bad decision, imposed without any consultation or evaluation. People will rightly look back on today's announcement and say it was a big mistake, driven by short-term thinking and political expediency. British film, which is one of the UK's more successful growth industries, deserves better.
>
> Our immediate priority now is to press the government to confirm that the funding levels and core functions that are needed to underpin British film are locked in, especially at a time when filmmakers and film companies need more support than ever as they make the challenging transition into the digital age. To that end, we will work with the DCMS over the summer to identify how they can guarantee both continuity and safe harbour for British film. (Bevan cited in Shoard 2010)

For his part, in a bitter article in reaction to Hunt's decision, published by *The Guardian*, the UKFC's CEO, John Woodward, wrote:

> On Wednesday, we were a valued DCMS agency; by Friday, we were on a list that enabled it to help meet the Treasury's targets for cutting UK public bodies, as part of the effort to reduce the country's

£156bn budget deficit over the next four years. It's blitzkrieg, but without any forward planning. (Woodward 2010)

The abolition of the UKFC was clearly a huge shock to its leadership and staff. As John Woodward subsequently recalled:

One Saturday morning,[5] Tim [Bevan] got a ... call from Ed Vaizey when he was in LA, I think, just saying, 'I am terribly sorry, but we decided yesterday we have to abolish the Film Council and we are announcing it on Monday.' (John Woodward, Interview, London, February 2013)

This was perceived as extraordinarily capricious inside the UKFC, where – following an encouraging meeting with Vaizey's staff – Woodward had been working with his policy team at the Minister's behest on the prospect of creating a Creative Industries Council (Interview 20, 2013).

Why did the UKFC Fall?

Our informants have offered three main explanations for the cut, and these are not mutually exclusive. They are: personal ambition, political revenge and lobbying by disaffected enemies.

According to the influential policy adviser John Newbigin, when the Coalition took office 'Jeremy Hunt wanted to be best boy' by demonstrating that he could undertake cuts. John Woodward was also inclined to think of personal ambition as the spur to the closure:

It tells you that film policy is not important in the UK and in the end it can be sacrificed on the altar of ... you know, one man's political ambition, not even in the long term, you know, just in terms of how he wants to be perceived in the next three weeks by the Prime Minister and the Deputy Prime Minister. That's what it tells you. (John Newbigin, Interview, London, February 2013)

In off-the-record comments, moreover, some key players have said that there were divisions between Hunt and Vaizey over the decision and one source maintained the latter had 'within days' of the decision said that the government had axed the wrong body (Interview 22, 2013). As Mr Hunt and Mr Vaizey were not available for interviews, we could not probe these contentions further with them.

However, although one informant close to the action thought Hunt to be ambitious, he also considered him to be 'absolutely pragmatic', once he had concluded that the UKFC was no longer needed (Interview 22, 2013). Our interviewee also thought that as the BFI had a Royal Charter, winding it down would have been 'a nightmare', although as we shall show in the discussion that follows, and as the BFI's former director Wilf Stevenson observed to us, it was the BFI's charitable status that seemingly proved more of an obstacle to ministers looking for rapid-fire abolition, although it may well be that the existence of a Royal Charter added to the perception of difficulty.

Once very close to government decision making as an adviser to Gordon Brown when Chancellor and then Prime Minister, and now an experienced Labour peer, Wilf Stevenson considered such obstacles to a government seeking rapid change to be awkward but not insuperable:

> What the Queen has given in the Royal Charter, she can also take away. It's not impossible. It's unusual but it's not impossible. That's part of the reason for having a Royal Charter, that slightly extra protection, but it's not much, but it does require additional formulas and formulations ... so it is tricky, but it's not impossible. More difficult is the fact that it was a charity, because you have to think through then very carefully what happens to the charitable ... possessions, and I am sure from charity law anything that's been created with charitable donation or funding has to be kept in future in case the beneficiaries from that charitable act ... may turn up and wish it ... So that is tricky. (Wilf Stevenson, Interview, London, February 2013)

That the situation could have been managed differently was certainly the view of one UKFC insider, who thought that the BFI, which sought its own legal advice, had played both its charitable status and the Royal Charter for all they were worth as appearing to offer major obstacles to take-over, thereby successfully deflecting attack. Certainly, as we have seen, these defences warranted attention in the Lords Communications Committee's report. An acerbic counter-view from within the UKFC camp was this:

> The BFI kept putting up the Royal Charter and kept putting up Charity Commissioner's blocks ... They say, 'Oh, we are an independent charity.' Well, of course you are not; you're totally dependent on government funding for your sustainability ... Your Royal Charter is governed by the Privy Council, which is, in effect, the Cabinet ... The BFI did, from time to time, put up these alleged roadblocks to structural reform. (Interview 18, 2013)

Furthermore, in retrospect, it was starkly clear that the UKFC's non-statutory status – on formation it had been constituted as a private company limited by guarantee – left it relatively vulnerable when it came to a crisis:

> We were not embedded anyway in statute, and I think that has made it both easier to destroy us in the end ... at a stroke of Jeremy Hunt's biro. So we had no statutory underpinning. (Interview 18, 2013)

Somehow, the UKFC had omitted to guard its flanks. The record shows, however, that the possibility of an executioner's axe being wielded was considered right at the start of its existence. In one of John Woodward's earliest reports to the Film Council's Board, the following point was made about a 'statutory basis' being sought for that body:

> The CEO reported that DCMS had indicated that there was a real possibility that a short bill might be passed placing the Film Council on a statutory basis before the end of the current Parliament. The main consequences would be to make the Film Council more embedded in government and would mean the appointment of the National Audit Office as the Council's auditors. (FC board minutes, 22 August 2000, minute 4)

Given his Labour Party credentials, it is perhaps not surprising that Wilf Stevenson saw the abolition as part of a much more far-reaching political plan:

> It felt to me and it still feels more like political spite ... moderated obviously by being in the Coalition. But there was an intention by the incoming government – what I think will become clearer in time – just to be one of the more radical governments of modern times. Think about hospitals, schools, you think about universities. You think about all these changes in the public realm and then you think about the Film Council. A quango ... It was done within a few days of coming into power. (Wilf Stevenson, Interview, London, February 2013)

A third view about the reasons for the closure, articulated by one leading independent film producer much in tune with other disaffected producers that we interviewed, is that the UKFC was not popular and that it had lost one of its key constituencies – significant film producers. One informant referred to the study undertaken for the Conservative Party by Maud Mansfield – mentioned above – as part of the essential background, and maintained that the Opposition DCMS team had been testing the waters among film industry leaders regarding the UKFC. Those soundings, it was held, had produced a highly unenthusiastic set of responses. If so, these negative views were not borne out by Mansfield's report, which did reflect producers' criticisms, notably of recoupment terms, but hardly denounced the UKFC. We cannot exclude the possibility that it played a background role along with a current of opinion that, in the end, may have exercised some influence.

In a similar vein, Peter Watson, another prominent producer, who had been very close to the action as he was then a member of the BFI board, defended the closure decision in the following terms:

> The DCMS had long been struggling to find a way to reform the UKFC, which they, and most of the industry, felt was more interested in serving its own interests than serving either government or industry ... Woodward had overplayed his hand in trying to 'take over' the BFI. The DCMS were furious. Greg Dyke was incandescent, the relationship with the BFI finally broken ... The DCMS's preference was reform but they hadn't the stomach for a public battle ... The BFI offered a rather palatable and much cheaper alternative ... It was the DCMS officials, not Jeremy Hunt, who really made the decision ... certainly made easier by the government's stated policy to scrap the quangos. (Peter Watson, film producer, personal communication, September 2014)

According to Bill Bush, who had been a special adviser to Culture Secretary Tessa Jowell (Interview, London, March 2013), the UKFC had made enemies in the Treasury, which saw it as 'captured' by the industry, particularly in its advocacy for tax relief when it was seen as not being sufficiently 'an expression of government policy'. Others, as we have shown, took a different view. Nevertheless, Bush considered that when in the end it came to the choice of which quango to be axed, the UKFC had no friends in the civil service. By contrast with the 'entrepreneurial, fast footed' UKFC, Bush believed, the BFI was seen as 'reliable' and 'solid'.

We have noted the injured reaction from the UKFC to which these last comments are a robust counterpoint. In other quarters, there was considerable support for the UKFC, as the Commons CMS Committee noted:

> The abolition of the UKFC attracted considerable criticism from representatives of the UK film industry and from abroad. In press reports, director and producer, Mike Leigh likened it to 'abolishing the

NHS' ... while actor Liam Neeson described the decision as 'deplorable' and Clint Eastwood agreed. (HC CMSC 2011: par. 116)

Other well-known figures, such as Steven Spielberg, joined the protests, adding to the more than fifty actors, including James McAvoy, Bill Nighy, Timothy Spall and Emily Blunt who had signed a letter of protest (Child 2010). The closure attracted media attention by the BBC and in *The Guardian* and *The Telegraph*, and there was also 'a broader campaign' that ran until late August 2010, involving 'industry bodies and the public critical of the decision', with online forums, a petition attracting more than 26,000 signatures, a public protest and criticism from the Broadcasting, Entertainment, Cinematograph and Theatre Union (BECTU) (Shrinking the state 2013: 3). Despite this support, reactions to the closure in the film industry were divided, with some, including Michael Winner and Julian Fellowes, standing up for the government (Macnab 2010; Shrinking the state 2013: 4).

Inventing a New Solution

On 28 July 2010, just two days after Jeremy Hunt's statement, the House of Commons Culture, Media and Sport (CMS) Committee launched an inquiry that delved usefully into the abolition, finally reporting in January 2011. The DCMS was far from pleased by the manifestations of support that the UKFC received. On 8 August 2010, Jeremy Hunt published an article in *The Observer* that was astutely focused on the sensitive spot of top salaries at the UKFC. He stated that it was 'simply not acceptable in these times to fund an organisation like the UK Film Council, where no fewer than eight of the top executives are paid more than £100,000'. He offered reassurances that Lottery funding and the film tax credit would remain in place. Also, in what proved to be an important straw in the wind for its future form of governance, he said that while guaranteeing the future of the BFI, he wanted to 'give them greater operational and artistic freedom' (Hunt 2010b). The following week, the DCMS's irritation was evident at what it saw as a disinformation campaign about the adverse effects of the UKFC's closure. Playing hardball, Ed Vaizey was reported as writing to Woodward to ask if public money was being misused:

> I am very concerned about what has come to light. It looks as though sources at the film council have been over-zealously briefing in order to protect their interests. As a result they may be damaging the film industry that they purport to represent. (Child 2010)

Even the Commons CMS Committee felt obliged to comment on the matter:

> The Government suggested that the UKFC had spent public money in orchestrating its campaign and the Committee heard evidence that the UKFC had employed a 'third party comms strategy'. Mr Bevan argued that this was a necessary response to a significant increase in the number of press inquiries. (HC CMSC 2011: par. 116)

Still on the attack in September 2010, Hunt subsequently told the CMS Committee:

> The Film Council spent 24% of the grant that it received on its own administration and we asked ourselves if there was a better way to support the UK film industry than having a large number of executives paid more than £100,000 and an office in LA. (HC CMSC 2011: par. 117)

Tim Bevan disputed Hunt's take on the UKFC's overhead expenditure in his own evidence to the CMS Committee, saying that the figure was 10 per cent (HC CMSC 2011: par. 118). But Ed Vaizey later disagreed with this, maintaining Hunt's line (HC CMSC 2011: Witnesses, Reply to Q396).

Inside the Film Council, the DCMS's attacks were viewed with considerable displeasure. A paper to the board, whose author is unclear, titled 'Abolition of the UK Film Council: Latest Position' engaged tersely (and plainly very hurriedly) with the accusations then flying around:

> Purpose
> This paper updates the Board on the latest news relating to the government's decision to abolish the UK Film Council.
> Latest position
> Since we last met there has been a great deal of heat but little light. We have been accused wrongly of employing a RP [sic] company to wage a 'save the UK Film Council' campaign. Our record and achievements and performance has [sic] been questioned by Ed Vaizey and I'm pleased to say that we have more than answered each [sic]. (UKFC 2010c)

The board's paper should be read in tandem with Tim Bevan's evidence to the CMS Committee where he acknowledged that some £50,000 had been spent on handling communications and that he had told Vaizey, on hearing of the closure decision, 'we may be a minnow of an industry but we pack a lot of punch in our PR' (HC CMSC 2011, Witnesses, Reply to Q127). Against the charge of wasting public money, he went on to explain that Jeremy Hunt – in their 'first conversation' since abolition – had asked him to stop the 'tide of bad press that was going on'. He had replied that he would do his best 'and part of that was to bring in an agency to help us'. He denied under repeated questioning that this assistance had been used in a campaign to save the UKFC (HC CMSC 2011, Witnesses: Replies to Qs 129–34; 162–6).

Although Vaizey had delivered the blow, Bevan told the CMS Committee: 'He was the bearer of the tidings. I don't know whether he fired the bullet or not' (HC CMSC 2011: Witnesses, Reply to Q150). Less equivocally, he told us: 'I entirely blame Jeremy Hunt, actually, because he made the policy decision and then got somebody else to go and execute it' (Interview, London, April 2013).

If Vaizey did have any private differences with Hunt, these were not apparent in his evidence to the CMS Committee. He observed: 'I think the merger of the Film Council with the BFI is an achievement and a renewed policy for British film' (HC CMSC 2011, Witnesses, Reply to Q399). He acknowledged that the decision had come as a 'bolt from the blue' and said the Friday telephone call to Tim Bevan had been intended to minimise leaks before the parliamentary announcement the following Monday (HC CMCS 2011: Witnesses, Reply to Q397).

In its conclusions, while accepting that the BFI was best placed to 'take over the role of film funding' the CMS Committee (HC CMSC 2011: par. 126) was otherwise damning of the error-strewn route taken:

> The abolition of the UK Film Council was handled very badly by the Government. We would not expect a decision with such significant implications for the film industry to be sprung on the UK Film Council with little discussion or consultation. It is extremely regrettable that a film-maker of the stature of Tim Bevan has, as a result, decided to take no further part in Government-sponsored initiatives. It also appears that little or no thought had been given as to who would take on its functions.

Parliamentary rumblings continued into the following year. On 7 March 2011, the Labour peer, Lord (Wilf) Stevenson of Balmacara, raised questions about the closure process in the House of Lords, when he accused the government of 'abolishing the UK Film Council by press release' (HL Public Bodies Bill 2011, Amendment 65A, Column 1413). Stevenson laid down an amendment to the Public Bodies Bill 2011 asking for further clarification as to which body would be responsible for the remaining UKFC activities, while also requesting the responsible minister to report to Parliament on the BFI's performance after one year. He explained his intervention as follows:

> The reason I went on about this is because we're talking about the proper processes that should exist for closing down a public body ... We [Labour] could hardly argue against because we had asked the BFI and the Film Council to consider merging themselves. So we weren't very far apart on it. [It was about] just the process, not the principle. (Wilf Stevenson, Interview, London, February 2013)

John Newbigin, who became the chairman of Creative England, the successor body to the Regional Screen Agencies, agreed that there had been scant concern for process. What came out of the merger, he said, was the BFI 'plus the Film Fund'. Moreover, he observed:

> The BFI was a delivery body. It archived and promoted British film and ran an education programme. It really wasn't a strategic body for the industry in the way the UKFC had been designed to be. So it simply didn't have the capacity, skillset or networks. And then the BFI was suddenly asked to do something different and to get to grips with this new remit needed heroic mind-shifts. It was unforgivably irresponsible of the government to push that change through. (John Newbigin, Interview, London, February 2013)

An Unplanned Closure

In its subsequent analysis of the closure decision, the National Audit Office drew attention to other procedural failings in a telling critique of the DCMS:

> [T]he Department announced the closure of UK Film Council in July 2010, but it had not performed sufficient analysis of the financial implications of the decision. It announced the transfer of functions four months later, but still had no formal arrangements in place as to which Film Council staff would transfer to other bodies. It had also not calculated the expected costs of closure, although it had decided the transfer of functions would take place on 1 April 2011. (NAO 2011: 1)

The lack of foresight was certainly borne out by the record of piecemeal transfer recorded by the two bodies concerned. Moreover, despite the undoubted bad feeling on each side, the creation of a new system depended hugely upon the goodwill of the UKFC's staff in ensuring the smooth transfer of functions.

During the closing months of the UKFC's life, the state of that body's morale may be judged from its uncorrected board minutes of 30 November 2010.[6] This was to be the last occasion on which the full board met. Of the fifteen members, nine were present (Greg Dyke was one of the absentees). A new smaller board with five members plus the chairman, Tim Bevan, was installed 'to steer the UK Film Council to close down' (UK Film Council, board minutes, 30 November 2010, p. 2).

Prior to this, in September 2010, the BFI board had noted that it 'would submit a proposal to adopt the production funds, and to suggest that it should lead the development of strategy on distribution and exhibition' (BFI board minutes, 2 September 2011, minute 8.2). Some two months later, the BFI discussed 'current proposals to transfer a significant number of current UK Film Council activities to the BFI. The paper dated 12 November 2010 that had been submitted by Greg Dyke and Amanda Nevill to DCMS – *Transforming the BFI: A New Organisation for Film* – was approved.'

It was then agreed that:

1) the Board of Governors wished the BFI to remain a registered charity;
2) it may be appropriate to offer greater scrutiny by the CMS Select Committee in exchange for reduced scrutiny by DCMS;
3) it would be unacceptable for DCMS to control appointments to the BFI's Board of Governors with the exception of the Chair and Deputy Chair;
4) it would be reasonable for DCMS to have the right to approve the appointment of the Chief Executive;
5) it would be unacceptable for DCMS to have control over the BFI's wider business plan. (BFI board minutes, 17 November 2011, minute 4)

Apart from this, the BFI was to assess the advantages and disadvantages of becoming a registered rather than an exempt charity.

In November 2010, just as the BFI was gearing up to take over, the UKFC board was preoccupied with its winding-up arrangements for the regional agencies Screen East and Screen Yorkshire, and with handing over responsibility to its successor for British Film Week 2012. Given John Woodward's imminent departure, the board authorised new arrangements for signing payments.

The UKFC's 'Abolition presentation', dated November 2010, gives us considerable insight into the detailed effects of closure on the organisation as well as the extent of what had to be done as a result of Jeremy Hunt's decision (UKFC 2010c). Under the title 'What We Know', the seven-slide presentation first noted that the BFI would become 'the lead organisation for Government's policy for film' and 'Lottery distributor for film in the UK'. It then listed the activities being transferred to the BFI: 'film development and production funding, film distribution and exhibition activity; film skills, training and edication [sic] funding, including support for Skillset, First Light; funding for England's Regional Screen Agencies (which will be recast as Creative England) and ongoing support for the Nations; Certification Unit; MEDIA Desk'. It further noted that all Lottery-funded activities would stay in place until 1 April 2012.

Under 'Financial considerations', it was observed that 'the DCMS have indicated that they have no funding to pay for the costs of closing the UK Film Council'. The scale of the financial obligations was estimated as redundancy costs of between £1.3 and £1.6 million; continuing operational costs for 2011/12 of £2.1 million; and closure costs of £3.8 million for pensions; and continuing leasing commitments of some £1.5 million – a total of between £8.7 million and £8.9 million.

The presentation then noted that Film London would become responsible 'for promoting the UK across the world as the best place to invest in film'. Furthermore, that it would work '[a]longside BAFTA, the BFI and BBC Worldwide to build on their existing capacities and connections to explore showcasing and promoting British films to the entertainment industry in the US'. Activities transferring to Film London would be '[i]nward investment work in a public/private partnership with the Production Guild, UK Screen, Pinewood Shepperton Studios and others in the industry'.

In the November 2010 presentation, under 'What We Don't Know' was listed 'current activity not funded', namely, 'film exports; research, statistics and market intelligence; work on intellectual property and combating film theft; co-production support; diversity initiatives; and impact on UKFC staff'.

Looking ahead to pre-Christmas 2010, the presentation envisaged 'detailed discussions with receiving organisations' as well as 'a process of due diligence, working with the relevant organisations on a smooth handover of film functions and expertise'. Post-Christmas, the main concern was what would happen to staff at risk of redundancy, with those staff that were transferring to 'receiving organisations' having done so by the end of March 2011, and most of those who were to be made redundant leaving by the end of May 2011.

The slide titled 'Paying the Bill' identified the UKFC's then 'under-spend or uncommitted accruals'. These figures are not presented unambiguously, but it would appear that £8 million was available under Grant-in-Aid (GIA) and £1.35 million from the Lottery. It is not clear how much of this funding was eventually transferred to the BFI, nor what proportion was used to wind up the UKFC, although according to *The Guardian*'s Freedom of Information request, the UKFC's annual administration cost was about £3 million whereas it cost £11.3 million to wind up the UKFC (Curtis and King 2010), a figure also discussed at the CMS Committee's hearings (HC CMSC 2011: Q154).

Finally, it was estimated that some thirty-five to forty staff would be subject to the Transfer of Undertakings (Protection of Employment) Regulations 2006 (TUPE). The presentation noted that the BFI would now need 'funding and industry expertise' and that its 'communication with the industry' was an issue, too. For its part, as late as December 2010, the BFI was still engaged in discussing the transfer of staff and 'Lottery and UKFC-funded activities' (BFI board minutes, 17 December 2010, minute 5). Its designation as a Lottery distributor was finally reported as agreed only in February 2011 (BFI board minutes, 22 February 2011, minute 6). Moreover, the structure of Creative England, it was reported, would be in place only by 1 October 2011 (BFI board minutes, 11 May 2011, minute 12).

Ed Vaizey set out the full official position on the new arrangements in a lengthy speech delivered on 29 November 2010. The 'New BFI' was the linchpin of the announcement. It would, he said, 'change fundamentally ... become more open to partnerships with others, more engaged with the nations and regions, more able to realise an exciting vision of a coherent, joined up film industry' (Vaizey 2010: 2).

The New Institutional Landscape

The UKFC's closure involved yet another redrawing of the institutional map. Most of the UKFC's functions (and forty-four of its seventy-three posts) were formally transferred to the BFI on 1 April 2011. This was a new influx equivalent to some 10 per cent of the BFI's existing workforce. As Vaizey indicated in his speech, the eight Regional Screen Agencies were closed and replaced by three 'regional hubs' under a new body intended to work alongside the BFI, Creative England. Film London – a curiously inapt name for a body intended to represent the UK as a whole – took over the role of attracting inward investment for film production.

In a paper written shortly after the abolition had been decided, the BFI had welcomed the restoration of its direct reporting to the DCMS, which would allow it 'to have a conversation at a departmental level alongside other national cultural bodies and collections, giving a much needed direct voice for film as an art form' (BFI 2010b: par. 7.2). The BFI, as we have seen, became the new lead agency, but not on the same operational terms as before. The government was set upon achieving a new deal in respect of the control it could exercise.

Thus, what 'direct reporting' meant for the BFI gradually became clearer as functions were progressively transferred from the UKFC. Amanda Nevill subsequently acknowledged the challenge in her evidence to the CMS Committee (HC CMSC 2011: Reply to Q168) when she said that the BFI 'would have to change quite fundamentally from the board down, because ... you're going to have to bring in new people and new skills into the additional organisation to do that'. At the December 2010 board meeting, 'The BFI's status with Government' was an item of major importance. The Board's Secretary reported on negotiations with the DCMS and the Treasury 'over the BFI's prospective status as a non-departmental public body, and the controls that government were seeking to impose'. It was noted that 'discussions were continuing in an attempt to find a solution to a seemingly intractable problem: reconciling the Board's duty to protect private charitable assets with Government's apparent desire to take control of them' (BFI board minutes, 17 December 2010, minutes 4.1, 4.2).

The BFI's charitable status, we have noted, had appeared to offer it some protection from the axe in the summer of 2010. However, the BFI's desire for a proximate 'conversation' with the DCMS mutated under evident government pressure into an acceptance of a new NDPB status, putting it back on the same footing as the UKFC. To safeguard its charitable assets, however, the board had decided to hive these off into 'an independent registered charity whose objects would mirror those of the BFI's and which would be analogous to a "Friends of ..." charity created by other cultural institutions' (BFI board minutes, 22 February 2011, minute 1). The following month, the creation of the BFI Trust was reported. Aside from a change of status the DCMS also required the BFI to be audited by the National Audit Office, which needed a special dispensation from the Charity Commission (BFI board minutes, 24 March 2011, minutes 5 and 6). A few months later, in May 2011, following the formal abolition of the UK Film Council, the BFI had to amend its Royal Charter.

The BFI's charitable status, which had buttressed its defence against closure in 2010, proved in the end to be no serious obstacle to changes that amounted to a de facto merger. In retrospect, it does appear that the outgoing Labour Government had foreclosed its merger options more than need be.

The BFI was anticipating that its new leading role could create problems in the future. It was counselled by its policy adviser, Neil Watson, who had previously occupied that role at the UKFC, not to 'seek to be a gatekeeper for the film industry in its relations with government'. Nor, he counselled, 'should the BFI seek strategic leadership on every issue that affected industry' (BFI board minutes, 22 February 2011, minute 13). This formulation quite expressly overturned the line taken by John Woodward, when he had distanced the UKFC from the film industry in his fateful speech of 2005. It is doubtless an indication of the BFI board's nervousness that its determination to maintain its autonomy was restated at the next meeting, with even more brio:

The Board reiterated its view that it would not seek leadership in all areas and, indeed, would positively resist the idea that the BFI should be either the mouthpiece of the film industry or a gatekeeper between the industry and Government – there had to be a space for a thriving set of trade and professional bodies to emerge – and nor would the BFI be a replacement for all the work undertaken by the UKFC since much of the funding had been withdrawn. (BFI board minutes, 24 March 2011, minute 10.2)

This stance evolved further as the BFI assumed the role of key public funder of film production. In yet a further step in taking over the UKFC's role in production, while signalling its own distinctive approach, the board approved the job description for a new head of the Film Fund in November 2011, while emphasising that this was seen as a 'creative' job (BFI board minutes, 16 November 2011, minutes 8.6, 8.7). This followed Tanya Seghatchian's decision, in September 2011, to depart from running the Film Fund.

In a similar vein, the board's view of the BFI's forward planning firmly stated:

[T]he purpose of the BFI should be determined with reference to the vital cultural importance of film rather than starting from market failure: the purpose may perhaps be related to the idea of the transformative power of film. A critical starting point was the idea that the BFI was rooted in public service. (BFI board minutes, 11 May 2011, minute 10)

At this point, it was clear that the Coalition Government was intending to have another review of the film sector, and the BFI sought to exert maximum influence on the inquiry's focus and deliberations. The board learned that '[s]everal liaison meetings had been held with DCMS officials and the Minister and with the Chair of the Review, Chris Smith. Three BFI Governors were members of the Review Panel, although they had been appointed in their own right as individuals, not as representatives of the BFI' (BFI board minutes, 16 June 2011).

On 24 May 2011, Ed Vaizey announced that Chris Smith, former Culture Secretary and now the Labour peer, Lord Smith of Finsbury – would lead an 'independent panel of film industry experts, reviewing the Government's film policy' (FPRP 2012: 1). The panel's report – *A Future for British Film: It Begins with the Audience* – was published in January 2012. It was a nice irony for the progenitor of the UKFC to re-enter the policy landscape after the demise of his erstwhile creation, only now to confer fresh blessings on the reborn BFI. The Film Policy Review (FPR) situated itself firmly in the digital age and inaugurated a new audience-focused phase in film policy, the analysis of which is beyond the scope of this book. Suffice it to say that the FPR extensively addressed the role of the BFI, which it recommended should be 'a single focused leadership body for UK Film, demonstrating transparency, accessibility and collaboration', carefully noting that 'it now has an industrial as well as a cultural brief' (FPRP 2012: 95, Recommendation 54). The government's response welcomed and largely endorsed the FPRP's wide-ranging recommendations, recognising the new challenges faced by the BFI (DCMS 2012).

The publication of the BFI's own revised strategy – *Film Forever: Supporting UK Film* – followed in October 2012. A clear statement of the BFI's new status headed the report: 'In 2011 the BFI became the lead organisation for film in the UK. It is now a Government arm's length body and distributor of Lottery funds for film'. But it also said: 'Founded in 1933, the BFI is a registered charity governed by Royal Charter' (BFI 2012a: 2). In their foreword, Greg Dyke and Amanda Nevill (BFI 2012a: 5) situated the BFI's thinking as a response to the Film Policy Review Panel. In light of the debate engendered by *Film Forever*, and the consultations it had conducted, the BFI identified three strategic priorities: the expansion of education, learning opportunities and boosting audience choice across the UK; investing in film development, production talent and skills; and also investing in preservation, digitisation, interpretation and access. In its *Triennial Review of the British Film Institute* (2014), the DCMS endorsed the BFI's new role and – with a focus on the organisational transition that had taken place – found that, on the whole, the new model was functioning efficiently. Although recommendations for further operational improvements were made, the BFI was seen by the government as having passed the necessary tests to remain an NDPB and as fitted to pursue the objectives set out in its Royal Charter.

The Post-UKFC Settlement

New Labour's creation of the Film Council under Chris Smith hardly came about in a transparent manner. Nevertheless, there was a public review process along with the inevitable private conversations and lobbying. By comparison, however, complete opacity prevailed when the UK Film Council was axed. Whatever the precise background factors in play, Jeremy Hunt's decision to abolish the UKFC was acted on rapidly and ruthlessly. The Council's decision makers were taken totally by surprise and there was no wider consultation to assess the consequences.

After a period of indecision following the closure announcement, by a nice irony the Conservative Culture ministers hit upon precisely the rationalisation that they had at first rejected: they opted for a closure that was in reality a merger because it meant shifting a good half of the UKFC's expertise into the BFI. The lack of due process – adversely commented on both in Parliament and by the National Audit Office, not to speak of across hostile sectors of the film industry – left an institutional succession problem for which urgent solutions had to be found and that took the best part of a year to complete.

In their reflections on the 'blunders' of British politics, Anthony King and Ivor Crewe (2013: 386–7) have argued that there is a 'deficit of deliberation' in much decision making. They characterise a deliberative approach as involving careful consideration, not being over-hasty, and conferring and taking counsel. None of these desirable criteria was met when the UKFC was axed.

The post-UKFC phase of film policy merits further research. Whether the BFI's shift back to NDPB status will prove to be fateful for its future survival and functioning is beyond the scope of the present study. Here, we would merely observe that the influx of a significant number of ex-UKFC personnel, coupled with the change of internal culture required for it to become a funding agency on a major scale, have indeed begun to constitute a 'new' BFI.

CHAPTER 10

Conclusions

I've never been certain whether the moral of the Icarus story should
only be, as is generally accepted, 'don't try to fly too high', or whether
it might also be thought of as 'forget the wax and feathers, and do a
better job on the wings'.

(Kubrick 1997)[1]

Introduction

In this book we have told the tale of the rise and unexpected fall of the
UK Film Council. It is a story rich in characteristically overweening
ambitions for the British film industry, of both deft and inept political
backdoors dealings, clashing egos and conflicting interests, falling over
hubristic tripwires and, in the end, as the decade-long outcome of the
banal organisational routines of strategising and decision making, some
genuine achievement.

We have found the brief history of the UKFC not only to be fascinat-
ing but also revealing about the challenges faced by cultural funding
bodies as they negotiate competing policy objectives over time, facing
uncertain navigation in the choppy waters of shifting economic and
political conditions. Our analysis of the history of the organisation has
highlighted the particular circumstances that precipitated the perceived
need, in the late 1990s, for a new body to support film in the UK. In
our account of the hidden history of its formation, we have examined
who drove the organisation's agenda, analysing which objectives were
prioritised and why their weighting changed over time. The Council's
performance has been assessed in a number of ways to probe how effective in fulfilling its remit this iconic – if, at times, controversial – body
proved to be. Like all bodies of this kind, it had to negotiate competing
economic and cultural objectives and satisfy the key constituencies of
interest that really count in the landscape of film-making and public
policy. Quite unlike, for instance, broadcasting, with its established regulatory apparatus and habit of provoking resonant debate, film policy
is not widely discussed outside the narrow circles of cognoscenti and
really does not engage that wider public that in the case of broadcasting
is variously constituted as citizens, consumers or audiences. The world

of film is one dominated by insiders. In this sense, our study reinforces earlier accounts of the closed nature of film policy formation in the UK (Dickinson and Street 1985).

Here, in concluding, and in the interests of showing why these issues matter to us all, we reflect critically on the political, policy and technological contexts that framed the UKFC's creation, existence and eventual demise. We ask how reasonable were the expectations articulated at the Film Council's inception and, with this in mind, how well it performed as the lead strategic support body for film. We reflect on the challenges characteristically faced by national film agencies as they necessarily relate to transnational political, economic and cultural spaces (Schlesinger 2015b) and seek to fulfil demanding and, at times, contradictory public remits. We also consider what strategic lessons there may be for the future design of film policy, based on the specific experience of the UK Film Council.

Context

Some who were involved in the Film Council's formation now look back on an exceptional chance to start afresh with 'a kind of carte blanche' (Interview 14, 2013) by using Lottery money to reshape the approach to support for film. However, the setting up of a new lead body for film took place against the background of historical, political and economic constraints that undoubtedly shaped the kind of organisation that emerged and, as discussed in Chapter 3, the invention of the Film Council actually followed closely on from events in the 1990s that left a strong impression on the newly minted organisation's initial sense of purpose.

The UK film industry had long been seen as a sector characterised by unfulfilled economic potential that, if provided with the right sort of supportive intervention, may flourish. The view that the UK film industry was in recurrent crisis may be traced back 'at least to the Cinematograph Films Act 1927 which imposed a quota for the exhibition of British films after it had been established that over 90 per cent of films shown in the UK were made in America' (Pratten and Deakin 1999: 1). There was a succession of reports and studies prior to the late 1990s, including one prepared by the investment banker Sir Peter Middleton of Barclays de Zoete Wedd (Middleton 1996), shortly before the celebrated Film Policy Review of 1998 that led to the setting up of the Film Council. Middleton had drawn attention to how their small size and vertically disaggregated structures meant that British film production companies were outclassed by the Hollywood majors, finding themselves unable to compete either at home or in international markets. A solution to the question of smallness of scale was needed but there was little consensus about what form that should take (Pratten and Deakin 1999).

A new Labour Government, anxious to demonstrate its commitment to promoting economic and industrial success and, distinctively, attaching a high priority to support for Britain's creative industries, was elected in 1997. The establishment of the National Lottery in the mid-1990s had created a new stream of public funding support for film. But, led by a hostile press, criticism was rife of the manner in which Lottery funds were being 'squandered' on obscure and unpopular film projects by the Arts Councils of England, Wales, Scotland and Northern Ireland (Hill 2012). When the incoming Labour Culture Secretary Chris Smith commissioned the Film Policy Review Group, led by the commercially experienced Stewart Till, at the time president of Polygram Filmed Entertainment International, the die was cast for new measures intended to overhaul Britain's approach to public support for film. Our analysis in Chapter 3 suggests that while there was certainly a public process, behind the scenes there was a political fix that led to recommending the creation of a new lead body for film.

In line with earlier diagnoses, the predominant concern that shaped the setting up of the Film Council was the UK film industry's commercial under-performance. This needed to be put right, so it was held, by promoting a more market-savvy and business-minded approach to film making. John Woodward, Alan Parker and Stewart Till, identified as suitable exemplars of the expertise and values needed to transform the film industry, were recruited and installed to lead the development of the new agency.

The new Film Council packed considerable clout as a public support body. It was intended to be a single well-funded entity that aimed to replace an array of previous bodies and, as such, it was meant to bring a more integrated approach to film support. As we have shown, however, there was a fatal fault-line from the very start in the unsettled relationship that the new body had with the veteran BFI. And, indeed, the intended simple design became a baroque accumulation of fiefdoms (or 'partnerships') – represented in Appendix 1 – that without a hint of irony was referred to inside the UKFC as its 'family'.

But, at the start, as a leading body charged with bringing greater strategic coherence to a factious and fragmented field, the organisation set up in 2000 looked sleek and rational as it assimilated its erstwhile rivals. In common with Ofcom, established a few years later in 2003, it represented what one interviewee described as 'an iconic New Labour creation' (Interview 18, 2013). Whether this perceived status served the organisation well over the longer term is questionable, as – to date, at least – the pivotal party political contest at Westminster has been between the Conservatives and Labour and, as we have shown, each has long dabbled in re-engineering the film support framework in its own distinctive way. The Coalition Government formed in May 2010 broke the post-war mould of two-party dominance but left the Conservatives in charge of cultural policy. As we have shown in Chapter 9, so far as the UKFC was concerned, as the DCMS was in the Conservatives' hands, politics as usual prevailed under the Coalition: this meant initiating institutional change, even though major elements of Labour's film policy were kept intact.

Mission

> Film matters. It matters because it is both a powerful engine of the creative economy, and a form of cultural expression which reaches huge audiences and influences lives. Yet without a well-structured set of interventions by Government, the UK film sector cannot begin to realise its potential. The UK Film Council was set up to provide a framework [for such] intervention[s]. (Woodward cited in UKFC 2004b: 4)

As a unified body, the UK Film Council's remit officially encompassed all aspects of promoting film and film culture. Even so, at the inception of the Film Council it was widely understood that its primary raison d'être was 'to create a self-sustaining commercial film industry' (FPRG 1998: 4). With such an all-encompassing agenda, key aspects of the organisation's remit needed to be devolved to partner agencies and cultural responsibilities were delegated largely to the BFI, whereas the Council focused on the key task of promoting industrial development.

But was it realistic to expect the Film Council to bring about a sustainable UK film industry? Given the unique historical circumstances and the well-established advantages of size and structure that have contributed to the singular success of the Hollywood-based US major production studios, the level of public intervention required to place independent producers in the UK on a similar competitive footing would have had to be enormous and unprecedented and, in any case, without ever offering any serious guarantee of success in what is an international cultural market economy. Equipped with Lottery funding of £17 to £20 million per annum, although the UK Film Council was empowered to influence levels of film-making and the culture of the UK independent sector, it really stood little credible chance of reproducing within Britain industrial conditions that may conduce to consistent commercial success in international film-making.

In the early 2000s, under the leadership of CEO John Woodward and Board Chairman Alan Parker, the Film Council took major steps to reorientate the ideological emphasis of public support. Under the new regime, this was shifted from culturally relevant film production – as had been the approach under the Arts Councils – to pursuing production with distributor, exhibitor and wider market appeal, as well as attracting greater inward investment. Despite progress in this direction, it did not go unnoticed at the Film Council that making the UK film industry commercially self-sustaining was a difficult challenge. According to John Woodward:

> It was Chris Smith who hung ['sustainability'] around our neck. Nobody at the Film Council wanted that, I have to say ... It's a very unhelpful word. It's a word that lacks any kind of clarity ... Where I come from, 'sustainable' would mean that you make some sort of investment in the film industry but in the end it ceases to need public money in order to support itself ... That was what people immediately thought the end-game was. So you terrify everyone because they can't see any pathway to that ... There's no historical precedent for film industries that are self-sustaining without public subsidy and support and policy. And people got very scared. And then that ghost gets pushed back on the organisation because you're there, saying, 'So how are you going to do this, then?' (John Woodward, Interview, London, February 2013)

This was a pregnant question that overshadowed the UKFC's short history.

Execution

However questionable 'sustainability' may have been as a founding remit, as Stewart Till noted, such rhetoric was effective in propagating a sense of the Council's strategic aspiration and of a new mood (Interview, London, March 2013). The aim of promoting a more 'professional' and 'business-minded' approach to film-making was inscribed in a pro-active programme of schemes and interventions carried out by the organisation during its lifetime and, indeed, this strong emphasis on industrial development was the chief distinguishing feature of the model of support that it offered (Dickinson and Harvey 2005: 422; Hill 2012).

But the objectives pursued by the Film Council and how it understood and projected its mission changed over time. As discussed in Chapter 4, the central focus of the Council's strategy shifted from, initially, promoting commercial sustainability and a distribution-led approach to, in its final years, pursuing greater support for both independent production and innovation. One of the key factors that determined how priorities were reweighted over time was the organisation's leadership. By all accounts, John Woodward was a decisive and highly effective CEO, if at times provoking controversy. However, the influence of successive chairmen, all of whom were film industry executives of exceptional international stature, is also reflected in how the organisation's sense of mission changed over time, with a gradual dilution in later years of the 'Atlanticist' orientation that had held greatest sway in the early years of the Council's life. Some sceptics have argued that a retreat from 'sustainability' was inevitable, given the impossibility of the task and a self-serving instinct for survival on the UKFC's part. However, it may be argued that any organisation worth its salt will learn through experience what is feasible and adapt accordingly, so that the gradual broadening and reinvention of the UK Film Council's remit over time could be seen as an evolutionary process still in train when its life was terminated.

The original objective of creating a commercially 'sustainable' industry was never achieved. Following more than a decade of intervention by the Council, when the organisation closed in 2011 the British film industry was still fragmented, consisting predominantly of small and under-capitalised firms. Nevertheless, the Council's period as lead support body for film is associated with a number of successes, including substantially increased levels of inward investment in UK film production, modest increases in box-office receipts for British-made films and achieving higher levels in the regional dispersion of film funds. In 2011, in an ironically timed tribute to its achievements, *The King's Speech*, one of the films to which the Council had awarded Lottery funding shortly before being closed down, became the highest-grossing independent British film of all time, as well as winning four Oscars (FPRP 2012: 5).

According to John Woodward (Interview, London, April 2013), even though in 2010 there were 'still a lot of things to be done', the organisation had played a decisive role as a 'change agent', and had 'grabbed British film by the scruff of the neck and forced it to raise its game and professionalise itself'. Somewhat in counterpoint, the UKFC's last chairman, Tim Bevan, has maintained that key aspects of the Council's remit (such as its response to digital distribution technology and the priority given to independent producers) still needed further development (Interview, London, April 2013). Furthermore, Bevan considered that aspects of how the organisation operated (for instance, its staffing levels and high salaries) also needed correction.

Potential Lessons for Film Support Bodies

Tim Bevan described the closure announcement by the new Conservative-led Coalition Government as 'a complete bolt from the blue'. Prominent industry figures, including the Labour peer David Puttnam (2010), immediately spoke out against this move, arguing that thanks to the Film Council the UK film industry finally had a unified and coherent industry body guiding public policy for film support. But in addition to the many messages of praise and support for the organisation that followed, the Film Council was also subject to criticism. Evidently, being a lead body was a mixed blessing and it was difficult for the Film Council to satisfy all of its contending constituencies of interest.

Other support bodies for film may learn from this experience. For one, it is important not to be associated with unrealistic or unattainable objectives. That the Film Council was initially steered strongly towards industrial sustainability is entirely consistent with the current governmental emphasis on 'growing' the creative industries (Dickinson and Harvey 2005; Hesmondhalgh 2013) as well as the 'defensive instrumentalism' that has characterised New Labour's approach to policies for supporting culture (Belfiore 2012). However, because of the persistent structural and competitive disadvantages faced by the domestic production sector in the UK and, for that matter, in all other European countries, it is simply not within the power of a national film support body to create a commercially sustainable production industry. Even though the UKFC eventually distanced itself from this objective in favour of a more rounded agenda, it was forever tainted by the impression that securing a sustainable industry was its primary *raison d'être*, which in the end proved to be mission impossible.

The coherence and strategic leadership that the Film Council, as a unified body, brought to bear assisted the organisation to move forward decisively in pursuit of its industry-focused agenda. But it also involved drawbacks. Unified film support bodies face the problem of meeting diverse expectations as to what priorities they should pursue. One fundamental challenge is how to reconcile inherent tensions between economic and cultural goals. Some models of support for film are prone to criticism for focusing excessively on artistic or socio-cultural merit to the exclusion of market imperatives, whereas others are denounced for placing too much emphasis on commercial rather than cultural aims (Bintliff 2011).

Even where the focus may be purely on promoting the industry's commercial performance, the task of providing support is complicated by the disparate nature of the film industry and the diverse sectors of which it is comprised; each has its own interests and all of these groups expect to be prioritised and respected. This was exemplified, for instance, in the dispute about tax breaks that began in 2004, when some producers wanted tax concessions to be framed so that cultural tests would not deter inward investment by the US majors; others, however, were opposed to directing public support towards major international players rather than small independent film-makers. Trying to satisfy all stakeholders with an interest in public support for film was well-nigh impossible, as Alan Parker has conceded:

[I]f there was a flaw in what we [at the Film Council] tried to do, [it] is that ... we had our finger in every single pie, trying to do a lot of things. (Alan Parker, Interview, London, March 2013)

Whereas a leading film support body may deploy more resources and influence than a scattering of smaller entities, it is more likely to be perceived as monolithic and excessively controlling – a pitfall for the UK Film Council. Independent producers critical of the Council's ideology and strategy also tended to take the view that it was too centralised, controlling and 'arrogant'. This points to another important lesson that emerges from the UKFC's experience, namely the importance of maintaining cordial relationships with all key interests, if at all possible, and especially those most likely to be the most articulate and energetic in airing their discontents. However, the present vogue for 'stakeholder management' has inherent limitations. Sweet talk cannot abolish real differences of interest.

Friction persisted between the Film Council and those who disagreed with its approach of favouring a distribution-led strategy, as opposed to supporting creative and culturally relevant film-making at home. However, all film bodies that occupy subordinate positions in the international cultural market-place face difficulties in negotiating not only their differing ideological stances but also the competing international influences over which approach to support to take. On the one hand, the example posed by Hollywood's economic success is an irresistible beacon. On the other, seeking to emulate the Hollywood approach without the key advantages of structure and scale enjoyed by the US majors is simply not going to work, as the independent producers' leader John McVay has underlined (Interview, London, March 2013). From this point of view, given the absence of a cultural rationale, public support for film may be judged to make little sense (Interviews 13 and 16, 2013). Herein lies the attraction of some European approaches to film support, characterised by a primary concern to ensure the production and circulation of culturally relevant content to the home audience.

For a number of players, disapproval of the Council's ideology and approach was reinforced by resentment at the manner and style in which the organisation treated those it was supposed to be serving. Moreover, the payment of high salaries to executives was a particular bugbear and contributed to an abiding perception of arrogance and hubris that eventually came about. In the transformed political context of the austerity economics that followed the banking crash of 2008, the payment of high salaries laid the Council open to the charge that here was a quango eminently suitable for cost-cutting – the key justification used by Culture Secretary Jeremy Hunt.

Criticism of high recoupment targets, of 'spin', and of senior executives at the Council who 'comported themselves … more like studio executives than people who were there with a public service ethos', according to producer Peter Watson (Interview, London, March 2013) were all symptomatic of the UKFC's failure to successfully maintain good relations with a significant portion of one key interest group: UK independent producers.

But for a public body, the kingpin is the government. The dispute about tax break reform that broke out in 2004 was an opportunity for the Film Council to state how it viewed its allegiance to the film industry. In his fateful conference speech in 2005, John Woodward made it clear that the Council's main job was to help government come up with sensible policies to advance the wider public interest surrounding film support – rather than support the industry. Although the Film Council's relations with government were prioritised and closely managed, as discussed in Chapter 9, in the end this proximity failed to save the organisation from being abolished.

In this regard, our study has strongly underlined the importance of how a statutory basis for a public body affords it some protection from precipitate and expedient political action. As we have shown, the need for such cover was recognised by the board right at the start of the

Film Council's existence. But, somehow, it was an insight that was never turned into a new status. We have shown how the fact that the BFI was a charity governed by Royal Charter worked protectively in its favour during the protracted merger showdown in 2009/10. By contrast, the UK Film Council was a company limited by guarantee. Closing down a body with a Royal Charter would have involved some legal complexity, and axing a charity even more. It may well be the case that, on grounds of expediency, the decision to close down the UKFC instead was shaped to some extent at least by the inconvenience of circumventing legal obstacles and the time needed for due process to take its course. Some, such as Alan Parker (2010), have been forthright in denouncing the abolition of the Film Council as essentially 'a hasty, petulant act of political vandalism executed by an arrogant and ignorant, right wing ideologue'. Be that as it may, the closure of the Film Council carries a strong message for other public support bodies of the importance of maintaining a protected statutory status, in a political culture where a change in the ruling party or coalition is as likely as not to bring about institutional volatility.

Implications for Public Policy

In his highly controversial landmark speech of 2002, Alan Parker observed that the UK film industry had had enough of 'quick fixes and Band-Aids' and it needed nothing less than 'radical re-invention' (Parker 2002). The policy intention that lay behind the setting up of the Film Council was to provide that fundamental overhaul. But throughout its lifetime the UK Film Council was confronted by an array of concerns and competing pressures that required continual negotiation, and this process caused it to change and widen its remit. The problem of competing pressures is, we would argue, both inescapable and symptomatic of wider challenges faced by national film support bodies everywhere. Many of the main challenges stem from the contradictory and multifaceted nature of public expectations and aspirations surrounding public support for film and the difficulty of successfully managing and satisfying different constituencies of interest over a sustained period of time. Against this inherently contentious background, a pertinent question for the future design of public policy is what can reasonably be asked of support bodies for film?

The Film Council's difficulty in managing the expectations of differing interest groups and stakeholders raises serious questions about whether setting up a single unified lead support body, as opposed to opting for more pluralistic models of support, is necessarily the best approach to take. A mature and grounded public policy needs to address the severe mismatch between harbouring world-beating ambitions for the UK film industry and the relative paucity of public finance made available to achieve that end.

Our analysis has pointed to deficiencies in procedures that led to the setting up and, especially, the closure of the UK Film Council. John Woodward remarked, in retrospect, that, having evolved and learned from its mistakes as it went along, he considered the UKFC to be 'in pretty good shape' by 2010, just as it was about to be abolished (Interview, London, April 2013). Not surprisingly, Woodward maintained that while he was in favour of public bodies being subject to renewal every decade or so, the procedures for undertaking a reappraisal ought to be rational and should rely on 'a clear set of objectives and some sort of evidence base about what has worked and what is needed' (Interview, London, February 2013). Setting aside Woodward's obvious personal interest in the case, the argument for taking a considered approach to closure appears to us to be irrefutable, and is shared by most of the key players that we have interviewed.

Clearly, the decision to abolish the Film Council and the lack of compelling grounds for doing so testify to the fact that, at times, film policy in the UK simply is not rational. Deliberation and due process were short-circuited by the immediacy of post-electoral political pressures and ideological commitments. While, especially in periods of austerity, it is by no means unusual for incoming governments to seek savings by merging or closing down public bodies seen as wasteful, such action requires a well-evidenced analysis of the relevant costs and benefits to convince the public of the integrity of the decision in question. However, according to views gathered from an extensive range of interviewees, including prominent UK film-makers, senior Film Council personnel, industry experts and policy analysts, the decision to close the UKFC took place without any prior consultation and without proper and transparent evidence-gathering or analysis of the consequences. That was also the verdict of the National Audit Office and of informed voices in Parliament.

The haphazard way the UK Film Council's existence was terminated forms part of a wider pattern of inconsistency in interventions to support film. Our conclusion supports earlier analyses of British film policy that have drawn attention to a disjointed and incoherent history of intervention (Dickinson and Street 1985; Hill 1996; Puttnam 2010). Contradictory approaches to policies for film support are by no means confined to the UK (Craik, McAllister and Davis 2003). What the UK simply does not have is a state policy for film. Rather than seek consensus for the longer term, those in power are subject to the vagaries of the politics of the moment. Hard though it may be to achieve, a different starting-point would be to develop an approach to film policy that transcends party politics and endeavours to accommodate, so far as possible, the plural nature of national aspirations regarding film support.

Notes

Chapter 3

1. Secretary of State from May 1997 to June 2001. Created Baron Smith of Finsbury in June 2005.
2. Secretary of State from May 2010 to September 2012.
3. The following section draws freely on Magor and Schlesinger (2009).
4. Recognised for his services to the British film industry by appointment as a Knight Bachelor in 2002.
5. Created Baron Stevenson of Balmacara in 2010.
6. Created Baron Puttnam of Queensgate in 1997.
7. Richard Attenborough was one of the producers interviewed by the Hydra team.

Chapter 4

1. A set of ethical guidelines for those in public office named after the first chairman (Lord Nolan) of the Committee on Standards in Public Life.

Chapter 6

1. Although set up as the lead body for film in the UK, the Film Council only assumed responsibility for the Arts Council of England's Lottery Film Department. The National Screen Agencies of Wales, Scotland and Northern Ireland received annual funding from the UKFC in the region of £0.36 million to distribute on their own terms.
2. In the UKFC's Annual Report for the year ending 31 March 2001, the figure reported for the average number of management and administration employees was fifty-four. This suggests that Smith's figure of seventy-three either represents the number of UKFC staff as of April 2000 or refers to functions outside of management and administration or employees on fixed or short-term contracts.

Chapter 8

1. The median is the middle figure within the population when ranked from largest to smallest, as opposed to the average. On account of the skewing influence that a small number of large-budget film projects will have on calculations of average budgets, the median provides a more reliable indicator of typical budgets.
2. Recoupment for the Prints and Advertising Fund is not included here.

Chapter 9

1. A Royal Charter is a formal document issued by the monarch, granting a right or power to an individual or a body corporate. The BFI's Royal Charter was originally granted in 1983 and amended in 2000.
2. From June 2009 to May 2010.
3. This letter has not been available to us.
4. www.bfi.org.uk/about-bfi/senior-staff-governors-bfi-fellows/board-governors-meeting-minutes
5. According to Tim Bevan, it was midnight on Friday (HC CMSC 2011: par. 120) but Ed Vaizey disagreed (HC CMSC 2011: Witnesses, Reply to Q397).
6. For instance, at the UKFC board meeting of 30 November 2010, the minutes with the self-same date were accepted as an accurate record. It could hardly be possible to accept minutes before the meeting itself had actually taken place!

Chapter 10

1. This is cited from film director Stanley Kubrick's acceptance speech for the Directors Guild of America's (DGA's) D. W. Griffith Award, in 1997.

Bibliography

Albertazzi, D. and Cobley, P. (2010), *The Media: An Introduction (Third Edition)*, Harlow: Pearson.

Aldgate, A. and Richards, J. (1994), *Britain Can Take It: British Cinema in the Second World War*, second edition, Edinburgh: Edinburgh University Press.

Aldgate, A. and Richards, J. (2002), *Best of British: Cinema and Society from 1930 to the Present*, London: I. B. Tauris.

Babington, B. (ed.) (2001), *British Stars and Stardom*, Manchester: Manchester University Press.

Bakhshi, H., McVittie, E. and Simmie, J. (2008), *Creating Innovation. Do the Creative Industries Support Innovation in the Wider Economy?*, London: NESTA, www.nesta.org.uk/publications/creating-innovation (last accessed 27 September 2014).

Balio, T. (2013), *Hollywood in the New Millennium*, London: BFI.

Barr, C. (1980), *Ealing Studios*, New York: The Overlook Press.

Barr, C. (ed.) (1986), *All Our Yesterdays: 90 Years of British Cinema*, London: British Film Institute.

BBC News (2010), 'Streetdance Beats Prince of Persia at UK Cinemas', 26 May, www.bbc.co.uk/news/10149644 (last accessed 23 July 2014).

Belfiore, E. (2012), '"Defensive Instrumentalism" and the Legacy of New Labour's Cultural Policies', *Cultural Trends*, 21: 2), 103–11.

Bellucci, L. (2010), 'National Support for Film Production in the EU: An Analysis of the Commission Decision-Making Practice', *European Law Journal*, 16: 2, (March), 211–32.

Bintliff, E. (2011), 'Britain's Got Talent But …', *Financial Times*, Life & Arts Section, 15–16 January, pp 1–2.

Birt, J. (2002), *The Harder Path*, London: Time Warner Books.

BOP Consulting (2014) *Review of the Film Sector in Scotland*, Edinburgh: Creative Scotland.

Bourdieu, Pierre (1984), *Distinction: A Social Critique of the Judgement of Taste*, London and New York: Routledge & Kegan Paul.

British Film Institute (BFI) Board Minutes (2009–11), British Film Institute, Board of Governors Meeting Minutes, dated 16 September 2009; 16 November 2009; 24 February 2010; 17 March 2010; 5 May 2010; 8 July 2010; 2 September 2010; 17 November 2010; 17 December 2010; 22February 2011; 24 March 2011; 11 May 2011, 16 November 2011, www.bfi.org.uk/about-bfi/senior-staff-governors-bfi-fellows/board-governors-meeting-minutes (last accessed 14 December 2014).

British Film Institute (BFI) (2010a), Business Plan 2010–11, PowerPoint Presentation, 27 Slides, March.

British Film Institute (BFI) (2010b), Written Evidence submitted by the British Film Institute (BFI) (arts 211), *Culture, Media and Sport Committee – Third Report. Funding of the Arts and Heritage*, printed 22 March 2011, www.publications.parliament.uk/pa/cm201011/cmselect/cmcumeds/464/46402.htm (last accessed 3 January 2014).

British Film Institute (BFI) (2011), *Statistical Yearbook*, London: BFI.

British Film Institute (BFI) (2012a), *Forever Film: Supporting UK Film, BFI Plan 2012–2017,* London: BFI.

British Film Institute (BFI) (2012b), *Statistical Yearbook*, London: BFI.

British Film Institute (BFI) (2014), *Statistical Yearbook*, London: BFI.

British Screen Advisory Council (BSAC)/Producers Alliance for Cinema and Television (PACT) (2005), Industry Working Group on Fiscal Policy for Film, *Response to HM Treasury Consultation Paper on the Reform of Film Tax Incentives*, London: BSAC.

Broche, J., Chatterjee, O., Orssich, I. and Tosics, N. (2007), 'State Aid for Films – A Policy in Motion?', *Competition Policy Newsletter*, 1 (spring), 44–8.

Brock, G. (2013), *Out of Print: Newspapers, Journalism and the Business of News in the Digital Age*, London: Kogan Page.

Buchanan, I., Chang, J.-H., Couto, V., Neilson, G., Pigorini, P., Saddi, J., Schaädler, J., Tan, E.-M. and Uchida, A. (2003), *Management Spans and Layers: Streamlining the Out-of-Shape Organization*, Chicago: Booz Allen Hamilton.

Burgess, S. and Ratto, M. (2003), *The Role of Incentives in the Public Sector: Issues and Evidence*, CMPO Working Paper Series No. 03/071, University of Bristol and CEPR

Caterer, J. (2011), *The People's Pictures: National Lottery Funding and British Cinema*, Newcastle upon Tyne: Cambridge Scholars Publishing.

Chibnall, S. and Murphy, R. (eds) (1999), *British Crime Cinema*, London: Routledge.

Child, B. (2010), 'Government Attacks UK Film Council for Lobbying to Stay in Existence', *The Guardian*, 17 August 2008, www.theguardian.com/film/2010/aug/17/government-uk-film-council-lobbying (last accessed 18 December 2014).

Clapp, P. (2014), '2014 – The Year of Digital Learning', *Cinema Technology*, 25: 2 (March), 18.

Cook, P. (1996), *Fashioning the Nation: Costume and Identity in British Cinema*, London: BFI.

Council of Europe (2014), *Eurimages: European Cinema Support Fund*, Council of Europe, www.coe.int/t/dg4/eurimages/About/default_en.asp (last accessed 14 October 2014).

Craik, J., McAllister, L. and Davis, G. (2003), 'Paradoxes and Contradictions in Government Approaches to Contemporary Cultural Policy: An Australian Perspective', *The International Journal of Cultural Policy*, 9: 1, 17–33.

Creative Industries Task Force (CITF) (1998), *Creative Industries Mapping Document*, London: Department for Culture, Media and Sport.

Creative Screen Associates (2013), *Comparison of French and UK Public Support Mechanisms for the Film Industry*, London: BECTU.

Culture, Media and Sport Select Committee of the House of Commons (HC CMSC) (2003), The British Film Industry, HC 667–1, *Sixth Report of Session 2002–03*, London: HMSO.

Culture, Media and Sport Select Committee of the House of Commons (HC CMSC) (2011), Funding of the Arts and Heritage, HC 464–1, *Third Report of Session 2010–11*, London: HMSO.

Curran, J. and Porter, V. (eds) (1983), *British Cinema History*, London: Weidenfeld & Nicolson.

Curtis, P. and King, M. (2010), 'Government's "Bonfire of the Quangos" Plan Will Cost as Much as it Saves', *The Guardian*, 7 October, www.theguardian.com/politics/2010/oct/07/quangos-government-multibillion-pound-bill (last accessed 18 December 2014).

Dawtrey, A. (2011), 'Best and Worst of Britain's Subsidised Film-makers Revealed', *The Guardian*, 29 July 2011, www.theguardian.com/film/2011/jul/29/subsidised-film-makers-james-marsh (last accessed 14 October 2014).

Department for Culture, Media and Sport (DCMS) (2012), *A Future for British Film: It Begins with the Audience*, London: DCMS.

Department for Culture, Media and Sport (DCMS) (2014), *Triennial Review of the British Film Institute*, 12 September, www.gov.uk/government/uploads/system/uploads/attachment_data/file/354106/140912BFI_TR_vFinal__3_.pdf (last accessed 22 December 2014).

Department for Culture, Media and Sport (DCMS) & Department for Business, Innovation and Skills (BIS) (2009), *Digital Britain Final Report, Presented to Parliament by The Secretary of State for Culture, Media and Sport and the Minister for Communications, Technology and Broadcasting*, June, London: HMSO.

De Vany, A. (2004), *Hollywood Economics: How Extreme Uncertainty Shapes the Film Industry*, London: Routledge.

Dickinson, H. (2010), 'If Partnership is the Answer Then What is the Problem? English Health and Social Care Partnerships and Service User Outcomes', Paper prepared for the 7th Biennial Conference of the Organisational Behaviour in Health Care (OBHC) 11–13 April, University of Birmingham.

Dickinson, H. (2012), 'The Making of the 21st Century Servant', *The Guardian*, Public Leaders' Network, 22 November, www.theguardian.com/public-leaders-network/2012/nov/22/21st-century-public-servant (last accessed 14 October 2014).

Dickinson, M. and Harvey, S. (2005), 'Film Policy in the UK: New Labour at the Movies', *The Political Quarterly*, 76: 3, 420–9.

Dickinson, M. and Street, S. (1985), *Cinema and State: The Film Industry and the British Government 1927–1984*, London: BFI.

Doyle, G. (2013), *Understanding Media Economics: Second Edition*, London: Sage Publications.

Doyle, G. (2014a), 'Film Support and the Challenge of "Sustainability": On Wing Design, Wax and Feathers, and Bolts from the Blue', *Journal of British Cinema and Television*, 11: 2–3, 129–51.

Doyle, G. (2014b), 'Audio-visual Trade and Policy', in C. Findlay, H. K. Nordas and G. Pasadillo (eds), *Trade Policy in Asia: Higher Education and Media Services*, Singapore: World Scientific Publishing, pp. 301–33.

Dupin, C. (2012), 'The BFI and Film Production: Half a Century of Innovative Independent Film-making', in G. Nowell-Smith and C. Dupin (eds), *The British Film Institute, the Government and Film Culture, 1933–2000*, Manchester and New York: Manchester University Press, pp. 197–218.

Durgnat, R. (1970), *A Mirror for England: British Movies from Austerity to Affluence*, London: Faber and Faber.

Eisenhardt, K. (1989), 'Agency Theory: An Assessment and Review', *Academy of Management Review*, 14: 1, 57–74.

European Commission (EC) (2014), *European Film in the Digital Era: Bridging Cultural Diversity and Competitiveness*, Communication from the Commission to the European Parliament, The Council, The European

Economic and Social Committee and the Committee of the Regions, Brussels: European Commission.

Film Council (FC) (2000a), *Film Council Board of Directors Minutes*, meeting held on 22 August.

Film Council (FC) (2000b), *Towards a Sustainable UK Film Industry*, London: Film Council.

Film Council (FC) (2001), *Working Together, Making a Difference: The Work of the Public Film Agencies in the UK*, London: Film Council.

Film Council (FC) (2003), *Three Years On*, London: Film Council.

Film Policy Review Group (FPRG) (1998), *A Bigger Picture*, London: TSO.

Film Policy Review Panel (FPRP) (2012), *A Future For British Film: It Begins with the Audience*, London: DCMS.

Film Policy Review Panel (FPRP) (2014), *It's Still about the Audience: Two Years on from the Film Policy Review*, London: DCMS.

Finney, A. (1996), *Developing Feature Films in Europe: A Practical Guide*, London and New York: Routledge.

Fowler, C (2002), *The European Cinema Reader*, London: Routledge.

Freedman, D. (2008), *The Politics of Media Policy*, Cambridge: Polity.

Gash, T. and J. Rutter (2011), 'The Quango Conundrum', *The Political Quarterly*, 82: 1, 95–101.

Geraghty, C. (2000), *British Cinema in the Fifties: Gender Genre and the New Look*, London: Routledge.

Gibson, O. (2005), 'Cinema Levy Call to Save Film Industry', *The Guardian*, 10 May, www.guardian.co.uk/uk/2005/may/10/film.media (last accessed 14 October 2014).

Gillett, P. (2003), *The British Working Class in Postwar Film*, Manchester: Manchester University Press.

Goodridge, M. (2010), 'UK Government Should Direct Lottery Funds to Arthouse Film', *Screen Daily*, 26 August, 1.

Greiner, L. E. and Schein, V. E. (1988), *Power and Organization Development. Mobilizing Power to Implement Change*, Reading: Addison-Wesley.

Hansard – Written Answers (1976), *House of Commons Debate*, 29 March, vol. 908 332–4W.

Hansard – Written Answers (2001a), *House of Commons Debate*, 4 April, Column 202W.

Hansard – Written Answers (2001b), *House of Commons Debate*, 10 July, Column 447W.

Hanson, P. (2007), '"Celluloid or Silicon?" Digital Cinema and the Future of Specialised Film Exhibition', *Journal of British Cinema and Television,* 4: 2), 370–83.

Harper, S and Porter, V. (2003), *British Cinema of the 1950s: The Decline of Deference,* Oxford: Oxford University Press.

Headland, J. and Relph, S. (1991), *The View from Downing Street,* UK Film Initiatives Series, London: British Film Institute.

Her Majesty's Stationery Office (HMSO) (1976), *Future of the British Film Industry: Report of the Prime Minister's Working Party,* London: HMSO.

Hesmondhalgh, D. (2013), *The Cultural Industries (Third Ed),* London, Los Angeles and New Delhi: Sage.

Higson, A. (1995), *Waving the Flag: Constructing a National Cinema in Britain,* Oxford: Oxford University Press.

Higson, A. (2003), *English Heritage, English Cinema,* Oxford: Oxford University Press.

Hill, J. (1986), *Sex, Class and Realism,* London: BFI.

Hill, J. (1993), 'Government Policy and the British Film Industry 1979–90', *European Journal of Communication,* 8: 2), 203–24.

Hill, J. (1996), 'British Film Policy', in A. Moran (ed.), *Film Policy,* London: Routledge, pp. 101–13.

Hill, J. (1999), 'Cinema', in J. Stokes and A. Reading (eds), *The Media in Britain,* London: Macmillan.

Hill, J. (2004), 'UK Film Policy, Cultural Capital and Social Exclusion', *Cultural Trends,* 13: 2, 29–39.

Hill, J. (2012), 'This is for the Batmans as well as the Vera Drakes: Economics, Culture and UK Government Film Production Policy in the 2000s', *Journal of British Cinema and Television,* 9: 3, 333–56.

Hjort, M. (2005), *Small Nation, Global Cinema: The New Danish Cinema,* Minneapolis: University of Minnesota Press.

House of Lords Select Committee on Communications (HL SCC) (2010), 'The British Film and Television Industries – Decline or Opportunity?', *HL 37-I, First Report of Session 2009–10,* Volume I: Report; London: The Stationery Office.

Humphries, A. (2004), 'If It's Too Smutty, You're Too Snooty', *The Guardian,* 27 February, www.theguardian.com/film/2004/feb/27/2 (last accessed 20 January 2014).

Hunt, J. (2010a), 'DCMS Improves Efficiency and Cuts Costs with Review of Arm's Length Bodies', DCMS press release 081/10, 26 July 2010.

Hunt, J. (2010b), 'I've Cut the UK Film Council So That Money Goes to the Industry', *The Observer*, 8 August, www.theguardian.com/business/2010/aug/08/film-council-quangos-cuts-jeremy-hunt/print (last accessed 18 December 2014).

Hydra Associates (1996), *Scotland on Screen: The Development of the Film and Television Industry in Scotland*, Glasgow: Scott Stern Associates.

Hydra Associates (1997), *A Review of Potential Structures of Government Support for the Film Industry in the United Kingdom*, London: Hydra Associates.

Iordanova, D. and Cunningham, S. (eds) (2012), *Digital Disruption: Cinema moves On-Line*, St Andrews: St Andrews Film School.

Jäckel, A. (2003), *European Film Industries*, London: British Film Institute.

James, N. (2001) 'Digital Deluge', *Sight & Sound*, 11: 10, 20–4.

Johnson, G., Scholes, K. and Whittington, R. (2011), *Exploring Strategy Text & Cases*, ninth edition, Harlow: FT/Prentice Hall.

Kilduff, M. and Krackhardt, D. (2008), *Interpersonal Networks in Organizations: Cognition, Personality, Dynamics, and Culture*, Cambridge: Cambridge University Press.

King, A. and Crewe, I. (2013), *The Blunders of our Governments*, London: Oneworld Publications.

Knell, J. and Taylor, M. (2011), *Arts Funding, Austerity and the Big Society: Remaking the Case for the Arts*, London: RSA.

Krietner, R. (2009), *Principles of Management*, eleventh edition, Belmont: Wadsworth Publishing.

Landy, M. (1991), *British Genres: Cinema and Society, 1930–1960*, Princeton: Princeton University Press.

Lay, S. (2002), *British Social Realism*, London: Wallflower.

Leach, J. (2004), *British Film*, Cambridge: Cambridge University Press.

Littoz-Monnet, A. (2007), *European Policy Studies: European Union and Culture: Between Economic Regulation and European Cultural Policy*, Manchester and New York: Manchester University Press.

Low, R. (1985), *Film Making in 1930s Britain*, London: Allen and Unwin.

Macnab, G. (1992), *J Arthur Rank and the British Film Industry*, London: Routledge.

Macnab, G. (2005), 'UK Film Boss Responds to "Unrealistic" Kuhn Speech', *Screen Daily*, 28 July.

Macnab, G. (2010a), 'The Life and Death of the UK Film Council', *Sight & Sound*, 20: 10, old.bfi.org.uk/sightandsound/feature/49647 (last accessed 21 March 2013), pp. 1–7.

Macnab, G. (2010b), 'UKFC/BFI Merger Called Off', *Screen Daily*, 22 June, www.screendaily.com/ukfc/bfi-merger-called-off/5015305.article (last accessed 24 February 2015).

Macnab, G. (2013), 'Thatcher's Film Legacy', *Screen International*, 16 April, www.screendaily.com/features/in-focus/thatchers-film-legacy/5053937.article (last accessed 4 July 2014).

MacPherson, R. (2010), *Is Bigger Better? Film Success in Small Countries – The Case of Scotland, Ireland and Denmark,* in 16th International Conference of the Association for Cultural Economics International, 9–12 June, Copenhagen Business School, Copenhagen, Denmark.

MacPherson, R. (2011) 'Film Success in Small Countries – from Scotland to Singapore', http://film.culture360.asef.org/magazine/film-success-in-small-countries-%E2%80%93-from-scotland-to-singapore (last accessed 6 November 2014).

Magor, M. and Schlesinger, P. (2009), '"For this Relief Much Thanks." Taxation, Film Policy and the UK Government', *Screen*, 50: 3, 299–317.

Mansfield, M. (2009), *A Report on the British Film Industry for Shadow DCMS*, London: DCMS, www.mansfieldwb.com/filmreportnov09.pdf (last accessed 14 October 2014), pp. 1–47.

Marquis, A. and Marquis, S. (1995), *Art Lessons: Meditations On The Creative Life*, New York: Basic Books.

Marr, A. (2007), *A History of Modern Britain,* London: Macmillan.

Meikle, G. and Young, S. (2011), *Media Convergence: Networked Digital Media in Everyday Life*, Basingstoke: Palgrave.

Middleton, P. (Chair) (1996), *Report of the Advisory Committee on Film Finance*, London: DNH.

Minns, A. (2001), 'UK's Film Council Says Spending Under Budget', *Screen International*, 24 August, www.screendaily.com/uks-film-council-says-spending-under-budget/406681.article (last accessed 23 September 2014).

Mintzberg, H. (1983), *Power in and around Organisations*, Englewood Cliffs: Prentice-Hall.

Mitchell, W. (2007), 'UKFC Development Fund Restructures Single-project Funding', *Screen International*, 1 October, www.screendaily.com/ukfc-development-fund-restructures-single-project-funding/4035020.article (last accessed 25 September 2014).

Mitchell, W. (2013), 'BFI Film Fund', *Screen International*, www.screendaily.com/territories/uk-ireland/bfi-film-fund/5057711.article (last accessed 25 September 2014).

Monk, C and Sargeant, A. (2002), *British Historical Cinema*, London: Routledge.

Moyne Committee Report (1936), *Report of a Committee Appointed by the Board of Trade to Consider the Position of British Films* (Cmnd 5320), Moyne Committee, November.

Mulgan, G and Paterson, P. (eds) (1993), *Hollywood of Europe?*, London: BFI.

Murphy, R. (1992), *Realism and Tinsel: Cinema and British Society, 1939–48*, London: Routledge.

Murphy, R. (2000), *British Cinema and the Second World War*, London: Continuum.

Murphy, R. (2001), *British Cinema Book 2nd Edition*, London: BFI.

Murphy, R. (ed.) (1996), *Sixties British Cinema*, London: BFI.

National Audit Office (2010), *Department for Culture, Media and Sport: Briefing for the Culture, Media and Sport Select Committee*, London: The Stationery Office.

National Audit Office (2011), *Department for Culture, Media and Sport: Financial Management*, London: The Stationery Office.

Nesta (2011), *Research and Policymaking for Film – A Symposium*, London: Nesta.

Newsinger, J. (2012), 'British Film Policy in an Age of Austerity', *Journal of British Film and Television, 9*: 1, 133–44.

Northern Alliance (2008), *Low and Micro-Budget Film Production in the UK*, London: UKFC.

Nowell-Smith, G. (2012a), 'Towards the Millennium', in G. Nowell-Smith and C. Dupin (eds), *The British Film Institute, the Government and Film Culture, 1933–2000*, Manchester: Manchester University Press, pp. 272–303.

Nowell-Smith, G. (2012b), 'Epilogue 2011', in G. Nowell-Smith and C. Dupin (eds), *The British Film Institute, the Government and Film Culture, 1933–2000*, Manchester: Manchester University Press, pp. 304–9.

Nowell-Smith, G. and Dupin, C. (2012), *The British Film Institute, the Government and Film Culture, 1933–2000*, Manchester: Manchester University Press.

Oakley, K., Hesmondhalgh, D., Lee, D. and Nisbett, M. (2014), 'The National Trust for Talent? NESTA and New Labour's Cultural Policy', *British Politics, 9*: 3, 297–317.

Olsberg SPI (2010), *A New Business Model for UK Film Producers*, London: PACT.

Olsberg SPI (2012), *Building Sustainable Businesses: The Challenges for Industry and Government*, London: Film i Väst, PACT and the Swedish Film Institute.

Olsberg SPI and Barratt, J. (2010), *UK Film Council Performance: Assessment*, London: UKFC.

Oxford Economics (2012), *The Economic Impact of the UK Film Industry (Third Edition)*, London: Oxford Economics.

Parker, A. (2002), *Building a Sustainable UK Film Industry*, Presentation to the UK film industry, 5 November.

Parker, A. (2010), 'UK Politics: The Muddy Waters of Eternity', Alan.Parker. com, www.alanparker.com/cartoon/uk-film-politics.(last accessed 14 October 2014).

Perkins, S. (2012), 'Film in the UK, 2001–10: A Statistical Overview', *Journal of British Cinema and Television*, 9: 310–32.

Perry, G. (1988), *The Great British Picture Show*, Boston: Little, Brown and Company.

Peters, B. G. (2014), 'Implementation Structures as Institutions', *Public Policy and Administration*, 29: 2, 131–44.

Petley, J. (2002), 'From Brit-flicks to Shit-flicks: The Cost of Public Subsidy', *The Journal of Popular British Cinema*, 5: 1, 37–52.

Pfeffer, J. (1981), *Power in Organisations*, Marshfield: Pitman.

Pratten, S and Deakin, S. (1999), 'Competitiveness Policy and Economic Organisation: The Case of the British Film Industry', *ESCR Centre for Business Research, Working Paper No 127*, Cambridge: University of Cambridge.

Prescott, M. (1991), *The Need for Tax Incentives*, UK Film Initiatives Series, London: British Film Institute.

Pulver, A. (2010), 'Film Council Axemen Could Murder an Industry', *The Guardian*, 26 July, www.theguardian.com/film/filmblog/2010/jul/26/uk-film-council-axe (last accessed 14 October 2014).

Puttnam, D. (2010), 'Directors' Cut: The End of UKFC', *New Statesman*, 14 October, www.newstatesman.com/film/2010/10/british-nffc-government (last accessed 14 October 2014).

Puttnam, D. with N. Watson (1997), *The Undeclared War: The Struggle for Control of the World's Film Industry*, London: HarperCollins Publishers.

Ratto, M. and Burgess, S. (2003), 'The Role of Incentives in the Public Sector: Issues and Evidence', *Oxford Review of Economic Policy*, 19: 2, 285–300.

Richards, J. (1997), *Films and British National Identity/From Dickens to Dad's Army*, Manchester: Manchester University Press.

Sandbrook, D. (2005), *Never Had it So Good: A History of Britain from Suez to The Beatles,* London: Little, Brown.

Sandbrook, D. (2006), *White Heat: A History of Britain in the Swinging Sixties,* London: Little Brown.

Schlesinger, P. (2007), 'Creativity: From Discourse to Doctrine', *Screen*, 48: 3, 377–87.

Schlesinger, P. (2009), *The Politics of Media and Cultural Policy*, Media@LSE Electronic Working Papers, 1 December, www.lse.ac.uk/collections/media@lse/mediaWorkingPapers (last accessed 18 December 2014).

Schlesinger, P. (2015a), 'The Creation and Destruction of the UK Film Council', in K. Oakley and J. O'Connor (eds), *The Routledge Companion to Cultural Industries,* London and New York: Routledge.

Schlesinger, P. (2015b), 'Transnational Framings of British Film Policy: The Case of the UK Film Council', in A. Böger and C. Decker (eds), *Transnational Mediations: Negotiating Popular Culture between Europe and the United States,* Heidelberg: Winter Verlag: 180–96.

Scott, A. J. (2000), 'French Cinema: Economy, Policy and Place in the Making of a Cultural-Products Industry', *Theory, Culture & Society*, 17: 1, 1–38.

Screen Daily (2009), 'UKFC and BFI Merger Proposed', *Screen Daily*, 21 August, www.screendaily.com/ukfc-and-bfi-merger-proposed/50004720.article (last accessed 18 December 2014).

Shoard, C (2010), 'Government to Axe UK Film Council', *The Guardian*, 26 July, www.theguardian.com/film/2010/jul/26/uk-film-council (last accessed 9 October 2014).

Shrinking the state (2013), 'UK Film Council', Shrinking the state, shrinkingthestate.group.shef.ac.uk/wp-content/uploads/2013/12/UK-Film-Council.pdf (last accessed 19 November 2014).

Slater, J. (2008) 'EDCF Workshop: The Strategic Implications of Digital Cinema for Film Distribution', *Cinema Technology*, 21: 2 (June), 36.

Stanbrook, A. (1984), 'When the Lease Runs Out', *Sight & Sound,* 53: 3, 172–3.

Stokes, J. (1999), *On Screen Rivals: Cinema and Television in the United States and Britain,* Basingstoke: Macmillan.

Street, S. (1997), *British National Cinema*, London: Routledge.

Street, S. (2012), 'Digital Britain and the Spectre/Spectacle of New Technologies', *Journal of British Cinema and Television*, 9: 377–99.

Teece, D., Pisano, G. and Shuen, A. (1997), 'Dynamic Capabilities and Strategic Management', *Strategic Management Journal*, 18: 7, 509–33.

The Economist (2014) 'Best State in a Supporting Role,' *The Economist*, 18 January, www.economist.com/news/united-states/21594301-should-california -hurl-more-money-its-footloose-film-industry-best-state (last accessed 12 December 2014).

The Telegraph (2013), 'Number of BBC Chiefs Earning £100,000 or More Rises Despite Pledge to Cut Salaries', 23 January, *The Telegraph*, www.telegraph .co.uk/culture/tvandradio/bbc/9820669/Number-of-BBC-chiefs-earning-100000-or-more-rises-despite-pledge-to-cut-salaries.html (last accessed 9 October 2014).

Throsby, D. (2004), 'Assessing the Impacts of a Cultural Industry', *Journal of Arts Management, Law and Society*, 34: 3, 188–204.

Tunstall, J. and Machin, D. (1999) *The Anglo-American Media Connection*, Oxford: Oxford University Press.

Ulff-Moller, J. (2001), *Hollywood's Film Wars with France: Film-Trade Diplomacy and the Emergence of the French Film Quota Policy*, Rochester, NY: University of Rochester Press.

Ulin, J. C. (2014), *The Business of Media Distribution: Monitizing Film, TV and Video Content in an On-line World*, second edition, New York and London: Focal Press.

United Kingdom Film Council (UKFC) (2002), *Statistical Yearbook*, London: UKFC.

United Kingdom Film Council (UKFC) (2003a), *Digital Technology Strategy: An Interim Position Paper*, April, London: UKFC.

United Kingdom Film Council (UKFC) (2003b), *Digital Technology Futures Seminar, 24 June 2003*, London: UKFC.

United Kingdom Film Council (UKFC) (2004a) *Digital Futures Seminar, 29 January 2004*, London: UKFC.

United Kingdom Film Council (UKFC) (2004b) *The Second Three Year Plan: Funding and Policy Priorities April 2004–March 2007*, London: UKFC.

United Kingdom Film Council (UKFC) (2005a), *New Cinema Fund October 2000–February 2005: An Overview and Report to the Board*, February, London: UKFC.

United Kingdom Film Council (UKFC) ((2005b), *Development Fund October 2000–March 2005: An Overview and Report to the Board*, March, London: UKFC.

United Kingdom Film Council (UKFC) (2005c), *The Digital Screen Network*, Paper presented to UKFC Board, January.

United Kingdom Film Council (UKFC) (2005/6), *Annual Review*, London: UKFC.

United Kingdom Film Council (UKFC) (2007a), *Film in the Digital Age: UK Film Council Policy and Funding Priorities April 2007–March 2010*, London: UKFC.

United Kingdom Film Council (UKFC) (2007b), *UK Film Council: Group Annual Report and Financial Statements*, 2006–7, London: UKFC.

United Kingdom Film Council (UKFC) (2008), *Statistical Yearbook*, London: UKFC.

United Kingdom Film Council (UKFC) (2009a), *Response to Digital Britain: The Interim Report, 12 March*, London: UKFC.

United Kingdom Film Council (UKFC) (2009b), *Scenario Planning for 2010–2013: Discussion Paper. How Effective Have our Policies and Interventions Been to Date?*, summer, London: UKFC.

United Kingdom Film Council (UKFC) (2009c), *Scenario Planning for 2010–2013 Discussion Paper. How the UK Film Council and 'UK Film Council Family' Operates*, summer, London: UKFC.

United Kingdom Film Council (UKFC) (2009d), *New Cinema Fund Update: Board Paper*, summer, London: UKFC.

United Kingdom Film Council (UKFC) (2009e), *Premiere Fund Update: Board Paper*, August, London: UKFC.

United Kingdom Film Council (UKFC) (2009f), *Delivering Digital Inclusion: An Action Plan for Consultation, A Response from the UK Film Council*, London: UKFC.

United Kingdom Film Council (UKFC) (2009g), *UKFC Response to Copyright in a Digital World – What Role for a Digital Rights Agency*, London: UKFC.

United Kingdom Film Council (UKFC) (2009h), UK Film Council Board of Directors Meeting Minutes, meeting held on 26 May 2009.

United Kingdom Film Council (UKFC) (2009i) UK Film Council Board of Directors Meeting Minutes, meeting held on 30 June 2009.

United Kingdom Film Council (UKFC) (2010a), *Digital Innovations and Creative Excellence*, London: UKFC.

United Kingdom Film Council (UKFC) (2010b), *Statistical Yearbook*, London: UKFC.

United Kingdom Film Council (UKFC) (2010c), Abolition of the UK Film Council: Latest Position, September, London: UKFC.

Vaizey, E. (2010), 'The Future of the UK Film Industry', 29 November, London, BAFTA, www.gov.uk/government/speeches/the-future-of-the-uk-film-industry accessed: (last accessed 18 December 2014).

Van Thiel, S. and Leeuw, F. (2002), 'The Performance Paradox in the Public Sector', *Public Performance & Management Review*, 25: 3, 267–81.

Walker, A. (1974), *Hollywood England: The British Film Industry in the Sixties*, London: Michael Joseph.

Wayne, M. (2006), 'Working Title Mark II', *International Journal of Media and Cultural Politics*, 2: 1, 59–73.

Wickham, P. (2003), *Producing the Goods? UK Film Production 1991–2001*, London: BFI.

Woodward, J. (2010), 'Why Scrapping the Film Council is a Catastrophe', *The Guardian*, www.guardian.co.uk/film/2010/jul/26/john-woodward-film-council (last accessed 18 December 2014).

World Trade Organization (WTO) (2010), *Audio-visual Services; Background Note by the Secretariat*, Geneva, 12 January, S/C/W/310.

Appendix: UKFC 'Family' of Partner Organisations

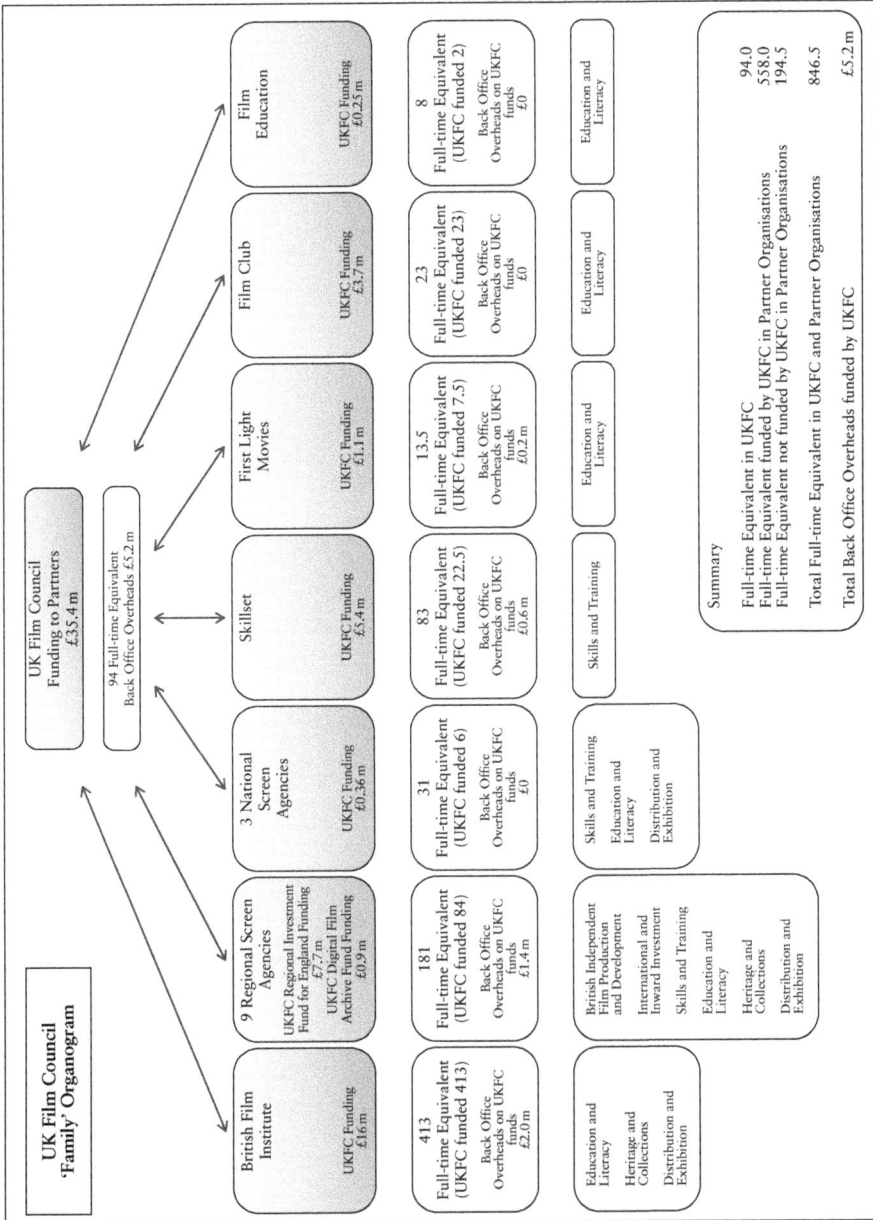

UK Film Council 'Family' Organogram

UK Film Council Funding to Partners £35.4m

94 Full-time Equivalent
Back Office Overheads £5.2m

British Film Institute	9 Regional Screen Agencies	3 National Screen Agencies	Skillset	First Light Movies	Film Club	Film Education
UKFC Funding £16m	UKFC Regional Investment Fund for England Funding £7.7m; UKFC Digital Film Archive Fund Funding £0.9m	UKFC Funding £0.36m	UKFC Funding £5.4m	UKFC Funding £1.1m	UKFC Funding £3.7m	UKFC Funding £0.25m
413 Full-time Equivalent (UKFC funded 413); Back Office Overheads on UKFC funds £2.0m	181 Full-time Equivalent (UKFC funded 84); Back Office Overheads on UKFC funds £1.4m	31 Full-time Equivalent (UKFC funded 6); Back Office Overheads on UKFC funds £0	83 Full-time Equivalent (UKFC funded 22.5); Back Office Overheads on UKFC funds £0.6m	13.5 Full-time Equivalent (UKFC funded 7.5); Back Office Overheads on UKFC funds £0.2m	23 Full-time Equivalent (UKFC funded 23); Back Office Overheads on UKFC funds £0	8 Full-time Equivalent (UKFC funded 2); Back Office Overheads on UKFC funds £0
Education and Literacy; Heritage and Collections; Distribution and Exhibition	British Independent Film Production and Development; International and Inward Investment; Skills and Training; Education and Literacy; Heritage and Collections; Distribution and Exhibition	Skills and Training; Education and Literacy; Distribution and Exhibition	Skills and Training	Education and Literacy	Education and Literacy	Education and Literacy

Summary

Full-time Equivalent in UKFC	94.0
Full-time Equivalent funded by UKFC in Partner Organisations	558.0
Full-time Equivalent not funded by UKFC in Partner Organisations	194.5
Total Full-time Equivalent in UKFC and Partner Organisations	846.5
Total Back Office Overheads funded by UKFC	£5.2m

Source: UKFC (2009b: 6).

Index